Biblical Theology
(For The Twenty-First Century Church)

Biblical Theology
(For The Twenty-First Century Church)

By
William L. Perry Th.D., Ph.D.

Theology for the 21st Century

Books may be ordered at Amazon.com or most any book dealer. Ask your local bookstore to order this book.

ISBN: 978-0-9909250-7-1

Newburgh Press
Newburgh, Indiana

Table of Contents

ACKNOWLEDGEMENTS

I would like to thank my Sons, Eric and Jim, and daughter Jennifer, who greatly encouraged me in writing this book. I want to thank Pastor Lester DeGroot of Nashville Baptist Church, who in 1972, lovingly led me to the Savior, where I was gloriously saved. John Duchardt for whetting my appetite for the Word of God, as well as, both Jack Wyrtzen of "Word of Life" ministry and Jerry Farwell of Liberty University for their encouragement in my beginning walk of service with the Lord Jesus Christ. All three have gone home to Glory, and are now at home with the Lord. I want to acknowledge Dr. Glenn Mollette and Newburgh Seminary and College of the Bible for their encouragement to delve deeper into the mysteries of God's Word. And a very special thanks to my wonderful wife Kathy, for her encouragement, guidance, patience, suggestions, and continual assistance. Without her this endeavor would not have been possible. Most of all I want to thank my Lord Jesus Christ for calling me into this blessed work.

Reaching Tomorrow By
Teaching God's Word Today!

Biblical Theology
For The Twenty-First Century Church

Introduction

Nearly two thousand years ago Jesus of Nazareth was put to death on the cross in an obscure corner of the Roman Empire. Today, worldwide faith in the risen Christ has grown as never before, not just in the so-called Christian West, but also in the new centers of Christianity; Africa, South-East Asia, and South America.

How has the belief of a handful of persecuted and frightened people in Jerusalem expanded into a faith capable of "turning the world upside-down?" How has it outlived the mighty Roman Empire – and outlived the more recent empires of the last century? How did the Christian churches, denominations, movements, doctrines and beliefs we know today come into being? How has the faith been passed on from generation to generation, and from country to country? These are some of the questions I hope will be answered in this book.

The Christian story, and the out-line of Systematic Theology is an exciting story. I hope not to over-simplify difficult questions, nor do I wish to over complicate the answers. I have in mind those who may be new believers, as well as those who may be veterans, with advanced Bible training. I pray that we will each be excited by the new discoveries, and gripped by the unfolding knowledge we uncover, wanting an account which is not so superficial as to be unsatisfying, but which wears its learning lightly; concerned not so much with academic theories, as with the true meaning of Biblical Theology.

If I had to select one memorable moment that stands out from the many, I would have to give that distinction to the Garden of Gethsemane. As I consider the garden late in the day I am struck at the imposing view from the Garden, of the pinnacle of the Temple wall in Jerusalem, that is still standing. And would have been visible to Jesus as He was in Gethsemane that day; the pinnacle where Satan took Jesus and tempted Him to cast himself down and be miraculously delivered. It dawned upon me how closely related; both geographically and spiritually, were these two great temptations. For Jesus to "cast himself down from the pinnacle", would have meant building his ministry on the spectacular – on demonstrations of power. In the Garden, Jesus had to choose again to build His ministry on love, sacrifice, and service.

INTRODUCTION TO SYSTEMATIC THEOLOGY

In the study of theology no substitute will ever be found for the knowledge of the Word of God. That Word alone deals with things eternal and infinite, and it alone has the power to convert human souls and develop a God-honoring spiritual life. The truly limitless, yet hidden spiritual content of the Bible cannot be understood by the natural, un-saved man, even though he may truly be an expert in other areas of learning. The divine message of the Bible is presented "not in words taught us by human wisdom but in words taught by the Spirit, expressing truths in spiritual words". (1 Cor. 2:13) [1]

In modern seminary education too often the study of the English Bible for its spiritual content is considered what is important and the studies of the original languages, Hebrew and Greek, may be considered unnecessary. A true systematic theology should include careful study of the original languages, in careful exegesis of each text, and additional insights coming from the study of the doctrinal, devotional, historical, prophetical, and all the practical aspects of divine revelation. The studies, however, should never degenerate into mere grammatical and theological study of the text with little attention to the spiritual content of the Scriptures. No seminary can even hope to give the student more than an introduction to the complete text of the Bible, a proper curriculum should provide a method and require the habit of study to encourage research of the text itself. The study of history in connection with the doctrine and the examination of any evidence that supports Scripture have great value in the study of theology and it should not be diverted from the task of determining the very truth of the Word of God.

The Bible goes far beyond any other written literature in presenting the truth to be incorporated in a systematic theology. As stated in 2 Timothy 3:16, "All Scripture is God-breathed and is useful for teaching, rebuking, correction, and training in righteousness." With

Scripture, "the man of God may be thoroughly equipped for every good work" (v.17) [2]. Accordingly, the Bible, even though it was written by the pen of man, surely claims to be influenced by the Spirit of God who influenced the writers as they put pen to paper, and wrote, just as true as if God Himself had spoken or had written the words. Accordingly, in the original writings, every sentence, line, word, even the smallest letter, or part of a letter is exactly as God desired to express His complete divine purpose and will.

The great purpose of systematic theology is to state the truths of the Bible in a systematic form that will classify and clarify the truth of God's words. In studying theology, it is important to always consider (1) the supernatural origin of the Bible and (2) the Bible's general structure at all times.

BIBLIOLOGY

In the study of theology the Bible must be recognized as the major book of study and the incomparable supreme Book that is above all other sources of information, and is to be considered an absolute authority, as the revelation of Almighty God, as a supreme piece of literature, and a Book of books that continues to claim the attention of millions upon millions of readers over the centuries. The reason the Bible has this supreme place is that it declares the truth concerning the infinite God, His infinite Holiness, the infinite character of human sin, and God's ultimate plan of infinite redemption.

The Bible is such a unique Book that the only explanation that seems to be at all logical, is, that it is in fact, the Word of God. It is not the kind of a book a person would write even if he could, and conversely, a person could not write it even if he would. No other writings, not even those designed to present God and religion can ever compare in their characteristics to the Bible, the many superhuman traits of this Book makes this very clear, that the Bible is The Word of God.

In the nature of systematic theology the Bible is the text that theologians refer to constantly. A preliminary study of Scripture, however, supports the doctrine of the Bible and may be considered as having many divisions. The structure of the Bible is most revealing as to God's purpose and plan in this revelation. Each of the Bible's 66 books has its peculiar character and is subject to analysis and study, paragraph by paragraph, verse by verse.

Created beings and their relationships is a major subject of divine revelation. The Bible exhibits the origin, present estate, and destiny of four classes of rational beings in the universe: Angels, Jews, Christians and non Jews or Christians, called Gentiles or Pagans, called out from the general masses of the world, into a relationship with the Son of God. As these beings appear in history, they also appear in prophecy.

Angels are presented as created beings (PS. 148:2-5; Col. 1:16); [3] their abode is heaven (Matt. 24:3); [4] their activity is both on earth and in heaven (Ps. 103:29; Luke 15:10; Heb. 1:14); [5] and their destiny is the celestial city, the New Jerusalem (Heb. 12:22; Rev. 21:12). [6] Angels remain angels throughout their eternal existence; they do not pro-create, nor do they die. Because some angels sinned against God, a division occurred between fallen angels and the holy angels who did not fall (Matt. 25:41). [7]

The great mass of humanity is classified as Pagans or Gentiles, having their origin in Adam and continuing throughout history into the prophetic future. They became partakers of Adam's fall into sin and are the subjects of prophecy that speaks of their part in history as well as prophecy.

In the present age, the Gospel is open to Gentiles on the same basis as to the Jews (Acts 10:48; 11:17-18; 13:47-48) [8] and from them God is calling out a company (15:14). [9] Gentiles appear in the Millennium (Isa.60:3,5,12; 2:2; Acts 15:17) [10] as well as in eternity in the new earth and New Jerusalem (Rev.21:24,26). [11]

God's program for the church on earth will be completed at the Rapture when the bodies of those who have died will be raised and living Christians will be translated (1 Cor. 15:20-57; 1 Thes. 4:13-18). [12] The Church will have a separate judgment at the Judgment Seat of Christ, where they will receive rewards for service (1Cor. 3:9-15; 9:18-27; 2 Cor. 5:10-11). [13] Their relationship to Christ is described as a marriage (Rev. 19:7-9), [14] and they will reign with Him (Luke 12:35-36; Jude 14- 15; Rev. 19:11-16). [15] Their distinct place will continue in eternity, (Heb. 12:22-24; Rev. 21:1-22:5). [16] In contrast to Israel, the Christian possesses no land (Ex. 20:12; Matt.5:5); no house (Matt. 23:38; Acts 15:16); no earthly capital or city (Isa. 2:1-4; Ps. 137:5-6); no earthly throne (Luke 1:31-33); no earthly kingdom (Acts 1:6-7); no Davidic king that he is subject to (Matt. 2:2), though Christians properly speak of Jesus the Christ as "the King" (1 Tim.

1:17; 6:15) and no other sacrifice other than the cross of Christ (Heb. 13:10-14). [17]

The history of the human race can be divided into 7 specific periods: (a) From Adam to Abraham (Gen. 9:24-27). (b) From Abraham to Moses, in which God's blessing to Israel was revealed (Gen. 49:1-27). (c) From Moses to Daniel including the time when the major portion of Old Testament prophecy was written and much of it was also fulfilled (Deut. 28:1-33). (d) From Daniel to Christ including the prophecy and much of the writings of Daniel, Ezekiel, Haggai, Zechariah, and Malachi. This period also included the Great Tribulation immediately preceding the second coming of Christ. (e) From the first to the second advent of Christ which includes most of the New Testament prophesy concerning Christ and the Apostles. (f) From the beginning to the end of the millennial kingdom. (g) The eternal state, which begins after the Millennium with the creation of the new heaven and the new earth and the descent of New Jerusalem to rest on the earth. [18]

The divisions of Scripture relative to the history of Israel in the land are important milestones in God's dealings with Israel. In the history of Israel's relationship to the land, they have been dispossessed and scattered three times and have been restored twice. Prophecy indicates, however, that they will be restored completely in connection with the second coming of Christ (Ezek. 39:25-29; Amos 9:11-15). [19]

Now the division of Scripture relative to the Gentiles can be itemized in the following 7 ways: (a) As outside of the Jewish covenants and government privileges. This has been their situation from Adam until the time of Christ (Eph. 2:12). (b) As receiving a dispensation of world rule at the time of Israel's last dispersion among the People of Assyria and Babylon (Dan. 2:36-44). (c) And now given the privilege to receive the Gospel of divine grace and to be saved as individuals and brought into this new relationship with Christ and His heavenly glory (Acts 10:45; 11:17-18). (d) As brought into judgment at the end of their dispensation of the world rule and with respect to their treatment of Israel (Matt. 25:31-46). (e) Are seen in prophecy as those who are to take place as a subordinate people in the millennial kingdom (Isa. 2:4; 60:3, 5, 12; 62:2; Acts 15:17). (f) As entering and continuing in Israel's kingdom (Matt, 25:34). (g) To be partakers in the glory of the celestial city after the creation of the new heavens and the new earth (Rev. 21:24-26). [20]

The Division of Scripture relative to the church in the present age may be recognized in 7 ways as well: (a) As seen in types seen as examples of brides of the Old Testament. (b) As anticipated directly in prophecy (Matt. 16:18). (c) As ones being called out from the world, and yet being a resident in the world (Acts 15:14; Rom. 11:25). (d) As being different and distinct from Judaism, the church is seen as distinct both in promise and course in history and prophecy. (e) As caught up into heaven by resurrection and translation, Church-Age believers are rewarded and married to Christ (2 Cor. 5:10; 1 Thes. 4:13-18; Rev. 19:7-9). (f) As being a part of the company with Christ as He returns to the earth to set up His 1000 year reign (Jude 14-16; Rev. 19:11-16). (g) As reigning with Christ and as partakers in the glory of the New Jerusalem, the new heavens, and the new earth (Rev. 20:6). [21]

REVELATION

When used in systematic theology, the term "revelation" is defined as the divine act of communicating to mankind what otherwise would not be known. Accordingly the proper concept of revelation it does not refer to what we can discover by rational process or by regular observation but rather to what God communicates to us.

Since God made man in His own image with the capacity to commune with God, it is truly reasonable to expect that God would communicate to man and disclose to him the truths that He wants him to know. This expectation has been fulfilled. God has disclosed truths concerning Himself and His purpose, the place of man in the divine plan of Creation, man's relationship to God, to eternity, to time, to virtue, to sin, and to redemption. It is part of our Christian faith that God has spoken and that the Word of God, the Bible, is God's revelation to man though communicated through human instruments.

Revelation and reason, are very important aspects of systematic theology, and require careful evaluation. By reason, various facts can be taken and inductions formed or conclusions drawn that truly relate to God and His Creation. However, reason by itself could never arrive at the infinite truths contained in the Word of God because revelation by its very nature transcends the human capacity to discover truth and is a direct communication from God concerning truths which no person could discover by himself.

The Bible is God's principal source of communication but God can reveal Himself through nature. In many instances in the Bible He revealed Himself in direct communication to individuals. Among the many illustrations of direct revelation is in the form of guidance as in the case of Joseph who was warned by God in a dream that he was to go to Egypt with Mary and the Child (Matt. 2:13). [22] In seeking to understand himself, his world, and events of the past, present, and future, mankind has instinctively sought an explanation of his world and sought information about its divine Creator. Human philosophy has attempted to answer these questions within the limited sphere of the natural man understanding the natural world, but this has always fallen short in fulfilling the longings of the human heart to know God.

Paul stated to the Athenians, "From one man, He made every nation of men, that they should inhabit the whole earth; and He determined the times set for them and the exact place where they should live. God did this so that men would seek Him and perhaps reach out for Him and find Him, though He is not far from each one of us" (Acts 17:26-27). [23]

This search for truth about God is much more evident in one who has been redeemed and born again. Paul wrote in Philippians, "But whatever was to my profit I now consider loss compared to the surpassing greatness of knowing Christ Jesus my Lord, for whose sake I have lost all things. I consider them rubbish, that I may gain Christ and be found in Him, not having a righteousness of my own that comes from the Law, but that which is through faith in Christ – the righteousness that comes from God and is by faith. I want to know Christ and the power of His resurrection and the fellowship of sharing in His sufferings, becoming like Him in His death, and so, somehow, to attain to the resurrection from the dead" (Phil. 3:7-11). [24]

The concept of revelation falls into two principal divisions: (a) general, natural, or original. (b) Specific, supernatural, or soteriological. The former incorporates revelation that is communicated through nature and history. The latter incorporates all that comes as an intervention into the natural course of things and is supernatural in its source and mode.

INSPIRATION

Before systematic theology can be studied in depth, or even logically presented, it becomes necessary to first recognize that the Bible is the ultimate authority and that each word contained in its original writings is factually true and without error. Though the Bible is written in normal forms of literature including figures of speech, narrative, parables, including other forms of divine revelation, we can know what the Bible affirms to be true is always true, and what the Bible affirms to be false is always false. It is by accepting the doctrine of inspiration as a supernatural work of God working through imperfect human instruments to present a prefect, infallible Bible that theology can be safely constructed.

It is absolutely futile to attempt to debate theology and the truths relating to it without first agreeing on the foundation and source of this truth. Though many have rejected the Scriptures in whole or in part, it is quite obvious that only by accepting the Scriptures as the Word of God can systematic theology be erected that is self-consistent, true, and in keeping with all God has revealed. Benjamin Warfield has stated with clarity this central truth in his writings on; Bibliotheca Sacra; "This church-doctrine of inspiration differs from the theories that would fain supplant it, is not the invention nor the property of an individual, but the settled faith of the universal church of God; in that it is not the growth of yesterday, but the assured persuasion of the people of God from the first planting of the church until today; in that it is not a protean shape, varying its affirmation to fit every new change in the ever-shifting thought of men, but from the beginning has been the church's constant and abiding conviction as to the divinity of the Scriptures committed to her keeping. It is certainly a most impressive fact – this well-defined, aboriginal, stable doctrine of the church as to the nature and trustworthiness of the Scriptures of God, which confronts with its gentle but steady persistence of affirmation all the theories of inspiration which the restless energy of unbelieving and half-believing speculation has been able to invent in this agitated nineteenth and twentieth centuries of ours. Surely the seeker after the truth in the matter of the inspiration of the Bible may well take this church-doctrine as his starting-point. [25]

Inspiration of the Scriptures is affirmed in many ways in the Bible as an explanation of its supernatural truth that reaches from eternity past to eternity future, far beyond the wisdom or discovery of mankind. The fact of its inspiration leads to the matter of the authority and the canonicity of the Scriptures as they have been handed down to us. Through revelation, inspiration, and authority are very closely related as Bible doctrines, they should not be confused. Each supplies an important part of the grand purpose of bringing the full message of God to man.

The early books of the Bible, written by Moses, obviously bring out the amazing events that have occurred from eternity past to the time of the writing of Scriptures. God committed Moses to the great task of recording the origin of the nation of Israel, as well as setting down in detail the Laws of God revealed at that time. Moses was given the inspiration to predict the future of Israel as a nation, which has already been partially fulfilled (Duet. 28) [26] and is yet to be fulfilled completely (Duet 11:24-25). [27]

The doctrine of inspiration was affirmed by Christ and the apostles. Though some have attempted to find a distinction between the beliefs of Christ and those of the apostles, the contention does not stand up under careful scrutiny as we examine the Scriptures. In the effort to discredit Scripture many have attacked the human authors and have attempted to prove discrepancies of the Bible, and, have been answered very satisfactorily by careful and spiritual scholarship. In His life on earth Christ, according to Scripture, affirmed the inspiration of Scripture many times. In dealing with critics in His lifetime, The

Lord Jesus Christ affirmed that the scribes were in error, saying, "You are in error because you do not know the Scriptures or the power of God" (Matt. 22:29). [28]

Christ repeatedly affirmed the inspiration of the Old Testament. In quoting Psalm 110:1 in Matthew 22:44, [29] He took the Scripture as being accurate even to the very words. In quoting this verse, Christ affirmed that it was written by inspiration of the Holy Spirit even though David was its human author. In Mark 12:36 He attributed the accuracy of David's quotation to the Holy Spirit. Jesus said, "I tell you the truth, until heaven and earth disappears, not the smallest letter, not the least stroke of the pen, will by any means disappear from the Law until everything is accomplished" (Matt. 5:18). [30]

The apostles gave similar testimony. In quoting Psalm 41:9 in Acts 1:16, [31] Peter affirmed that what David said was by the Holy Spirit. In quoting Psalm 2:1-2 in Acts 4:25,[32] Peter attributed the truth in those two Old Testament verses to the fact that God had spoken. Paul quoted Isaiah 6:9-10 in Acts 28:7 [33] to indicate that the Holy Spirit had spoken through Isaiah. May other references to the Old Testament in the New can be found. The contention that Christ and the apostles were not in agreement on the subject of inspiration is not supported by a reading of the New Testament.

Because the inspiration of Scripture is supernatural and a work of God through men, it is impossible for men to explain it fully. None-the-less, theologians have often attempted to analyze inspiration with the obvious intent of qualifying or limiting the accuracy of Scripture and reducing its absolute authority. From these attempts have come a number of various theories of inspiration, each attempting to explain how the Bible can have the dual authorship of man and God.

A study of Scripture makes it clear that human authors brought with them into Scripture their vocabularies, their thoughts, their investigations into facts, and often their feelings and spiritual struggles. Some of the Psalms, in particular, as they begin with a recital of the psalmists' unbelief or struggle with life, would lose all their meaning if the writers were merely the stenographers to whom God dictated the Scriptures. Paul wrote regarding Israel, "I have great sorrow and unceasing anguish in my heart. For I could wish that I myself were cursed and cut off from Christ for the sake of my brothers, those of my own race, the people of Israel" (Rom. 9:2-4). [34] These statements would lose their meaning if the Apostle Paul were merely the stenographer of what God said. In Scripture evidence is frequently given of the human characteristics of the author.

It is also true that as men wrote by inspiration, often what they wrote was beyond their knowledge, and they often did not understand the full importance of what they wrote. Daniel, for instance, at the close of his book wrote, "I heard, but I did not understand. So, I asked, 'My lord, what will the outcome of all this be?' He replied, 'Go your way, Daniel, because the words are closed up and sealed until the time of the end'" (Dan. 12:8-9). [35] Though Daniel was guided in writing the inspired Scriptures of the prophecies his book contains, he did not understand it as well as we can understand it today because we have the benefit of having seen many of his prophecies fulfilled.

Because of these human characteristics of the Bible, it is clear that they were written by men, but it is also very evident that they were guided by the Holy Spirit in what they wrote. This is truly the inspiration of the Scriptures, the dictation or mechanical theory of divine inspiration.

Mystical inspiration is offered by some liberal theologians as another possible theory of how the Bible was written. An appeal is made to the statement of Paul, "For it is God who works in you to will and to act according to His good purpose" (Phil. 2:13). [36] Though this is obviously a true statement that God works in believers, the problem is that even though He does accomplish this in Christians, their actions are not infallible or without sin. Divine power transmitted to man does not bring with it perfection. The concept of mystical inspiration is sometimes traced to E.D. Schleiermacher (1768-1834), [37] one of the forerunners of modern liberalism. For him, inspiration was merely a supernatural heightening of man's natural abilities.

Dr. Benjamin Warfield has given us an excellent analysis of this mystical view in his writings; bibliotheca Sacra 51 (1884): pp. 623-24).

"Very varied forms have been taken by this conception; and more or less expression has been given to it, in one form or another, in every age. In its extreme manifestations, it has formerly tended to sever itself from the main stream of Christian thought and even to form separate sects. But in this past century (the nineteenth), through the great genius of Scheleiemacher it has broken in upon the church like a flood, and washed into every corner of the Protestant world. As a consequence, we find men everywhere who desire to acknowledge as from God only such Scripture as they "find in them," – who cast the clear objective enunciation of God's will to the mercy of the currents of thoughts and feeling which sweep up and down to their own souls,- who "persist" sometimes, to use a sharp but sadly true phrase of Robert Alfred Vaughan's, "in their conceited rejection of the light without until they have turned into darkness their light within…". Despite these attempts to introduce lowered conceptions, the doctrine of plenary inspiration of the Scriptures, which looks upon them as an oracular book, in all its parts and elements, alike, of God trustworthy in all its affirmations of every kind, remains today, as it has always been, the vital faith of the people of God, and the formal teaching of the organized church". [38]

The problem with mystical inspiration is that it falls short of assuring that the Bible is the true Word of God. For this reason, it is rejected by orthodox theologians who assert that the Bible is fully inspired and is the very Word of God.

In the Scriptures, as also, in the person of Christ, the perfection is attributed to the supernatural power of God. All agree that if ordinary human men had written the Bible and were able to do so without supernatural direction, it would surely be imperfect. The element of doubt about inerrancy necessarily relates to the human elements in Scripture. Basically the question is whether one recognizes the supernatural character of the writings of the Bible.

Both the Bible and Christ are called the *logos*, translated "Word". It is used several hundred times in the New Testament to refer to the Bible and seven times to refer to the Son of God as the Living Word (John 1:1; 14; 1 John 1:1; 5:7; Rev. 19:13). [39] In many respects, Christ as the Living Word is similar to the written Word. That both are the truth (John 14:6; 17:17; Ps. 119:19; Matt. 24:34-35; 1 Peter 1:25; John 11:25; Acts 16:31). [40] Just as a written word expresses a fact, so the Living Word expressed truth. Both are divinely intended channels of revelation to man. The many similarities between the Living Word and the written Word support and sustain the concept that both are perfect and without error.

Though there are many parallels, there are also differences between Christ as the Living Word and the Bible as the written Word. Christ in His incarnation continued in this state forever. The written Word does not require personal union. The human nature of Christ was unfallen in contrast to the fallen natures of the human authors. The writers of Scripture, though kept perfect in their writings, were not kept perfect in their lives; this contrasts with Christ's perfect nature. These differences, however, do not introduce error in either the written Word or the Living Word. In the study of the person of Christ, as in the study of the Bible, there is an observable tendency to go to extremes. This is seen in the written Word in the incorrect theory of dictation and in the person of Christ in the emphasis on Deity and the disregard of His humanity. The same error could be observed if Christ's humanity was recognized at the expense of His Deity or if the human nature of the Bible were acknowledged at the expense of its divine inspiration. A balance in doctrine so often is necessary to arrive at the truth, and extremes become departures from the truths.

The possible variations of opinion with respect to inspiration fall into four classes: (1) The Bible is of divine authorship almost exclusively. (2) The Bible is of human authorship almost exclusively. (3) The Bible is in some parts almost exclusively divine and in other parts almost exclusively human. (4) The divine and human authorship are both without impairment to either, wholly present in every word from first to the last. The fourth of these classifications is the true representation of the fact of inspiration.

The doctrine of inspiration is stated fully in 2 Timothy 3:16-17. "All Scripture is God-breathed and is useful for teaching, rebuking, correcting, and training in righteousness, so that the man of God my be thoroughly equipped for every good work." [41] The expression "God-breathed" is a translation of the Greek *theopneustos* and appears only here in the Bible. This states clearly that the Bible was given by the "outbreathed" of God and by God even though it was written by men. The words "all Scripture", called "the holy Scriptures" in verse 15, [42] are clearly limited to biblical books. Verse 16 indicates that all Scripture is equally inspired though all of it may not be equally important. Regardless of the form in which Scripture is presented, whether dictated by God as in some instances, the summation of human investigation as in the Gospel of Luke, or the personal experience of the psalmists, all Scripture is equally inspired of God.

The reference to "all Scripture" also clearly includes both the Old and New Testaments. Peter referred to the writings of Paul as "Scripture" (2 Peter 3:16). [43] Paul quoted Deuteronomy 25:4 in 1 Timothy 5:18 and also in Luke 10:7, [44] indicating that the Old and New Testaments were equally inspired. The writers of Scripture were quite conscious of the supernatural process of their writings. Their claim for its accuracy was not based on human authorship.

Because the Scriptures come from God, they are essential to divine communication to man. Paul made this clear in itemizing that the

Scriptures are useful for "teaching, rebuking, correcting, and training in righteousness," making it possible for "the man of God" to "be thoroughly equipped for every good work". Accordingly, there is no room for human correction or addition to the Scriptures. They are accurate and complete in their declaration of the will of God for man.

In the abundant theological writings dealing with the inspiration of the Scriptures, objections to the doctrine of verbal, plenary inspiration have been sufficiently answered.

The progress of doctrine observable from Genesis to Revelation does not mean that earlier and partial revelation were erroneous. Progress is an essential fact of Scripture but is never an indication that previous Scripture was in error. The inspiration in the Book of Genesis is just as clear and inerrant as the inspiration of the Book of Revelation. Some variations do occur, as in the Gospel where the superscriptions over the cross of Christ was written in three languages, Latin, Greek and Hebrew. Accordingly the different Gospels translating different superscriptions varied in their wording without contradiction. It is also true that in quoting the Old Testament, the Holy Spirit sometimes quoted freely rather than the precise words but without contradiction of the original writing. Though there may seemingly be difficulties in harmonizing Scripture, the problem is always one of incomplete understanding. When all the facts are in, the Scriptures do not contradict themselves.

The claim for verbal, plenary inspiration is made only for the original writings and it does not extend to any transcriptions or translation. Though the problem that we do not have the original manuscripts is often raised, the science of lower criticism which deals with manuscripts has reached such accuracy that there is little doubt that essentially we have the Word of God as it was originally written. The debate on passages such as Mark 16:9-29 and John 7:53-8:11,[45] which are omitted in some manuscripts, does not change essential biblical doctrine.

Wescott and Hort have summarized the whole problem of lower criticism, reducing it to its proper dimension:

"With regard to the great bulk of the words of the New Testament, as of most other ancient writings, there are no variations or other ground of doubt, and therefore no room for textual criticism; and here therefore an editor is merely a transcriber. The same may be said with substantial truth respecting those various readings which have never been received, and in all probability will never be received into any printed text. The proportion of words virtually accepted on all hands as raised above doubt is very great, not less, on a rough computation, than seven-eights of the whole. The remaining eighth therefore, formed in great part by changes of order and other comparative trivialities, constitutes the whole area of criticism. If the principles followed in the present edition are sound, this area may be very greatly reduced. Recognizing to the full the duty of abstinence from peremptory decision in cases where the evidence leaves the judgment in suspense between two or more readings, we find that, setting aside differences of orthography, the words in our opinion still subject to doubt only make up one sixtieth of the whole New Testament. In this second estimate the proportion of comparatively trivial variations is beyond measure larger than the former; so that the amount of what can in any sense be called substantial variation is but a small fraction of the whole residuary variation, and can hardly form more than a thousandth part of the entire text". [46]

Philip Schaff has also stated how limited are the problems in the matter of the biblical text.

"This multitude of various readings of the Greek text need not puzzle or alarm any Christian. It is the natural result of the great wealth of our documentary resources; it is a testimony to the immense importance of the New Testament; does not affect, but rather insures, the integrity of the text; and it is a useful stimulus to study. Only about 400 of the 100,000 or 150,000 variations materially affect the sense. Of these, again, not more than about 50 are really important for some reason or other; and even of these 50 not one affects an article of faith or a precept of duty which is not abundantly sustained by other and undoubted passages, or by the whole tenor of Scripture teaching. *The Texus Receptus* of Stephens, Beza, and Elzevir, and of our English Version, teach precisely the same Christianity as the uncial text of the Sinaitic and Vatican manuscripts, the oldest versions, and the Anglo-American Revision". [47]

Though the Scriptures have been attacked time and time again, even as the Word of God was attacked by Satan in the Garden of Eden, the evidence in support of its supernatural revelation and inerrancy of statement is overwhelming and intelligent men thoroughly familiar with the field of scholarship relating to the problem have had complete confidence in the Bible. Whether questions are raised about the nature of inspiration of Scripture or about the exact text of the original, the evidence is that for all practical purposes we have the infallible and full revelation of God in Scripture. The abundant evidence is the declaration of biblical canonicity and authority.

CANONICITY AND AUTHORITY

In the history of the church, the 66 books of the Bible were gradually recognized as constituting the Scriptures. Individual books, however, were widely recognized as soon as they were received. The Roman Catholic Church has added several books to those recognized by Protestants, but generally speaking, the canon refers to the 66 books that are received by all branches of Christendom. Though the church by its recognition confirmed the authority of the Bible, the Scriptures stand on their own merit quite apart from church recognition. Except in liberal theology, the 66 books commonly recognized as Scripture have stood the test of time as inspired writings distinct from all other literature.

The Old Testament was written by men who in many cases were in authority over the religious and civil life of the people. Moses was accredited as God's representative and Law-giver. His writings, like those of other writers in the Old Testament, preserved what was first proclaimed by word of mouth as authoritative and then was written for the benefit of later generations.

The New Testament was also written by men specially chosen for the task, most of whom were chosen by Christ Himself. Many books of the New Testament were addressed to local churches, but their truth was intended for the church at large. As copies of the books of the New Testament were completed and circulated in the first century, most were accepted by the church. As the books came into the possession of various churches, they were recognized as the inspired Word of God, and their message was received as the very inspired Word of God. Though a few books were questioned by some, such as Hebrews, 2 Peter, and Revelation, the entire Bible was recognized early in the second century.

Though churches recognized the authority of the biblical books, it should be emphasized that the Bible is its own authority, and no person or group of persons was ever authorized to select the books of Scripture. Even a casual examination of the Bible compared to other literature of the time reveals its distinctive character both in the way it was written and in the subject matter it presents. Though the Old Testament closed with obvious anticipation of what was yet to come, the Book of Revelation, probably the last of the New Testament books to be written, brought God's written revelation to a close. It's true that some in the early Church Age attempted to claim inspiration equal to that of Scripture; their claims were discarded quickly by the majority of believers. Because the Bible as a canon is the Word of God, it has absolute authority in all matters of faith and practice. This truth can be traced to the facts that make the Bible a distinctive book.

When we recognize the inspiration of the Bible as "God-breathed", we automatically assign to the Scriptures the supreme authority that belongs only to God. This authority proceeds from God immediately and without reduction or complications. The entire Bible is the very Word of God and therefore has divine authority behind all that is written in it.

In inspiring the Bible, God supernaturally guided His chosen men who wrote it so that they wrote the Scriptures exactly as God wished. Though the human element is present, the fact of dual authorship including divine direction makes it possible to recognize the infinite worthiness and holy excellence of the God-breathed message. Though the Word of God would have been true even if delivered orally, its written form constitutes an abiding statement that also possesses divine authority.

The entire Bible is properly refereed to as "the Law of God." Though the Bible is fully authoritative because it is "God-breathed," the evidence of its approval by Jesus Christ adds confirmation and recognition to the authority of the Bible. The four Gospels contain about 35 direct reference and quotations by the Son of God to the Old

Testament Scriptures. In this way Christ gave His own confirmation that the Old Testament is the Word of God. The listing of these many references in itself is overwhelming proof that Christ recognized the inspiration of the Old Testament.

In addition to His references to the Bible as the Word of God, Christ also declared, "I am the way and the truth and the life." [49] In this statement Christ not only declared that He is truthful but also that He is the truth. He was "the faithful Witness, the Firstborn from the dead, and the Ruler of the kings of the earth" Rev. 1:5.[50] In Revelation 3:14 He was described as "the Amen, the faithful and true Witness, the Ruler of God's creation."[51] In John 18:37, responding to Pilate, Jesus said, "You are right in saying I am a King. In fact, for this reason I was born, and for this I came into the world, to testify to the truth. Everyone on the side of truth listens to Me".[52] It may be concluded that Christ clearly affirmed that the Old Testament is the Holy Scripture. In appointing and commissioning the writers of the New Testament, He added His confirmation to what was yet to be written Rev. 22:18-20.[53]

The prophets of the Old and the New Testaments were divinely appointed spokesmen for God. The Prophets were among the distinctive leaders of the new order (Eph. 4:11); the church was built on them (2:20), and they spoke to the edification, exhortation, and comfort of believers (1 Cor. 14:3).[55]

Having originated and transmitted the Scriptures by chosen prophets, the Spirit employed the Scriptures as His own language in speaking to men. This further confirms the authority of the Scriptures. The Bible, being the very Word of God, is suitable for perfect expression in every situation in which the Spirit functions. The Scriptures are "the sword of the Spirit, which is the Word of God" (Eph. 6:17). In a sense the phrase in 1 Timothy 4:1, "the Spirit clearly says" might with entire justification be applied to all of the Word of God.

We can see that three of the exhibitions of the authority of the Scriptures are primary.

(1) The Bible as the outbeathing of God is seen in the transmission of that message to chosen prophets and in the recognition and acknowledgement of sacred canon by those to whom it first came. Its authority is not due to human recognition but rather to the fact that it was inspired by Almighty God. (2) The confirmation given by Jesus Christ as the second Person of the Trinity and the greatest of the prophets link the accuracy of the written Word with the truthfulness of the incarnate Word. (3) The use of the Scriptures by the Holy Spirit demonstrates their power and authority. This can be summarized in three actualities: The Scriptures are the out breathing of God- His own Word to man. The Scriptures are attested to by the Son of God. They originated with and are employed by God the Holy Spirit.

ILLUMINATION

Though the Bible provides accurate information of God's message to man covering the vast field of truth, the ability of man to understand Scripture was severely limited by Adam's fall. Apart from the Spirit of God, man is not able to understand the things of God (1 Cor. 2:14).[56] Man is blinded and in darkness as far as spiritual truth is concerned. So a special work of God is necessary to cast light on the Scriptures to make them understandable.

The period between the two advents of Christ is often designated "the age of the Holy Spirit" because it is a time when the Holy Spirit of God is resident in the world and especially in the child of God. Christians are indwelt by the Holy Spirit with the special purpose of providing supernatural enablement in all areas of the spiritual life including that of understanding truth. The Spirit of God can even reveal "the deep things of God" (1 Cor. 2:10).[57] This truth opens up a vast horizon of spiritual knowledge to the spiritual Christian with its corresponding warning to Christians who are not walking with God and who are not being taught by the Spirit. Even as Christ revealed the Scriptures to His companions on the Road to Emmaus on the day of His resurrection (Luke 24:13-35),[58] so today the Holy Spirit can open the minds of spiritual Christians to understand and accept the limitless truth of God revealed in the Bible.

These great truths relating to the illumination of the Spirit are especially applicable to those who seek to teach the Scriptures and minister to the spiritual needs of others. Students of Scripture must maintain a spiritual life in conformity to the will of God, and such a spiritual walk is determined and is crucial for their ministry. Just as it is imperative for one to have the new birth to see things of God, so there can be no full or worthy apprehension of God's revealed truth by the Christian who is unspiritual or fleshly.

INTERPRETATION

A student of Scripture who wants to determine the truth must give himself unrelentingly to the study of the Bible. Though the conclusions of various schools of thought should be studied, the task is to arrive at what the Bible actually teaches. The science of interpretation called hermeneutics is the art of determining the true meaning of Scripture. Hermeneutics must be distinguished from exegesis, which is application of the laws or principles of interpretations.

As a work of man, hermeneutics is necessarily imperfect, but this fact does not free students of Scripture from the arduous task of seeking to determine the actual teaching of Scripture.

Though the books of the Bible form a single unit of 66 books, each book has its own peculiar character which must be determined by careful study. Even books that are quite similar – as are the four Gospels[59] – offer an illustration of this. Matthew's Gospel relates especially to the kingship of Christ, Mark's Gospel relates especially to the servanthood of Christ, Luke's Gospel describes the humanity of Christ, John's Gospel emphasizes the deity of Christ. In the study of each book its specific purpose should be kept in mind as well as its contribution to the whole structure of the Bible.

Accurate understanding of a given Scripture passage depends on distinguishing its primary interpretation and secondary application. Though "all Scripture" is for Christians and "is useful for teaching, rebuking, correcting, and training in righteousness" (2 Timothy 3:16),[60] all Scripture may not necessarily be addressed to the individual who is studying Scripture. Though the Bible contains revelation concerning angels, it is not addressed to them. In like manner, all Scripture is not addressed only to Gentiles, Jews, or Christians. It is important that the one addressed be kept in mind as the text is interpreted.

After a primary interpretation is attained, often a secondary application of a given Scripture to order classes of people is appropriate. For instance much valuable truth may be gained by a Christian from the extensive body of Scripture relating to the Jews though at the same time recognizing that the Christian is not necessarily required to keep all the rules of life that applied to Jews in the Old Testament. Christians do not advocate that Sabbath-breakers be stoned to death (Num. 15:32-36).[61] Likewise judgments pronounced on the unsaved such as the danger of hell fire (Matt. 5:29-30)[62] as Judgments of God are surely and necessarily applicable. Of a Christian it is said that he "will not be condemned" (John 5:24). Likewise an unsaved person will not appear at the Judgment Seat of Christ to be rewarded for his works (2 Cor. 5:10-11).[63] Only by careful attention to the direct application of a Scripture passage and possible indirect applications can a text be properly understood.

A student of Scripture must determine the contextual boundaries of each chapter and verse of the Bible for the context is often a determining factor in understanding its meaning. The text of Matthew 16:28, though separated by chapter division from Matthew 17:1-13, must be understood as belonging to chapter 17.[64] The promise of 1 Corinthians 2:9 relative to the revelation of God for believers is stated in verse 10 to be applicable now, not in some distant time. Also 1 Corinthians 9:27 relates to rewards of Christians, not to loss of salvation. Most misinterpretations of the Bible arise from misunderstandings or neglecting the context.[65]

An interpreter of the Bible necessarily comes with some preconceived ideas, but he must avoid any personal prejudices that would make it impossible for him to allow a text to state what it actually says. Interpretation of the Word of God must be honest and sincere. Paul stated this standard in 2 Corinthians 4:2, "Rather, we have renounced secret and shameful ways; we do not use deception, nor do we distort the Word of God. On the contrary, by setting forth the truth plainly we commend ourselves to every man's conscience in the sight of God."[66]

It cannot be overemphasized that the basic laws of hermeneutics must be observed in all correct interpretation. Differences of opinion in the interpretation of Scripture almost always arise from neglect or faulty use of hermeneutical principles. It is especially important that no interpretation of the Bible attempt to explain a text in a way that no one else has ever explained it. In every case where truth is presented, more than one interpreter will agree on the meaning of the text.

ANIMATION

In studying Scripture it soon becomes evident that the Bible is different from all other writings because it possesses a living quality which comes from its divine inspiration. Animation refers to this inimitable element of vitality of life that is in Scripture as in no other book. This fact is variously presented in Scripture. Seven attributes of the Bible are stated in Psalm 19:7-9, "The Law of the Lord is perfect, reviving the soul. The statutes of the Lord are trustworthy, making wise the simple. The precepts of the Lord are right, giving joy to the heart. The commands of the Lord are radiant, giving light to the eyes. The fear of the Lord is pure, enduring forever. The ordinances of the Lord are sure and altogether righteous".[67]

In a similar way, seven attributes of the Bible are in Psalm 119. These are: "trustworthy" (v.86), "boundless" (v. 96), "right" (v.128), "wonderful" (v.129), "thoroughly tested" (v. 140), "eternal" (v. 160), "righteous" (v.172).[68] The New Testament adds that the Word of God is "truth" (John 17:17), "useful" (2 Tim. 3:16), and "living and active" (Heb. 4:12).[69] The living character of the Word of God is brought out by the Greek word *zon* meaning "living" and the word *energes* meaning "active" or "powerful." The attribute of "living" is used 13 times in reference to "the living God." A central text is Hebrews 4:12, "For the Word of God is living and active. Sharper than any double-edged sword, it penetrates even to dividing soul and spirit, joints and marrow; it judges the thoughts and attitudes of the heart." Just as there is life in Jesus Christ as the incarnate Word, so there is life in the written Word. A similar thought is presented in 1 Peter 1:23, "For you have been born again, not of perishable seed, but of imperishable, through the living and enduring Word of God."[70] Though the Word of God does not partake of personality or the constitution of a living creature, because it is "god-breathed" it has active power in the mind and heart of the reader.

The true proclamation of divine truth means obeying the command, "Preach the Word" (2 Timothy 4:2).[71] The reason for this is found in Romans 10:17: "Faith comes from hearing the message, and the message is heard through the word of Christ."[72] Paul described "the Holy Scriptures" as being "able to make you wise for salvation through faith in Christ Jesus (2 Timothy 3:15).[73] According to 2 Peter 1:4 individuals through the Word of God "may participate in the divine nature and escape the corruption in the world caused by evil desires."[74] The Word of God works with the Holy Spirit in the accomplishment of the new birth (John 3:5; Titus 3:5; 1 Peter 1:23). People become Christians as they are born again as stated in 1 Peter 1:23, "For you have been born again, not of perishable seed, but of imperishable, through the living and enduring Word of God."[75]

In His High Priestly Prayer in John 17, Christ requested that those the Father had given might be sanctified through the truth: "Sanctify them by the truth; Your Word is truth" (John 17:17).[76] Likewise, the Word of God is pictured as nourishing a believer and imparting spiritual strength and growth as stated in 1 Peter 2:2, "Like newborn babies, crave pure spiritual milk, so that by it you may grow up in your salvation."[77] Paul, in his prayer for the Thessalonians, thanked God for them because "when you received the Word of God, which you heard from us, you accepted it not as the word of men, but as it actually is, the Word of God, which is at work in you who believe".[78] In a similar way Paul prayed for the Ephesians elders when he was about to leave them, "Now I commit you to God and to the word of His grace, which can build you up and give you an inheritance among all who are sanctified" (Acts 20:32).[79] Christ uses the Word to make His bride "holy, cleansing her by washing with water through the Word".[80]

It should be clear from these and many other passages that the Word of God has a unique, living quality which makes it effective in accomplishing God's purposes. Isaiah stated this in Isaiah 55:10-11, "As the rain and the snow come down from heaven, and do not return to it without watering the earth and making it bud and flourish, so that it yields seed for the sower and bread for the eater, so is My word that goes out from My mouth: It will not return to Me empty, but will accomplish what I desire and achieve the purpose for which I sent it."[81] Likewise, Jeremiah wrote, "Is not My Word like fire,' declares the Lord, 'and like a hammer that breaks a rock in pieces?" [82]The Word of God is efficacious in the hand of the Holy Spirit in accomplishing supernatural results. This is the underlying reason for Paul's exhortation to Timothy to "preach the Word".[83]

THE PERSONALITY OF GOD

Problems of interpretation of the Bible are recognized in systematic theology, but within orthodoxy there is no problem of the trustworthiness of Scripture. In a similar way the fact of the existence of God established by reason in naturalistic theism is in no way open to question as one approaches biblical theism. The Bible clearly reveals the existence of God who has all the attributes properly recognized in Deity.

In the account of Creation given in Genesis 1:26 God said, "Let Us make man in Our image, in Our likeness, and let them rule over the fish of the sea and the birds of the air, over the livestock, over all the earth, and over all the creatures that move along the ground." Because of the subsequent fall of man into sin this image to some extent has been marred, but man even in his sinful state reflects some of the elements found in the personality of God though such similarity is imperfect. In mental and moral attributes, a correspondence in the nature of them found in both God and man may be observed though they are incomparable as to degree of perfection that belongs to both God and man, and though the degree to which God and man possess them differs greatly, the nature of these characteristics is the same in each sphere.

In comparing God and man one does not assert that man's corporeal or physical nature is involved since God is Spirit.[84] However, as Scripture reveals the nature of God, anthropomorphisms are often used. In Deuteronomy 33:27 Moses stated, "The eternal God is your refuge, and underneath are the everlasting arms."[85] In John 10:29 Jesus said, "My Father, who has given them to Me, is greater than all; no one can snatch them out of My Father's hand." In Isaiah 66:1, earth is referred to as the "footstool" of God. In 2 Chronicles 1:9 it is revealed, "For the eyes of the Lord range throughout the earth to strengthen those whose hearts are fully committed to Him." Isaiah wrote, "Surely the arm of the Lord is not to short to save, nor His ear too dull to hear" (59:1). Isaiah also wrote, "The mouth of the Lord has spoken" (58:14). References to the "face" of God (Ex. 33:11, 20) and His "nostrils" (2 Sam. 22:9, 1) also illustrate anthropomorphisms.[86] Since physical members of the human body are attributed to God in this way these statements indicate that God is able to perform similar functions. Anthropomorphic representations of God are so numerous in the Bible that one must obviously accept this as a part of scriptural revelation and part of God's effort to communicate to man in a way that God is pure spirit.

The weakness and sin of man cannot be expressed in terms of human life. But man's mental and moral properties do serve to demonstrate the significant and momentous fact in their degree of perfection, are resident in both God and man.

John Miley has summarized the fact of the personality of God in these words:

"If God is not a personal being, the result must be either atheism or pantheism. It matters little which. The dark and deadly implications are much the same. There is no God with self-consciousness or the power of rational and moral self-determination, no personal divine agency in the universe. A blind, necessitated force is the original of all. The existence of the world and the heavens is without reason or end. There is no reason for the existence of man, no rational or moral end. God has no interest in him, no rational or moral rule over him. The universal since of moral obligation and responsibility must be pronounced a delusion. There should be an end of worship, for there is wanting a truly worshipful being. All that remains is the dark picture of a universe without divine teleology or providence".[87]

Because God has personality, it is possible for man to have fellowship with Him as stated in many Scriptures.

THE ATTRIBUTES OF GOD

In the Scriptures God is not specifically defined in any one assertion, but His existence and attributes are assumed and appear in Scripture in various places and in many terms giving us a pretty good idea as to what He is and what He does. A true biblical definition of God is an induction from all Scripture that relates to a definition.[88] Though God is revealed sometimes in human terms, as previously mentioned, man can only partially understand God in all His infinity. In speaking of man's understanding of God, David wrote, "Such knowledge is too wonderful for me, too lofty for me to attain" (Ps. 139:6).[89] Speaking in similar words of appreciation Paul said, "God, the blessed and only Ruler, the King of kings and Lord of lords, who alone is immortal and who lives in unapproachable light, whom no one has seen or can see. To Him be honor and might forever: (1 Tim. 6:15-16). Similar expressions are found in Colossians 1:15 and 1 Timothy 1:17. In Christ, some of the attributes of God were revealed (John 1:14, 18). In recognition of the excellence of God, people are exhorted to be holy and perfect as God is (Matt. 5:48; I Peter 1:16).[90]

A comprehensive statement of God is found in the Westminster Confession of Faith:[91]

"The attributes of God presents themes so vast and complex, so interrelated and interdependent that to classify them is difficult if not completely impossible. Theologians generally have separated attributes into divisions under varying terminology. One group of attributes represents those characteristics that are said to be within God and not found elsewhere in creation; the other group represents those characteristics in God that to a limited degree are found in angels and human spirits. The twofold divisions of attributes are variously stated as incommunicable and communicable; natural and moral; immanent and emanative; passive and active; absolute and relative; negative and positive".

Attention has been given to the reality of the personality of God; but this subject is now addressed as it forms a logical starting point for the investigation into certain essential actualities concerning God. Though personality is a constitutional attribute, it sometimes also has been characterized as an attribute of God. Personality in this sense may be analyzed by its component parts: Intellect, sensibility, and will. These qualities of personality in turn relate to certain attributes of God.

Omniscience is related to God as intellect is related to man. A vast difference exists between the two in that man acquires knowledge only in a limited way, while the understanding or knowledge of God is all-inclusive and infinite.

Another element in personality is sensibility, which means, capacity for sensation or feeling.[92] God in Scripture is presented with the highest form of emotion illustrated in love and patience. His emotions are always in keeping with His attributes of holiness, justice, goodness, mercy, and faithfulness. Man's emotions derive from the fact that he is made in the image and likeness of God even though his emotions through sin have become less than perfect. Of a special force is the fact that God has loved us from eternity past and will love us throughout eternity future.[93]

As we observe the sensibility of Holiness in God, we can observe it as an active attribute that incites all He does. Accordingly, God is righteous in all His ways and though infinitely holy, He maintains a relationship to fallen creatures. His holiness is not what is sustained by effort or preserved by segregation from other beings. The holiness of God is intrinsic, uncreated, and untarnishable. It is observable in every divine attitude and action. Holiness not only includes His devotion to what is good but also is the very basis and force of His hatred of evil. Like other attributes the holiness of God is sustained by many Scriptures.[94]

Justice is another of God's sensibilities. Justice is a legal term, which refers to the essential character of God's government which is maintained at the point of highest excellence. God is absolutely right in His authority over His creatures. If man rebels against God, he is questioning the Creator's right and authority. God has the absolute right to dispose of all His works as it may please Him. His actions are always in keeping with His infinite wisdom and holiness.

God is also described in Scripture as "spirit" (John 4:24), 'light" (1 John 1:5) and "love" (4:8).[95] These three comprehensive descriptions refer to the entire nature of God. God is revealed as a God of infinite love, and this is His primary attitude toward all His creation. Accordingly the Bible clearly indicates that God loves Israel and He loves Christians and all those who put their trust in Him. Long before Creation, infinite love existed between the Persons of the Godhead, and God may be conceived as loving Himself supremely. This divine love is not selfish or misguided but is in keeping with all the perfections of God Himself.

God is knowable; Leith Anderson sums this up in a very few words in his book: Becoming Friends with God.

"God is great; God is good; God is holy; God is love; and God is knowable. You can know Him. Really know Him through faith in Jesus Christ".[96]

The good of God is an attribute that is related to His Holiness. God's infinite goodness is an aspect of perfection in His being that characterizes His nature and is the source of all in the universe that is good. Other terms are used to describe God's goodness (1) benevolence, which is goodness in its generic sense as embracing all creatures and securing their welfare; (2) complacency, which is that in God which approves all His own perfections as well as all that conforms to Himself; (3) mercy, which is God's goodness exercised on behalf of the needs of His creatures; and (4) grace, which is God's free action on behalf of those who are meritless, which freedom to act has been secured through the death of Christ.

The truth of God is manifested because all that He does confirms that He is true and that His faithfulness supports every promise and executes every threat or warning He has made. Because God is absolute in truth, what He reveals can be accepted as true in contrast to the lack of truthfulness in men (Rom. 3:4).[97] The Bible is the supreme setting forth of God's truth; it is the Word of God in all its parts. A vast array of truth, themes, and subjects that go beyond human knowledge support the concept of the absolute truthfulness of God.[98] As a truthful God, He is faithful to all His promises. All fulfilled prophecy tends to confirm the absolute truthfulness of God.

Will is another essential element in a personality. By His will God decides to put into effect all He has designed. Because He is omnipotent He is able to do all He wills to do, but His actions are always in keeping with His character. The will of God is free, meaning He can do as He pleases at all times, but His free will is always exercised in keeping with the wisdom and purpose of Himself as God. In theology distinction is sometimes made between the decretive will of God and the perceptive will of God.

The attribute of omnipotence represents the infinite power of God to realize all that He wills to do. This omnipotence is seen in the Creation of the world and His directing of human history. By contrast man is not free to accomplish all he wills to do. God had the ability to bring the universe into existence out of nothing and He is able to do whatever He wills. What He wills is always in keeping with His attributes.

Infinity is a "negative" attribute of God in the sense that God is infinite and therefore not finite. This quality relates to all attributes in that they are all infinite in degree and without termination. God transcends all limitations in time or space. In His knowledge He knows all things perfectly. In His power He is able to bring things to pass according to His will. In every moral quality He is complete to infinity.

Eternity, meaning (without beginning or end),[99] is the relation that God sustains to duration. God being the Author of time is in no way conditioned by it. He exists through all times past to all times future.

The immutability of God is the state or quality that He is not subject to change. In God there is no increase or decrease, no variation in His being, and what God is continues forever. This is stated in Psalm 102:24-27, in Isaiah 46:9-10, and in James 1:17.[100] The changelessness of the character of God means that there is no change in His moral principles. Though there are differences in dispensations and progression in divine revelation, through them all God remains unchanged in His Person.

The attributes of God, the personal ones and the constitutional ones, form an interwoven and interdependence communion of facts and forces, which harmonize in the person of God. Any omission of any of these qualities or undue emphasis on one at the expense of the other would distort what the Scriptures present as our mighty God.

All false conceptions of God arise from either omitting or falsely emphasizing one attribute at the expense of the other. Hence such deviations as polytheism, deism. pantheism, idealism, materialism, and evolution present a picture of God that is not in correspondence with Scriptures. Of all the attributes, love is the most pervasive and characterize all that God does. Those who accept the scriptural revelation can only bow in submission to our God who is perfect in all His being, acts, and ways.

DIVINE DECREES

The doctrine of divine decree assigns to God the position of being the first cause of all that exists. The Westminster Shorter Catechism states a decree is "His eternal purpose, according to the counsel of His will, whereby, for His own glory, He hath foreordained whatsoever comes to pass".[101]

Excluded from the decree of God are all things relating to His own existence, His attributes, His subsistence in three persons, His intimate relationships, or His responsibilities. All decree of God relates to His own acts that are not immanent and intrinsic and that are outside His own being. Though it is common to speak of the decrees of God, the one decree is divided into distinct decrees or acts of God. Because His plan is eternal there is no possibility that it will be altered by omission or additions. The fact of its eternal nature is stated in Acts 15:17-18, "These things …have been known for ages".[102] Certain qualities and descriptive terms can be used to define the decree of God. The decree of God is eternal through its execution is in time. All of the parts of the decree of God were in God's mind from eternity past even though they are fulfilled in history.

In addition to being eternal, the decree of God is wise, since it is a product of the infinite wisdom of God. Even His permission of evil will ultimately be a demonstration of His glory and will bring praise to Him Ps. 76:10.[103] The wisdom of God is expressed as infinite in Romans 11:33, "Oh, the depth of the riches of the wisdom and knowledge of God! How unreachable His judgments, and His paths beyond tracing out!"[104]

The divine decree is free. As stated in Isaiah 40:13-14, "who has understood the Spirit of the Lord, or instructed Him as His counselor? Whom did He consult to enlighten Him, and who taught Him the right way? Who was it that taught Him knowledge or showed Him the path of understanding?"[105] His determination of the decree was not influenced by any other because when the decree existed in eternity past, there was none in existence except God Himself. As a perfect God, He could not do otherwise than determine His decree in keeping with His Person. The freedom of God is conditioned only by His infinite attributes and He will not decree or do anything that is contrary to His nature.

The fact of sin is the major problem in the doctrine of God's decree. If sin had not entered the universe, there probably would have been no possibility of challenging the sovereignty of God. Within our limited comprehension as human beings it is perhaps difficult to see how God would sovereignty adopt a plan in which terrible acts of sin take place. Yet that is the universe in which we find ourselves and the universe to which Scripture addresses the truth of God's sovereignty.

Derek W.H. Thomas said it very well in his book; How the Gospel Brings Us All the Way Home: Published by; Reformation Trust, 2011.

"The assertion of Providence in Romans 8:28 is specific and directed only to Christians. God rules over everything and everyone believers and unbelievers – but his oversight is different in the case of believers. To them – and to them only God's providence works "for good." The unwritten logical implication is that providence confirms the blessing of some and the doom of others. For those "who love God," providence is directed to achieve "good." Who are "those who love God"? They are "those who are called according to (God's) purpose." The promise is given for those who are "called" by God into fellowship with Jesus Christ. Writing to the Corinthians, Paul addresses them as "the church of God that is in Corinth,… those sanctified in Christ Jesus, called to be saints" (1 Cor. 1:2).[106]

In examining the fact of sin, consideration must be given to the fact of God's grace toward the fallen and the sinful. No demonstration of grace is possible unless there are objects that need grace, objects that know the experience of sin. Sin must be brought into final judgment.

Dr. Greg Gilbert, senior pastor of Third Baptist Church in Louisville, KY in his 2010; What is the Gospel, September/October, brings out some very good points in his paper;

"Over and over the Bible makes this point. When God reveals Himself to Moses, He declares Himself to be compassionate and loving, but he also says, "Yet he does not leave the guilty unpunished." The Psalms declare that "Righteousness and justice are the foundation of His throne." What an amazing statement! If God is to continue being God he cannot simply set justice aside and sweep sin under the rug. He must deal with it – decisively and with exacting justice. When God finally judges, not one sin will receive more punishment than it deserves. And not one will receive less than it deserves, either.

We may not understand it fully now, but one day hell itself will declare God's glory. It will – even in its horror – testify together with the psalmist, 'Righteousness and justice are the foundation of His throne.'"[107]

In conclusion, it must be said that God's primary divine purpose was not to avoid the presence of sin. He could have prevented it if He had willed to do so. To achieve His purposes, which were holy, just, and good, God had to permit sin in order to demonstrate His glory – especially His righteousness, love, and grace.

THE NAMES OF DEITY

In the Bible individuals' names have meaning that go beyond the desires of the parents, or respect to "Uncle Jim" or "Aunt Tabatha", that usually were to convey some impression as to the intrinsic character of the one who bore the name. This is brought out especially when names are changed, as for example changing Abram to Abraham, Jacob to Israel and Solomon to Jedodiah.

In the beginning Adam gave names to all things that were created by God without necessarily intending a meaning behind each name. But the names of God are intended to reveal the nature of God. In studying the character of God the names by which God identifies Himself in the Scripture are an important avenue of divine revelation.

The occurrence of the names of Deity in the Old Testament – *Yahweh, Elohim,* and *Adonai.* (2) The three major compounds with Yahweh –*Yahweh Elohim, Adonai Yahweh,* and *Yahweh Sabaoth.* (3) Three compounds with El –*El Shaddai, El Eloyon,* and *El Olam.* (4) Three general classes of divine names – one proper and peculiar name, *Yahweh,* appellative such as *Almighty* and *God of hosts.*(5) The full title of Deity in the New Testament – *Father, Son,* and *Holy Spirit.* (6) The full title of the second Person – *the Lord Jesus Christ.*[108] (7) The trinitarian distinction as taught in theological terms – *the first Person, the second Person, and the third Person -* though these titles as such do not appear in Scripture.

Yahweh is the distinctive name of the God of Israel. Its original pronunciation has been lost due to the unwillingness of Jews to pronounce the name they considered too holy to be voiced.[109]

It is generally agreed that *Yahweh* means "I AM THAT I AM," according to Exodus 3:14-15.[110] The idea is that of self-existence or eternal existence. This seems to be the main idea of the term.

Elohim is the appellation most frequently used in the Old Testament for God and sometimes appears in abbreviated forms such as *El*, or *Eloah*. This common word for God is found in other literature as well as the Bible, and the name seems to have belonged to the whole Semitic world.

God is mentioned metaphorically in the Old Testament under various titles such as King, Law-giver, Judge, Rock, Fortress, Tower, Refuge, Deliverer, Shepherd, Husband, Husbandman, and Father.

In the New Testament what is intimated in the Old Testament is continued and given full revelation.

The final name for Deity is Father, Son, and Holy Spirit, sometimes made more explicit as God the Father, God the Son, and God the Holy Spirit. Titles of the first Person are largely combinations associated with the word "Father." Hence God is declared to be "God, the Father of our Lord Jesus Christ" Col. 1:13, "the Father of compassion" (2 Cor. 1:3, and is addressed as "Abba, Father' Romans 8:15), "Heavenly Father" (John 17:11), "righteous Father" (v. 25), "Father of the heavenly lights" (James 1:17), and "the glorious Father" Eph. 1:17.[111]

In all there are some 300 titles or designations in the Bible that refer to the second Person of the Trinity. His full and final name is Lord Jesus Christ. He is Lord because He is God, Jesus because of His humanity, and Christ because of His office as Prophet, Priest, and King and the Messiah of the Old Testament period. The usage of the various titles and names obviously has divine purpose and manifests divine wisdom in their selection.

Only a few names of the Holy Spirit are revealed and are very descriptive titles; the Spirit of God, the Spirit of Christ, and the Comforter. There are about 20 such designations in all.

For those who put their trust in God, it is clear that God exists not as a hypothesis but as the Object of divine revelation in Scripture as well as in nature. It is impossible to arrive at a rational understanding of the universe or what the Bible teaches without recognizing that it discloses the God who is both singular and plural and who has all the attributes properly belonging to Deity.

INTRODUCTION TO TRINITARIANISM

In orthodox Christianity it is generally agreed that God subsists as a Trinity of three Persons – the Father, the Son, and the Holy Spirit. Though the word "Trinity" does not appear in Scripture, the detailed revelation concerning the Father, Son, and Holy Spirit make clear that God is three Persons while at the same time remaining one God. The doctrine of the Trinity is the only way of explaining the person of Jesus Christ, His incarnation, and His work, as well as the person, nature, and work of the Holy Spirit.

The Bible reveals that each person of the Trinity has divine attributes as well as the properties of personality. On the other hand, in the Bible are disclosures equally plain and numerous that God is essentially one. To some extent it is possible to define these distinctions and what they imply, but the human mind must confess that it can only partially comprehend the infinity of God in all His attributes and revelations as Persons. The doctrines of Scripture though they are believable are not fully explainable. This is true of much that God does which is superhuman and beyond naturalistic expectation.

The Bible as the only trustworthy account of the nature of God clearly maintains the doctrine of the Trinity. If one accepts the inerrancy of the Bible and the supremacy of divine revelation over human reason, he must accept the doctrine of the Trinity as well.

There are partial illustrations of plurality in unity. In the human personality there is intellect, sensibility, and will, and yet the resulting person is one. It remains true however, that the doctrine of the Trinity is without parallel in human experience or observation, and apart from its divine revelation in the Bible, man would never be able to understand that God exists in three Persons.

The doctrine of the Trinity falls into four major divisions: (1) The fact of the Trinity; (2) God the Father, the first Person; (3) God the

Son, the second Person; and (4) God the Holy Spirit, the third Person. Though it is impossible to separate the Persons of the Trinity from their divine works, full attention should be given to the works of the Trinity as soteriology, ecclesiology, and eschatology are considered.

The doctrine of the Trinity may be summarized in the fact that there are three substances properly identified in God, though each possesses the same intelligence and will. It is not proper therefore to refer to God as being in "modes" of existence. Each of the Persons of the Trinity has a divine nature with all the attributes of God. Though the Trinity has three substances, they have but one and the same divine nature as one God.

The three Persons also have relationships that cannot be reversed in that the Son is properly the second Person in relation to the Father as the first Person, the Holy Spirit is the third Person in relation to the Father and Son. This numerical distinction, however, does not imply any inferiority what-so-ever. This relationship of the Son to the Father was called generation though not in the same sense as human generation.

These facts about the Trinity are an important part of orthodox Christianity, and any denial of the three Persons results in dishonor to the Trinity.

A denial of the doctrine of the Trinity inevitably raises questions about the absolute deity of Christ as the second Person and the Holy Spirit as the third Person of the Trinity. Denials of the doctrine of the Trinity must either adopt a modalistic point of view – that the Son and the Spirit are simply modes of existence of the Father – or they must affirm that the Son is a created Being. In either case serious questions are raised about how Jesus Christ could be the Savior, die on the cross for our sins, and rise from the grave. This could not be accomplished if He were only a mode of divine existence. If the Son be considered a created Being, following the Arian error of the fourth century, it is also a departure from Scripture. If Jesus Christ were a created Being, then He would not be suitable to die on the cross and pay an infinite price for the redemption of man.

Equally involved in the problem of the trinity is the deity of the Holy Spirit as One who exercises every power and function of God. Though generally there has been little tendency to identify the Holy Spirit as a created Being, Unitarians in their denial of the Trinity affirm that the Holy Spirit is only a mode of divine existence. This would require a fundamental change in the doctrine of divine grace and assistance since the Holy Spirit is said to have all the qualities of a person including intellect, sensibility, and will. The work of the Spirit as a whole is brought into question when Trinitarianism is denied.

In asserting that the Scriptures teach the divine ability subsisting in three Persons, Trinitarians are not begging the question. It is rather an affirmation that Unitarians deny biblical testimony which clearly support the concept of the Trinity. It is quite common for those who are Unitarian also to deny the inerrancy and accuracy of the Bible.

As the doctrine of the Trinity is a major doctrine of biblical orthodoxy, and carries with it the affirmation of many other important doctrines, especially in the area of salvation, I am giving it additional consideration.

In attempting to define the Trinity, two extremes should be avoided. On the one hand, the Bible does not teach polytheism, that is, that there are many gods; nor on the other hand does it teach tritheism, that is, that there are three gods. The Bible also denies Unitarianism, which teaches that God is one and exercises His interests and powers in various ways but not as three Persons. The Bible supports the concept of monotheism – that God is one- and yet it also affirms that God subsists in a plurality of three Persons. It is significant that the main supporters of orthodoxy since the early church have been Trinitarian in their interpretation of Scripture.

Though many definitions of the Trinity have been advanced by various theologians, orthodox theology on the one hand affirms that

God is one, and on the other hand that He exists in three eternal distinctions of subsistence – the Father, the Son, the Holy Spirit – with each Person of the Trinity possessing all of the attributes of God. Every definition of the Trinity must be tested by this definition.

It should also be observed that though the Father, Son and Holy Spirit are one God and have the same attributes Each also has properties which are incommunicable to the Others. The Father is always the first Person, the Son is always the second Person, and the Holy Spirit is always the third Person. It must be also be affirmed that each Person of the Trinity is essential to God, and the other Persons of the Trinity are an incomplete definition of what God is. At the same time, each with the other is God.

The Nicene Creed states the matter as it has been held by orthodox Christians since early centuries:

"I believe in one GOD THE FATHER Almighty; Maker of heaven and earth, and of all things visible and invisible.

And in one Lord JESUS CHRIST, the only-begotten Son of God, begotten of the Father before all worlds (God of God), Light of Light, very God of very God, begotten, not made, being of one substance [essence] with the Father; by whom all things were made; who, for us men and for our salvation, came down from heaven, and was incarnate by the Holy Ghost of the Virgin Mary, and was made man; and was crucified also for us under Pontius Pilate; He suffered and was buried; and the third day He rose again, according to the Scriptures; and ascended into heaven, and sitteth on the right hand of the Father; and He shall come again, with glory, to judge both the quick and the dead; whose kingdom shall have no end.

And [I believe] in the Holy Ghost, the Lord and Giver of Life; and proceedeth from the Father [and the Son]; who with the Father and Son together is worshiped and glorified; who spake by the Prophets. And [I believe] in one Holy Catholic and Apostolic Church. I acknowledge one Baptism for the remission of sins; and I look for the resurrection of the dead, and the life of the world to come. Amen".[112] From the Anglican Book of Common Prayer.

W.L. Alexander has summarized the essential differences between the Persons of the Trinity as they exist in properties peculiar to each: "That as respects the distinction in the one Godhead it is real and eternal, and is marked by certain properties peculiar to each Person and not communicable. These properties are either *external* or *internal*; the latter relating to the modes of subsistence in the divine essence, the former to the mode of revelation in the world. The *Notae internae* are personal *acts* and *notions*; the former being (1) That the Father generates the Son, etc., and breathes the Spirit; (2) That the Son is begotten of the Father, and with the Father breathes the Spirit; (3) that the Spirit proceedeth from the Father and the Son. The Personal *notions* are (1) Unbegottenness and paternity as peculiar to the Father; (2) Spiration as belonging to the Father and Son; (3) Filiation as peculiar to the Son; (4) Procession *(sptratio passiva)* as peculiar to the Spirit. The *external* notes are (1) The works in the economy of redemption peculiar to each; the Father sends the Son to redeem and the Spirit to sanctify; the Son redeems mankind and sends the Spirit; the Spirit is sent into the minds of men and renders them partakers of Christ's salvation. (2) The attributive or appropriative works, *i.e.*, those which, though common to the three Persons, are in Scripture usually ascribed to One of Them, as universal Creation, conservation, and gubernation to the Father through the Son; the Creation of the world, raising of the dead, and the conduct of the last judgment to the Son; the inspiration of the prophets, etc., to the Spirit (*System of Biblical Theology*. Edinburgh: T. & T. Clark, 1888, 1:104).[113]

Though the doctrine of the Trinity is one that boggles even the most careful theologian, its general truths as revealed in the Word of God are essential to a proper base for theology as a whole.

In approaching the theme of the Trinity as theological we must be prepared to confront the deep mysteries we find in the Scriptures that are not fully explainable to the finite mind. The fact that the doctrine is shrouded with mystery tends to restrict the theological inquiry to those who by spiritual illumination believe the testimony of God relative to things unknowable with the same assurance as one would the things that are clear. A simple confidence in the Word of God and what it affirms even if it does not conform to patterns of thought that are common in human thinking is essential to true Christian faith as it relates to the doctrine of the Trinity.

PROOF OF THE
TRINITARIAN DOCTRINE

Attempts to illustrate the Trinitarian doctrine only lead to frustration as there is no counterpart in human life or nature to the doctrine of the Trinity. The triune existence of God is more than the exercise of three primary functions such as power, intellect, and will or correspondence to three divisions of human being into a body, soul, and spirit. Likewise, suggestions coming from observations of motion, light, and heat as related to the sun or the three tones blending in one single chord also fall far short. A single ray of light may be decomposed by a prism into three primary colors, red, yellow, and blue, but they remain irrelevant as far as explaining the doctrine of the Trinity. As a result, one must rely primarily on revelation rather than reason though the use of reason in forming inductions from the facts of divine revelation is also proper.

In turning to reason a theologian must assume that there can be no real conflict between reason properly exercised and divine revelation. Reason does contribute a series of propositions in support of the doctrine of the Trinity.

Since God exists eternally, His attributes must also exist eternally and are not acquired. Attributes such as all-sufficiency, immutability, omnipresence, omniscience, omnipotence, goodness, love, and holiness are attributes of God now and must always have been in the past.

The thought that God has always been creating fails because it is based on the fallacy that God's activity is confined to the creation of material things. Creation according to Scripture had its beginning and is not eternal. In affirming eternal attributes it should be understood that there has never been a time when God was not completely omniscient or a time when God could not exercise omnipotence. God likewise has been eternally holy, just, and good even if there were no activity at the time relative to these attributes. An activity though the attributes of God which lead to that activity have always been a part of God's being.

Attributes such as power, love, and a disposition for communion necessitate both agent and object. This exercise relates to the activity between the Persons of the Godhead in which there was communion, love, and fellowship from eternity past. Reason indicates that if God did not exist in three Persons, there would have been no way by which God could have exercised some of these attributes before the Creation of the universe. This leads to the conclusion that God is not dependent on creation as an object for the exercise of His qualities or attributes as He depends on nothing beyond Himself.

God has existed from eternity past He has always been sufficient within Himself without creating any external object. Hence, there must have been perfect harmony and satisfying fellowship within the Persons of the Trinity.

Since the divine nature includes plurality, the Godhead must be a plurality of Persons. Such a plurality could not be predicated of the divine Essence, as is one God.

As the Persons of the Trinity are equally God, they are therefore equal though they may differ in their relationships to each other. All Persons of the Trinity must be equal in power, glory, wisdom, benevolence, dignity, and disposition to communion. Such attributes must have been eternally active in each Person. It is impossible for a finite mind to comprehend the intimate and enduring affection that infinite love has generated within the Godhead. Each was loving and each received love in return. Each with infinite understanding appreciated the perfection of the Others. The holy will of the One is in absolute agreement with the holy will of the Others. While on earth, Jesus Christ always did the will of God (John 8:29).[114]

Though the limits of reason can be observed, there is no rational basis for denying the doctrine of the Trinity. On the other hand there are rational basis for affirming it. Though the doctrine of the Trinity rests for the most part on divine revelation, reason to some extent can support divine revelation and can justify it as the intellectually justifiable conclusion.

The fact that the Father loves the Son is affirmed in John 17:24.[115] Love as it existed in God describes the relationship between the Persons of the Trinity in eternity past before Creation had been brought into being. Having been loved by the Father in eternity past, Christ is loved by the Father in time.

The exercise of mutual glory is also an eternal exercise of God. In John 17:5 Christ stated, "And now Father, glorify Me in Your presence with the glory I had with You before the world began".[116] The Son of God who shared the glory that belongs to Deity in eternity past, having hid this glory while on earth, was then going to return to the manifestation of the glory that is proper for Deity in heaven. The glory of Christ in eternity past will also be revealed in eternity future as stated in Revelation 21:23.[117]

A plurality in Persons of the Godhead provides for a mutual communion in knowledge between the agent and the object. The Father is stated to have known the Son (John 10:15), and the Son is said to know the Father (Matt. 11:27). In like manner the Holy Spirit is said to have knowledge on an infinite scale (Romans 8:27; 1 Cor. 2:10).[118]

There never was, nor could ever be anything except mutual communion which would be all-satisfying to both agent and object between the Persons of the Godhead. Hence in Scripture Christ is said to be in the Father, and the Father is said to be in Christ John 14:11.[119]

To the extent finite reason can be used it affirms what is revealed by the Word of God – that a Triune God exists from all eternity and that the attributes of God were active in the reciprocative agent and object as indicated in mutual love, glory, knowledge, and communion from eternity past.

In summary, the New Testament provides overwhelming proof for the Trinity in almost every line of doctrinal investigation, and anyone who accepts the Bible as the inerrant Word of God will find that Trinitarianism is intrinsic in biblical revelation.

GOD THE FATHER

The concept of God the Father held by orthodox Christianity is quite different from the monotheism of Unitarianism, Judaism, and Mohammedanism. The point is that a denial of the deity of Jesus Christ and the Holy Spirit necessitates a denial of the Word of God in its revelation concerning the second and third Persons. To say that a study of God the Father is similar to the concept of God as held by those who deny the Trinity is correct.

The very designation "Father" implies a Son, and the designation "first Person" implies a second Person as well as a third Person. A concept of God which is basically Unitarian is therefore faulty and insufficient to account for divine revelation. As indicated in Ephesians 3:14-15,[120] God as Father established a relationship between father and son as it occurs in the human race. By the term "Father" a number of major relationships are indicated.

The thought of fatherhood as an act of creation is also embodied in Malachi 2:10, "Have we not all one Father? Did not one God create us"?[121] God is the Father of all creation in the sense that He gave creation physical life and substance. Paul refers to this same concept in his message on Mars Hill when he said, "Therefore since we are God's offspring, we should not think that the divine Being is like gold or silver or stone" (Acts 17:29).[122] Paul again stated in 1 Corinthians 8:6, "Yet for us there is but one God, the Father, from whom all things came and for whom we live."[123]

In the Old Testament, God had an intimate relationship to Israel, which was likened to a relationship between a father and son. God instructed Moses, "this is what the Lord says: Israel is my firstborn son, and I told you, 'Let my son go, so he may worship Me.' But you refused to let him go; so I will kill your firstborn son" (Ex. 4:22-23).[124]

Though God claimed a fatherhood relationship over Israel, this does not support the concept that all Israelites were regenerated or redeemed in the sense of eternal salvation. It was rather fatherhood by close relationship. The same thought was indicated in God's relationship to Solomon. God had said to David, "I will be his Father, and he will be My son" (2 Sam. 7:14).[125] The Psalmist David also wrote concerning God, "As a father has compassion on his children, so the Lord has compassion on those who fear Him." (Psalm 103:13).[126] Fatherhood by intimate relationship is a step beyond Fatherhood as Creator but falls short of sharing eternal life as the Father does in the case of those who are born again.

The title "the God and Father of the Lord Jesus" (2 Cor. 11:31)[127] is the full title of the first Person of the Trinity, incorporating as it does the title of the second Person as well. It is also true that God the Father is the Father of all who believe, but this relationship begins in time whereas His relationship to the Son has been from all eternity.

In human relationships a son is generated in time later than the father, but the divine relationship is an eternal one because in the nature of the Godhead each Person of the Trinity must eternally be what He is. On the cross Christ referred to God as "My God": "My God, My God, why have You forsaken Me?" (Matt. 27:4).[128] And after His resurrection Christ said to Mary Magdalene, "I am returning to my Father and your Father, to My God and your God" (John 20:17).[129] Christ was speaking from His humanity, but this was no contradiction of His relationship to the Father as God from eternity past as the eternal Son.

In a distinctive sense God is the Father of those who believe and who have received eternal life by being born again. This is beyond all other distinctions such as the Father as Creator, the Father by intimate relationship, or the Father in relation to Jesus Christ. This describes an everlasting relationship beginning at new birth which is true for each Christian. The fact that God is the Father of those who believe is brought out in many familiar passages such as John 3:16;

20:17; and 1 Peter 1:23.[130] As stated by Peter, "For you have been born again, not of perishable seed, but of imperishable, through the living and enduring Word of God". This new relationship assures to those who have been born again that they will spend eternity in the presence of God justified, forgiven, and transformed. By contrast all other men, being unregenerate, are completely lost. The Scriptures make clear that the difference between a believer and a nonbeliever is the element of faith or confidence in God to do what He has promised to do for those who put their trust in Him. Salvation is "by grace" and "through faith," "the gift of God" rather than by works (Eph. 2:8-9).[131] The sonship of a believer in Christ is an exalted position whereby he becomes an heir of God and a joint heir with Christ Himself. The concept of God as Father to those who put their trust in Him is one of enduring comfort and eternal promise.

GOD THE SON:
HIS PREEXISTENCE

In the study of Jesus Christ as the Son of God, one is impressed at the outset by the Limitations of the finite mind to express in proper words the glories and excellencies of His person and work. One can share the thoughts expressed by that great hymn writer, Charles Wesley in his famous hymn:

> O for a thousand tongues to sing
> My great Redeemer's praise,
> The glories of my God and King,
> The triumphs of His grace.

How can words describe the person of Christ from eternity past, the glories of His work in Creation, His revelation and ministry in the Old Testament, the wonders of His incarnation and life on earth, the inexhaustible depths of the truth relating to His death and resurrection, and the eternal glory which is His in heaven? Impossible as it is to do justice to the extensive revelation concerning Jesus Christ, it is nevertheless profitable to allow all who study it to make clear the facts revealed in Scripture concerning the second Person of the Trinity. This must necessarily begin with a study of Christ in His preincarnate state and the eternity of His existence from eternity to eternity.

In beginning the study of Jesus Christ as the Son of God, the essential fact that the second Person is intrinsically equal in every respect to the other Persons of the Godhead must be kept constantly in mind. He is the eternal God though there was added to His Person the full humanity involved in the Incarnation.

Though theology proper is normally limited to the study of the person of Christ in contrast to His works; the birth of Christ, His life on earth, His death on the cross, and His resurrection as well as His present ministry in heaven and His second coming and reign on earth all contribute to the knowledge of His person. Though not at all attempting to present a complete Christology, we do need to consider (1) His preexistence, (2) His deity, (3) His incarnation, (4) His humanity and life on earth, (5) the kenosis, (6) the hypostatic union, (7) His person as revealed in His second coming and future reign on earth. An obvious consideration preliminary to studying the facts of Jesus Christ, the Son of God, is the scriptural revelation of His eternal preexistence.

Though preexistence in its strict definition means only that Christ existed before He was born, in theology it is usually referring to and is considered to be synonymous with His eternity. An exception to this was the Arian heresy which taught that Christ was the first of the created beings.[132] This was refuted in the early church and is not a factor in theology today. If one asserts that Christ is preexistent, it automatically carries with it that He existed from eternity past.

The evidence for this is both direct and indirect. There are many references to Christ that imply His preexistence. He said of Himself that He was sent into the world and wasn't of the world (John 17:18) and was from above (8:23); and "came from heaven" (3:13). It is recorded that He became flesh (1:14); that He shared humanity (Heb. 2:14); that He became a man (Phil. 2:18). Many other Scriptures imply His preexistence (John 1:15. 18, 30, 3:16-17, 31, 33, 42, 50-51; 7:29; 8:23, 42; 9:39.[133]

Even more direct biblical assertions can be found that state the fact of His preexistence. In John 1:1-4 and 14,[134] He asserted that He was both in the beginning and was with God and was God, that He was God, that He was the Creator, that in Him was life, that He became flesh, and that He came from the Father. These qualities could not be stated of any other than the second Person of the Trinity, and this passage states both His deity and the fact that He is distinguished from God the Father.

Seven times in John, He affirms that He came from heaven (John 6:33, 38, 41, 50-51, 58, 62).[135] He stated that He came "from above" and "is above all" (John 3: 13, 31). In references to His preexistence in John 6, Jesus stated very clearly, "What if you see the Son of man ascend to where He was before!" (6:62).[137]

Another assertion of Christ's preexistence is found in His dealing with the Jews who wanted to stone Him. Christ had said "Your father Abraham rejoiced at the thought of seeing My day; he saw it and was glad" (John 8:56).[138] Then Jesus said even more abruptly, "Before Abraham was born I am!" The Jews rightly understood this to be a claim to eternity and a claim to be God.

In His Priestly Prayer in John 17:5 Christ said, "And now, Father, glorify Me in Your presence with the glory I had with You before the world began."[139] The thought of His preexistence is also revealed in the Pauline Epistles. Christ, "being in very nature God, did not consider equality with God something to be grasped, but made Himself nothing, taking on the very nature of a servant" (Phil. 2:6-7).[140] In this personage Christ is revealed as being God before He became man. The whole passage of Philippians 2:5-11 implies the preexistence of Christ. In these many passages, both direct and indirect revelation of Christ's preexistence leave no room for doubt that this is the teaching of the Word of God.

In the Old Testament, the Angel of *Yahweh* was also clearly seen to be the second Person of the Trinity. The identification of the Angel of *Yahweh* as God is a declaration of His deity. When He is distinguished from God the Father, it is evident that He is one of the Persons of the Godhead. Inasmuch as the second Person is the One who is the visible representation of God in the New Testament, it seems clear that He is not to be identified with the Holy Spirit.

This is confirmed by the fact that the Angel of *Yahweh* in the Old Testament did not appear after the incarnation of Christ. The Angel of *Yahweh* was sent by God, which is similar to the fact that Christ was sent by the Father. Taking all of the evidence together, it is clear that the Angel of *Yahweh* is in fact the second Person of the Trinity and therefore a proof of the preexistence of Christ. Other theophanies or appearances of God in the Old Testament are probably also references to Christ. Among these instances could be several cases where He appeared as a man on earth (Gen. 18:1-33; 32:24-32; ex. 24:9-11.[141] The cloud of the Lord and the cloudy pillar of the Book of Exodus is a similar form of appearance of Christ in the Old Testament (Ex. 33:9-23).[142] Any earthly appearance of God in bodily form therefore should be identified with Christ (Josh. 5:13-15; Ezek. 1:1-28; Dan. 10:1-21).[143] All of these evidences tend to confirm and support the doctrine of the deity of Christ and His preexistence.

GOD THE SON:
HIS NAMES

The names of Christ in Scripture are an important medium of divine revelation concerning His person and His work. Major names include that of Lord or *Yahweh*, *Elohim* or God, and Son of man, and His full title Lord Jesus Christ. Many other designations of Christ can be cited which are not formal names.

As Christ is commonly called *Yahweh* in the Old Testament, it is evident that He is God in the full sense of deity of the Father and the Holy Spirit. This title was given only to the God of Israel and was applicable to each of the Persons of the Trinity (Ps. 83:18; Isa. 42:28).[144] The name *Yahweh* was specifically assigned to Christ in Zech. 12:10, "And I will pour out on the house of David and the inhabitants of Jerusalem a spirit of grace and supplication. They will look on Me, the One they have pierced, and they will mourn for Him as one mourns for an only child, and grieve bitterly for Him as one grieves for a firstborn son."

In the Old Testament the most common name for God is *Elohim*. Though occasionally used for beings other than God, its primary reference is to God, and the use of the name affirms Deity. In the New Testament the corresponding term is *Theos*. Both of these names for God are used for the Trinity and also for Jesus Christ as the second Person, thereby affirming His complete deity. Isaiah for instance anticipated the mission of John the Baptist when he wrote, "A voice of one calling; 'In the desert prepare the way for the LORD; make straight in the wilderness a highway for our God'" (Is. 40:3).[145] Matthew states that this applies to the ministry of John the Baptist in preparing the way for Christ (Matt. 3:1-5).[146] In referring to "our God"[147] Isaiah was indicating that Jesus Christ was the God of the

Old Testament as well as the New, and this would support His eternal deity.

In the Gospels Christ referred to Himself as "Son of man" about 80 times. By this common designation He was pointing out that He fulfilled the Old Testament anticipations of a coming Man, born of a woman, who would be the Jewish Messiah and the Savior and God of those who trust Him (Matt. 11:19; Luke 19:10). The term is used of His death and resurrection (Matt. 12:40; 20:18; 26:2) and likewise of His second coming (24:37-44; Luke 12:40).[148] Typical of Christ's references to Himself is His conversation with Nathaniel when He stated, "I tell you the truth, you shall see heaven open, and the angels of God ascending and descending on the Son of man" (John 1:51).[149] In commanding His disciples to go as witnesses to the "lost sheep of Israel" He affirmed, "You will not finish going through the cities of Israel before the Son of man comes".[150] In John 5:22-27 Christ asserted that He was given universal judgment of all men as the Son of man.

The full title of the second Person of the Trinity is Lord Jesus Christ. In the New Testament the word "Lord" (*Gr. Kyrios*) affirmed His deity and authority even though the same title was sometimes used of men. The name Jesus meaning Savior is His human name and refers to His humanity and His redeeming sacrifice on the cross. The title "Christ" (*Gr. Christos*) means the Anointed One and refers to Christ as the Messiah of the Old Testament and implies His office of Prophet, Priest, and King.[151] The title "Christ" appears often in Scripture in relation to the Father and affirms that Christ is equally God.[152]

GOD THE SON:
HIS DEITY

The evidence for the deity of Christ in Scripture is so complete in both the Old and New Testaments that one has to marvel that scholars would ever attempt to give a different answer. In affirming the deity of Christ, one is asserting that He is all that God is.

The *Westminster Confession of Faith* provides for us a comprehensive statement of what Deity means:

"There is but one only living and true God, who is infinite in being and perfection, a most pure Spirit, invisible, without body, parts, or passions, immutable, immense, eternal, incomprehensible, almighty, most wise, most holy, most free, most absolute, working all things according to the counsel of His own immutable and most righteous will, for His own glory; most loving, gracious, merciful, long suffering, abundant in goodness and truth, forgiving iniquity, transgression, and sin; the rewarder of them that diligently seek Him; and withal most just and terrible in His judgments, hating all sin, and who will by no means clear the guilty. God hath all life, glory, goodness, blessedness, in and of Himself; and is alone in and unto Himself all-sufficient, not standing in need of any creature which He hath made, nor deriving any glory from them, but only manifesting His own glory in, by, unto, and upon them: He is the alone fountain of all being, of whom, through whom, and to whom, are all things; and hath most sovereign dominion over them, to do by them, for them, and upon them, whatsoever Himself pleaseth. In His sight all things are open and manifest; His knowledge is infinite, infallible, and independent upon the creature, so as nothing is to Him contingent or uncertain. He is most holy in all His counsels, in all His works, and in all His commands. To Him is due from angels and men, and every other creature, whatsoever worship, service, or obedience He is pleased to require of them".[153]

No more comprehensive declaration of the nature of God could probably be framed than this statement and yet all that is affirmed of God can also be affirmed of Christ. Questions about His deity arose from the fact that He also became man in the Incarnation. This introduced the complication of joining infinity with finity, and theologians have wrestled with this problem through the centuries in attempting to define the exact nature of the relation of Deity to humanity. It should be obvious to any student of Scripture that any questioning of the deity of Christ or any lessening of His divine qualities is destructive to the Christian faith and a contradiction of Scripture. Many lines of evidence support that Jesus Christ is all that God is. Every attribute which can be assigned to Deity is also declared to be true of Christ. The attributes include all of the common attributes of God.

Various prerogatives that belong to Deity are assigned to Christ. He is declared to be the Creator of all things and the Preserver of them. He has authority over His creation. He forgives sins, He will raise the dead, and He will judge the world. True worship is offered to Him and is received by Him. He is honored as Deity by the inspired Scriptures as well as by those who put their trust in Him.

Three major passages support this declaration. The Apostle John affirms, "Through Him all things were made; without Him nothing was made that has been made" (John 1:3). In verse 10 John added that "the world was made through Him." Colossians 1:16 says, "For by Him all things were created; things in heaven and on earth, visible and invisible, whether thrones or powers or rulers or authorities; all were created by Him." Verse 17 affirms that He existed before all created matter and that the world is held together by the power of Christ: "He is before all things, and in Him all things hold together." Hebrews 1:10-11, quoting Psalm 102:25, states, "In the beginning You laid the foundations of the earth, and the heavens are the work of

Your hands. They will perish, but You remain."[154]

All objections to the deity of Christ inevitably involve a conflict with the Bible as the inerrant Word of God. The witness of the Scripture is entirely clear that Christ is presented as Deity with all that that term implies.

B.B. Warfield answers the objection of Oskar Schmiedel, 1887-1959, Higher criticism of the deity of Christ.

"Proceeding after this fashion Schmiedel fixes primarily on five passages which seem to him to meet the conditions laid down; that is to say, they make statements which are in conflict with the reverence for Jesus that pervades the Gospels and therefore could not have been invented by the authors of the Gospels, but must have come to them from earlier fixed tradition; and they are preserved in their crude contradiction with the standpoint of the evangelists, accordingly, only by one or two of them, while the others, or other, of them, if they report them at all, modify them into harmony with their standpoint of reverence. These five passages are: Mark 10:17. "Why callest Me good? None is good save God only"; Matt. 12:3 "blasphemy against the Son of Man can be forgiven"; Mark 3:21, "His relations held Him to be beside Himself"; Mark 13:32, "Of that day and of that hour knoweth no man, not even the angels in heaven, neither the Son but the Father" Mark 15:34; Matt. 27:46, "My God, My God, why hast Thou forsaken Me?".[155] To these he adds four more which have reference to Jesus' power to work miracles, Mark 8:2, "Jesus declines to work a sign" Mark :5, " Jesus was able to do no mighty works in Nazareth" Mark 8:14-21, "The leaven of the Pharisees and of Harod" refers not to bread but to teaching. Matt. 11:5; Luke 7:22. (the signs of the Messiah are only figuratively miraculous). These nine passages he calls "the foundation-pillars for a truly scientific life of Jesus." In his view, they prove on the one hand, that "He (Jesus) really did exist, and that the Gospels contain a least some trustworthy facts concerning Him," – a matter which, he seems to suggest, would be subject to legitimate doubt in the absence of such passages; and, on the other hand, that "in the person of Jesus we have to do with a completely human being. And that the divine is to be sought in Him only in the form in which it is capable of being found in a man." From them as a basis, he proposes to work out, admitting nothing to be credible which is not accordant with the nonmiraculous, purely human, Jesus which these passages imply".[156]

It is obvious in reading criticisms of the deity of Christ that they proceed from presuppositions, not from facts as stated in Scripture. The Bible presents a supernatural world with a supernatural God, and one who rejects these concepts necessarily rejects the Bible itself.

GOD THE SON:
HIS INCARNATION

The incarnation of Jesus Christ is one of seven major events in the history of the universe: (1) The creation of the angelic host (Col. 1:16); (2) the Creation of material things, including man (Gen. 1:1-31); (3) the Incarnation (John 1:14); (4) the death of Christ (19:30); (5) the resurrection of Christ (Matt. 28:5-); (6) the second advent of Christ (Rev. 19:11-16); and (7) the creation of the new heaven and the new earth (Isa. 5:17; Rev. 21:1).[157] These great events are not only major divine undertakings, but also the beginning of the divinely ordered programs for the world. Among these the Incarnation was one the greatest major events. In it the second Person partook of the human elements of body, soul, and spirit with the distinct purpose of remaining a partaker of all that is human for all eternity (Eph. 1:20-21; Phil. 29:9-11; Heb. 1:3.[158]

The Incarnation introduced the unique situation in which God and man became one without depriving either of their essential qualities. In understanding the Incarnation it is necessary to examine several issues: (1) The Old Testament anticipations, (2) Who become incarnate? (3) How did He become incarnate? (4) For what purpose did He become Incarnate?

Who became Incarnate? The Scriptures are abundantly clear in both the Old Testament prophecies and the New Testament fulfillment that Jesus Christ, the eternal Son of God became incarnate by being born of the virgin Mary. In a sense Christ occupies a unique role in the Christian faith in contrast to the role of leaders of various heathen religions. Few of them ever claimed deity, and their message was that they had discovered the way of salvation according to their point of view. In Christianity Christ occupies the central place not only as the

Savior but also as the Son of God. In the Incarnation, Jesus Christ was perfect God and became perfect man being all that God is in His deity and all that man is apart from sin. The Incarnation became a major part of God's plan and purpose for the world whereby He provided salvation through Christ the God-Man.

Though the virgin birth of Christ has been challenged by unbelievers, there is no other satisfactory explanation of how Christ could be both the eternal God and man in one Person. The fact of His Incarnation is stated in John 1:1-2, 14.[159] In these verses it is clear that the One who became incarnate was the eternal God and that He partook of human flesh and nature.

Philippians 2:6-8,[160] another major passage on the Incarnation, speaks of how Christ, though existing from eternity past as God, was willing to make Himself a humble servant and became obedient even to death on the cross. The Philippians passage makes it plain that Christ was originally in the form of God, that He was equal with God, and that in the Incarnation He became like men. This important doctrine will be considered later under the subject of the *kenosis*.

In Colossians 1:13-17 the eternity of Christ and His work on the cross delivering us from sin is fully supported. First Timothy 3:16 indicates that God became flesh, lived among men, and then was received up into glory.[161]

The book of Hebrews abounds with Christological revelation. Christ is seen as the Creator in chapter 1, as the partaker of flesh and blood in chapter 2, and as our High Priest and sacrifice in chapters 2-10 He fulfills what was anticipated in type in the Old Testament sacrifices.[163] We will be looking more into the Old Testament prophecies later.

How did the Son become Incarnate? Though Scripture cannot explain what is supernatural, the result of Christ's incarnation is made clear. Christ was born into the human family and possessed His own identifiable body, soul, and spirit. He was not simply a man indwelt by God, but God who took on a human nature as a part of His person.

He was like other men except that He had no fallen nature. He was declared to be holy. In the announcement to Mary (Luke 1:35), the virgin Birth is the divine explanation of how Christ became incarnate. Because Christ had a human body, which was ultimately resurrected, Christianity can anticipate the same experience. In brief, Christ became incarnate by virtue of conception of the Holy Spirit and birth through His mother Mary.

The Incarnation is at the very center of God's purpose for the world. At least seven major reasons are given for the divine purpose in the Incarnation: (1) that He might manifest God to man, (2) that He might manifest man to God, (3) that He might be a merciful and faithful High Priest, (4) that He might destroy the works of the devil, (5) that He might be Head over a new creation, (6) that He might sit on David's throne, and (7) that He might be the kinsman-Redeemer.

The New Testament redemption followed the Old Testament types in that Christ redeemed by His blood and be delivered from the bondage of sin by the power of the Holy Spirit.

In the case of Christ as Kinsman-Redeemer, He had to be a kinsman, He had to be able to redeem, and He had to be willing to redeem. Christ on earth did everything to please His Father (John 8:29),[164] including going to the cross. Other facts relating to Christ including His humanity and life on earth, His deity, the hypostatic union, and *kenosis* shed further light on the Incarnation.

GOD THE SON: HIS HUMANITY AND LIFE ON EARTH

The early church had more difficulty asserting the humanity of Christ than the deity of Christ. Though it is true that the physical world weighted with the sin of man and under the divine curse, the humanity of Christ is distinct in that it is perfect and has the same moral quality that is in God Himself. By contrast many people in the modern church have more difficulty asserting the deity of Christ than His humanity. The tendency has been to reduce Christ's deity to a level where it is compatible with ordinary men.

The Scriptures declare that Christ possessed a human body (Hebrews 10:5), soul (Matthew 26:38), and spirit (Mark 2:8).[165] Theologians have discussed at length whether Christ had two wills – one human and one divine. As ultimately even in the person of Christ there had to be one deciding factor, is it best to consider that Christ had human desires and divine desires but that His ultimate determinative will brought these two together so that they were always in perfect harmony with the will of God.

Because the life of Christ on earth, His death, and His resurrection are intrinsic in the eternal purposes of God, it is clear that it was determined long before Creation that Christ would be "the Lamb that was slain from the Creation of the world" Rev. 13:8. Though Christ was slain in time when He was crucified on the cross, the fact of His death was recognized in the plan of God from eternity past.

Though the Old Testament fully anticipated that when Christ came He would be Immanuel (Isa. 9:6-7),[166] it also anticipated that He would be a human being who would suffer and die and who ultimately would reign on the throne of David as the promised King.

Both types and prophecy emphasize these facts. As has been

considered, types are an important vehicle for illustrating the truth, but one must turn to biblical prophecy for specific information about the coming Messiah as recorded in the Old Testament. In the Old Testament two types of messianic prophecy are found. First, there is general messianic prophecy, that is, prophecy expressed in language that only a Messiah could fulfill.[167]

The second is a personal messianic prophecy which can be identified by some specific term, as for instance "Immanuel" in Isaiah 7:14, or other titles that identify Him as God.

Apart from being a man, Christ could not have shed blood. Believers are redeemed by the blood of Christ (Acts 20:28). The blood of bulls and goats could cover sin (Hebrews 10:4-10) but not deal with sin in a complete way. Being man, He could die; and being God, He could raise Himself from the dead (John 2:19). Both His death and His resurrection are proof of His genuine humanity.[168]

His death and resurrection also fulfilled the many prophecies of the Old Testament predicting His death and resurrection. Both Psalm 22 and Isaiah 53 are major passages in the Old Testament anticipating the death of Christ.[169]   In regard to resurrection, Psalm 16:10 anticipated the fact that His body would not see corruption but would be resurrected. All the passages that speak of Christ's kingdom reign in the Millennium as well as His present session in heaven support the fact of His bodily resurrection.

As the disciples conferred with Christ, according to Acts 1, they saw Him go bodily from earth to heaven. Peter testified that after Christ went to heaven He was seated at the right hand of the Father (Acts 2:33; 5:31; 7:55-56; Romans 8:34). These passages make clear that Christ is now in heaven bodily, seated at the right hand of the Father, and fulfilling His role as the believers' High Priest (Hebrews 7:25). The fact of His ascension and His continued human body in heaven are further evidence of His humanity.[170]

According to the announcement of the angels at the ascension of

Christ (Acts 1:11), He will come again to reign. When He returns in His second coming, He will sit on the throne of His ancestor David (Luke 1:32; Isa 9:7). This throne will be a glorious throne from which He will judge the nations (Matt. 25:32). From these many evidences it can be seen that the humanity of Christ is beyond question and that it is an essential fact relating to the exercise of His offices of Prophet, Priest, and King as well as making it possible to die on the cross to be the Savior of the world.

GOD THE SON:
THE *KENOSIS*

The key to understanding the doctrine of the *Kenosis* is the expression "made Himself nothing" in Philippians 2:7.[171] The problem centers in the Greek verb kenoo,[172] which means, "to empty." From this concept some theologians have presented Christ as being completely human without some of the divine attributes, especially the relative attributes of omnipotence, omniscience, and omnipresence.

As devout scholars have studied this problem, they have concluded that Christ retained His omnipotence, His omniscience, and even His divine omnipresence while He was in a physical body on earth. Instead of emptying Himself or removing these central attributes of Deity, Christ willingly did not use His divine attributes to make His life on earth easier.

The problem of adopting a view that Christ gave up some attributes of God is that if this were true, then He was not actually God. This would cast reflection on His person as well as His work on the cross and His resurrection. Every attribute of God is essential to His deity, and God cannot cease to be what He has always been from eternity past. Though Christ had self-imposed human limitations, He could on occasion use His power to accomplish miracles, and this He commonly did in His life on earth. Three major areas of study emerge from the exegesis of this passage; namely, (1) "the form of God", or "in the very nature of God" (v.), (2) the condescension in which He "made Himself nothing" (v.7), and (3) "the form of a servant: or "taking the very nature of a servant" (v. 7).

To accomplish His purpose in the Incarnation, Christ had to veil His glory and use His attributes only for the good of others and not for Himself. In Philippians 2: 6 Christ was said to have the very nature of

God before His incarnation. On earth He took the form of a servant and performed humble tasks such as washing the disciples' feet (John 13). As a servant He was "Faithful and True," a title that will be given Him at the time of His second coming (Rev. 19:11). He continued to submit to the wickedness of men even to the extent of His crucifixion, and at the moment of death, He was able to say, "It is finished" (John 19:30).[173]

Christ empted Himself of self-interest. He did not attempt to hold on to His previous exalted estate, which was rightfully His. He condescended to become a lowly person like a servant. His glory was veiled, and He was despised and rejected by men. Even though He was incarnate when He died on the cross, "God was reconciling the world to Himself in Christ" (2 Cor. 5:19).[174]

In the history of the doctrine of Christology, Thomasius adopted the concept that Christ gave up His relative attributes. This is not supported by Scripture. Another view, held by such men as Gess, Godet, and Newton Clark, is that Christ became a purely human soul and that His eternal consciousness ceased. This is clearly refuted by the Gospels. The third theory held by Ebard is that Christ exchanged His divine mode of existence for a human mode of existence. This is also inadequate to explain the continued deity of Christ. The only concept of the *kenosis* that is true to the Scriptures is the view that Christ as the incarnate Logos possessed all the divine attributes though He operated with self-restricted use of them.[175] Though Christ's act of becoming incarnate is beyond human comprehension, as a careful student of Scripture one soon arrives at the truth that Christ never gave up His deity, but gave up the exercise of certain attributes which would conflict with His earthly purpose.

GOD THE SON:
THE HYPOSTATIC UNION

The term "hypostatic" is derived from the word *hypostasis*,[176] which refers to the union of the human and divine of Christ. The term is used only of Christ and of the two natures in a believer.[177] The fact that His human and divine natures, each complete in themselves, were united in one Person has raised a number of theological questions, which require definition. If Christ at the same time was all that God is and all that man is apart from sin, how do the attributes of both natures affect the person of Christ? The specific theme of the hypostatic union is approachable under two main divisions: (1) the structure of the doctrine and (2) the relationship of the theanthropic Person.

Four vital factors constitute the structure of the specific doctrines of the hypostatic union: (1) Christ's deity, (2) His humanity, (3) the complete preservation of each of these two natures without confusion or alteration of them and their unity, and (4) the unity of the theanthropic Person.

Christ's death has already been established in previous discussion and is evidenced not only in His preincarnate existence and His future glorious estate but in His life on earth when He demonstrated in one way or another all the attributes of God Though Christ in His deity is similar to the Father and the Spirit. In His human form He is distinguished from the other Members of the Trinity and by the Incarnation He took His place in the human family. Though the Trinitarian unity of the three Persons of the Godhead continued without interruption after the Incarnation, the addition of the humanity did bring in certain complicating factors.

Humanity is also and important part of the person of Christ, and its existence in the incarnate Christ has been demonstrated in previous discussions also. Though His deity is eternal, the humanity of Christ was gained at His conception.

The hypostatic union refers to the complete preservation of each of His two natures without confusion or alteration and their unity in one Person. The natures of the hypostatic union was such that it was not a matter of Deity possessing a human body or a human individual possessing God, but rather both natures existing undiminished and yet united in one Person. No parallel to this exists in any other situation in the universe. The importance of this doctrine can be seen in its support of the deity of Christ but also its support of what could be accomplished only by a man, namely, His earthly sufferings, death, and resurrection. The hypostatic union assures that both the deity and the humanity of Christ exist in one Person, not a correlation of two Persons.

Some of the attributes of both the human and the divine natures can be attributed to the whole Person. This was seen in His role as Redeemer, Prophet, Priest, and King. In each of these situations Christ had to be both human and divine.

The unity of the anthropic person of Christ is affirmed by the historic orthodox creeds. The view of the hypostatic union presented here follows the thinking of the early church fathers, which was crystallized in several centuries of discussion. The Chalcedonian Creed has been considered the norm of orthodox thinking since it was drafted in the fifth century. It reads:

"We, then, following the holy Fathers, all with one consent, teach men to confess one and the same Son, our Lord Jesus Christ, the same perfect Godhead and also perfect in manhood; truly God and truly man, of a reasonable (rational) soul and body; consubstantial with the Father according to the Godhead, and consubstantial with us to Manhood; in all things unto us, without sin; begotten before all ages of the Father according to the Godhead, and in these latter days, for us and for our salvation, born of the Virgin Mary, the Mother of God (the mother of Jesus, not the mother of God{my insert}), but only according to Manhood; one and the same Christ, Son, Lord, only begotten, to be acknowledged in two natures, *unconfusedly, unchangeably, indivisibly, inseparably*; the distinction of natures being by no means taken away by the union, but rather the property of each nature being preserved, divided into two persons, but one and the same Son, and only begotten, God the Word, the Lord Jesus Christ; as the prophets from the beginning (have declared) concerning Him, and the Lord Jesus Christ Himself has taught us, and the Creed of the holy fathers has handed down to us."[178] This is also stated in the Chalcedonian Creed and incorporated in the Westminster Confession of Faith and in other orthodox creeds.

A summary of Christian thought through the centuries can be found in the work by John Miley.[179]

In conclusion, the subject of the person of Christ in its nature, its relationship to other Persons of the Trinity, and its relationship to the human nature of Christ is a subject that extends far beyond human understanding. Much of the doctrine must be accepted by faith, but at the same time it is obvious that the situation could not be other than it is in order for God to accomplish what He intended to do through Christ. Because of the central nature of Jesus Christ in His Person and work in Christian theology, it is not too much to say that the central theological questions are, "Who is Jesus Christ, and how does His work in time and eternity relate to the Christian?" Even the Apostle Paul testified to the complexity of the doctrine of Christ when he wrote, "Beyond all question, the mystery of godliness is great: He appeared in a body, was vindicated by the Spirit, was seen by angels, was preached among the nations, was believed on in the world, was taken up in glory" (1 Tim. 3:16).[180]

GOD THE HOLY SPIRIT

Though the study of the doctrine of the Holy Spirit in theology proper is often limited to His person, some reference to His works is necessary in order to establish His person and relationship to the world and to the Christian.

The title "the Holy Spirit" is in itself an affirmation that He is God. This is brought out in the various titles which are given to Him and in the nature of His work as God. The threefold name of Deity indicates that the Holy Spirit is just as much God as the Son or the Father. This is illustrated in the command Jesus gave His disciples to baptize believers in all nations "in the name of the Father and of the Son and of the Holy Spirit" (Matt. 28:19).[181]

The scriptural titles given to the Holy Spirit also support the concept of His deity. Though His former name is "the Holy Spirit," all other descriptions of the Holy Spirit confirms the essential deity of the third Person. In relation to the Father, He is declared to be "the Spirit of the Lord" (Luke 4:18); "the Spirit of our God" (1 Cor. 6:11); "His Spirit" (Nom. 11:29); "the Spirit of the Lord" (Jud. 3:10); "Your Spirit" (Ps. 139:7); "the Spirit of the Sovereign LORD" (Isa. 61:1); "Spirit of your Father" (Matt. 10:20); "Spirit of the living God" (2 Cor. 3:3); "My Spirit" (Gen. 6:3); "Spirit of Him who raised Jesus from the dead" (Rom. 8:11); "Spirit of God" (v.9); "Spirit of Jesus Christ" (Phil. 1:19); "Spirit of Christ" (1 Peter 1:11); "Spirit of the Lord" (Acts 16:7); "Spirit of His Son" (Gal. 4:6); and" Spirit of the Lord" (Acts 5:9; 8:39).[182] The titles that relate the Holy Spirit to Christ could be interpreted as referring to the Spirit of the second Person, but it is probable that they refer to the Holy Spirit.

Other titles of the Holy Spirit relate divine attributes to Him: "one Spirit" (Eph. 4:4); "seven spirits" (Rev. 1:4; 3:1), which could refer to angels but more probably refers to the Holy Spirit in His perfections;

"the Lord, who is the Spirit" (2 Cor. 3:18); "eternal Spirit (Heb. 9:14); "Spirit of glory" (1 peter 4:14); "Spirit of life" (Rom. 8:2); "Spirit of holiness: (1:4). The formal title of the Holy Spirit was frequently used: "Holy Spirit" (Ps. 51:11; Matt. 1:20; Luke 11:13); "holy One" (1 John 2:20); "Spirit of wisdom" Eph. 1:17); "the Spirit of wisdom and of understanding" (Isa. 11:2); "the Spirit of truth" (John 14:17); "Spirit of grace" (Heb. 10:29); and "Spirit of sonship" (Rom. 8:15)[183] . The Holy Spirit is also called the "Comforter" in John 14:16, 26; 15:26; 16:7 (kjv). Another translation He is called "Counselor." The thought is that the Holy Spirit is always with believers to help them. Taken together the various names of the Holy Spirit gives evidence of an unqualified Deity, of His relationship to the other members of the Trinity, and the work He undertakes for believers.

The Scriptures ascribe every attribute of God to the Holy Spirit and affirms His whole personality in the same sense that God the Father or God the Son are Persons. It is therefore incorrect to think of the Holy Spirit as merely a mode of operation of God the Father or God the Son. The references to His works confirms the fact that He is absolute God.

In conclusion, we see that the many works of the Holy Spirit demonstrate His personality and His deity because none of these great undertakings could be accomplished by anything other than the power of God. The works of the Spirit combine with other evidences to demonstrate that the Holy Spirit is a Person and one of the three Persons of the Godhead.

THE HOLY SPIRIT IN
THE OLD TESTAMENT

Prophecy in its larger meaning includes both forthtelling and foretelling, thereby including the entire revelation from God.

As previously concluded, the Holy Spirit is the One who inspired the Bible, and the writers of both the Old and New Testaments were able to produce the Bible without error because of this ministry of the Holy Spirit. Even passages where the Father or the Son are quoted were written under the guidance of the Holy Spirit. Because of the work of the Holy Spirit directing the writers of Scripture, they could write the Word of God without eliminating their human intelligence, their individuality or literary style, or their personal feelings. The point is that the Scriptures were written with perfect accuracy, and the very words have the stamp of divine authority.

The Holy Spirit as the Subject of predictive prophecy has been generally neglected in standard theological works. This is due in part to the confusion that exists among various views of the Millennium. The Scriptures prophesy that when Christ returns to set up His kingdom on earth the Holy Spirit will be evident in ministry to believers as in the present age. In the Millennium believers will be indwelt by the Spirit (Ezek. 36:25-27).[184] The Holy Spirit will be omnipresent and will operate much as He did in the Old Testament.

In the Millennium believers will be regenerated. Renewal of believers by regeneration is true in all dispensations and accounts for the presence of believers in the Old Testament as well. In the Millennium when Christ will be reigning on earth, there will be a full display of the work of the ministry of the Holy Spirit (Isa. 32:15; 44:3; Ezek. 39:29; Joel 2:28-29).[185] The Spirit also will rest on Christ fully in the Millennium (Isa. 11:2).[186] The revelation of the future ministry of the Holy Spirit is an integral part of the prophetic program of God, which is revealed in the Scriptures.

THE PRESENT WORK OF THE HOLY SPIRIT IN THE WORLD

In the present age a new divine purpose is being fulfilled, namely, that of forming from both Jews and Gentiles, a new entity called the church. The church is formed as the body of Christ by the baptism of the Holy Spirit (1 Cor. 12:13).[187] Since the Day of Pentecost the deity of the Holy Spirit is indicated in His works of regeneration, indwelling, sealing, and baptism into the body of Christ. To these works, accomplished once and for all at the time of the new birth are added repeated experiences of being filled with the Spirit.

In the present age believers in Christ are exhorted to preach the Gospel to the whole world (2 Cor. 5:18-19)[188] in contrast to the emphasis in the Old Testament on the people of Israel. During the present age there is no progress as far as the prophecies of Israel in the Old Testament are concerned. The fact that in the 20th century, and until the present, Israel has once again occupied her ancient land is a sign of the imminence of the Rapture of the church and the end of the present age.

In Matthew 13, which covers the whole period from the first coming of Christ to His second coming, special revelation is given concerning the character of evil. The darnel seed portrays profession of Christ short of faith; the birds in the mustard tree represent the work of Satan; and the leaven in the meal, speaking of evil in the church, indicates that good and evil will appear in the church as a sphere of profession. The present age in a special sense is a contest between God and the devil and the believer and the devil. Satan is recognized as the "god of this age" (2 Cor. 4:4).[189]

Gentiles have a special blessing referred to in Romans 11:25 in the present period ending with the Rapture of the church, but this will change when God begins to deal with Jews and Gentiles once again as separate people.

In His role as the One sent by Christ into the world following the ascension of Christ to heaven, the Holy Spirit according to Christ's own prediction will bring conviction to the world and help the unsaved understand the Gospel. The Scriptures make clear that under normal conditions the world is blinded to the truth of God (2 Cor. 4:3-4).

In recognition of man's need, Christ sent the Holy Spirit to reveal the truth of the Gospel to the unsaved as recorded in John 1:7-11.[190] This enlightenment had to do with the fact that sin and unbelief blocked the work of salvation. The Holy Spirit will reveal the righteousness of God both as a requirement and as a gift of God to those who trust Him. Satan will be judged and those who do not believe in Christ will be judged with Satan. The Holy Spirit's work of conviction obviously proves His deity and His important ministry to the world in leading people to Christ.

THE HOLY SPIRIT IN RELATION TO CHRISTIANS

The great events recorded in the Gospels and the early chapters of the Book of Acts mark the tremendous changes that took place with the first advent of Christ. The important events which brought this about can be enumerated: (1) the introduction of a new and unforeseen age with specific revelation concerning its character; (2) the death of Christ with all the new realities and relationships which it secures; (3) the resurrection of Christ with its new creation headship; (4) the present session of Christ with its limitless provisions; (5) the coming of the Spirit at Pentecost with His limitless blessings for all those He indwells; (6) the inauguration of a new divine purpose in the calling out of heavenly people from both Jews and Gentiles into one body; and (7) the introduction of a new ethic or governing code adapted to a people who are perfected in Christ, clothed in divine righteousness, justified forever, and filled with the fullness of the Godhead.

Though it is apparent from Scripture that regeneration was experienced by the saints in all dispensations, in the present age it is given a prominence and clarity which it lacked in the Old Testament. The work of the Holy Spirit in regeneration gives eternal life to believers in Christ. Regeneration means being born again by the Spirit.

The necessity of regeneration is brought out in the words of Christ to Nicodemus in John 3:5, "I tell you the truth, unless a man is born of water and the Spirit, he cannot enter the kingdom of God."[191] It was not enough for a Jew to have a genuine relationship to Abraham through Jacob which was a matter of race. Nor was it sufficient to take part in the religious rites of Israel. Each individual, being dead in sin was/is in need of eternal life.

One of the marvelous facts that distinguishes the present age from the Old Testament is that every believer is indwelt by the Holy Spirit. This is clearly brought out by the words of Christ in John 7:38-39 where He predicted, "Whoever believes in Me, as the Scripture has said, streams of living water will flow from within him.' By this He meant the Spirit, whom those who believed in Him were later to receive, Up to that time the Spirit had not been given, since Jesus had not yet been glorified."[192]

The baptism of the Holy Spirit is a very important work of the Spirit that occurs at the time of salvation. The baptism of the Holy Spirit refers to the act of God in placing a believer in the body of Christ and in Christ Himself (1 Cor. 12:13). Since baptism of the Spirit is obviously a work which only God can do, it testifies to the deity of the Holy Spirit. The baptism of the Holy Spirit is sometimes represented in the Bible as something Christ did with the Holy Spirit serving as the Agent, and other times it is said to be a work of the Holy Spirit directly. The Holy Spirit's work as an Agent relates to passages dealing with the period when Christ was on earth.[194] Other passages make the Holy Spirit the immediate Actor and the One who forms the body of Christ .

The baptism of the Holy Spirit is distinguished from the filling of the Holy Spirit in that the baptism of the Spirit occurs once and for all and is true for all Christians (1 Cor. 12:13), whereas the filling of the Spirit can occur more than once as illustrated in the Book of Acts.

The work of the Holy Spirit in salvation, in which the church, and in the future work constitute proof of the deity of the Holy Spirit because they can be accomplished only by Christ Himself.

Once we become aware of the tremendous work prepared in Scripture by God the Holy Spirit in His plan of salvation, we are then prepared to face our response to what God has done. This involves the whole realm of the spiritual life. Though properly an aspect of ecclesiology, this is introduced here to demonstrate that this work of the Spirit truly demonstrates His deity.

The work of the Spirit in a believer at the time of his salvation introduces the infinite power of God that is available to Christians to enable them to overcome evil. This has both a negative aspect – overcoming evil – and a positive aspect – accomplishing what is good. The need for power to overcome sin is evident in every believer's spiritual experience.

On being saved, a believer is given a second nature, a sinless nature, even though the old nature remains to be contended with. An unsaved person has only one nature and that nature is sinful. Paul's experience before he was saved is entirely contrary to what he described in Romans 7:15-15.[195] There the two natures are seen in constant struggle. But at the end of the chapter Paul confessed that his only possibility of victory is through Jesus Christ. In verse 25 Paul affirmed that he could be delivered only through "The law of the saving work of the Lord Jesus". Then in 8:2 he declared, "The law of the Spirit of life set me free from the law of sin and death."[196] Victory over the sin nature begins with salvation and continues in the power of the Holy Spirit.

This great truth can be summarized in four statements: (1) Every Christian, still possessing the flesh, is called on to wage a ceaseless warfare against the old nature. (2) Every Christian is indwelt by the Spirit and is equipped with power to be victorious over the flesh. (3) Christ's death was the judgment God required against the sin nature. (4) Deliverance from the power of the flesh is possible depending in faith on the Spirit rather than on any of one's own resources.

The central truth of power to do good is revealed in Galatians 5:22-23 where the new life in Christ is described as the fruit of the Spirit. "But the fruit of the Spirit is love, joy, peace, patience, kindness, goodness, faithfulness, gentleness and self-control. Against such things there is no law."[197] The God honoring characteristics of a Christian life described, as the fruit of the Spirit are possible only by the indwelling presence of the Persons of the Trinity. This ministry of the Holy Spirit affirms His absolute deity and omnipotence.

The fruit of the Spirit are superhuman qualities impossible for a person in his own strength to achieve. They can be acquired only as he walks by faith and depends on the Holy Spirit. By the power of the Spirit a believer's human character can be renewed and transformed so that he can be like Christ and evidence the fruit of the Spirit in his life. This shows that walking with God is more than a negative approach to life. It is more than simply not doing certain things; it is also a manifestation of positive qualities that are in God Himself.

The works of the Spirit that are related to the believers' salvation are accomplished once and for all. By contrast the filling of the Spirit relates to believers' experiences and can be a repeated spiritual condition. The Bible specifies certain steps a believer should take in order to be filled with the Spirit. It is unnecessary to pray for the filling of the Spirit. Instead a believer should seek to be obedient to the revelation of God regarding the conditions He has set forth in His Word. If he meets those conditions, he will be filled with the Spirit.

Charles Ryrie, in his book; Balancing the Christian Life brings it out pretty clear:

"To be spirit-filled, then, is to be Spirit-controlled. And to be thus controlled requires the yielding of a dedicated life and of a daily dependence on the power of the Spirit. Prayer and human effort may be involved in meeting these conditions, but when met the control of the Spirit (and thus the filling) is automatic."[198]

The first condition for being filled with the Spirit is stated in the command in Ephesians 4:30, "And do not grieve the Holy Spirit of God, with whom you were sealed for the day of redemption."[199] What grieves the Holy Spirit is sin. Sin is a barrier to the unhindered ministry of the Spirit of God and prevents the Holy Spirit of God from filling the believer. The cure of the effects of sin in the spiritual life of a child of God is repentance, which leads to making a genuine confession of his sin. Because sin is such a common problem in Christians' lives, the

Bible suggests three ways it can be prevented.

A study of the Word of God and hiding it in the heart helps to prevent sin as is stated in Psalm 119:11, "I have hidden Your Word in my heart that I might not sin against You."[200] As stated in Hebrews 4:12, the Word of God has power to make a child of God understand the nature of his sin.

The indwelling Holy Spirit Himself can enable a Christian to resist sin before it happens. A Christian who is walking in fellowship with God has the power within him to prevent sin from occurring.

In his book; The Tozer Pulpit, A.W. Tozer covers this with-

"Contrary to what professing Christians like to think, many of God's people are not willing to walk in perfect agreement with Him, and this may explain why so many believers do not have the power of the Spirit, the peace of the Spirit and many of the other qualities, gifts and benefits which the Spirit of God brings.

The question is: Are we willing to walk with Him in love and obedience?

The answer is that we cannot walk with Him unless we are agreed and if we are not agreed, we will not walk with Him in harmony and fruitfulness and blessing."[201]

The intercession of Christ as the believers' High Priest in heaven strengthens them and helps keep them from sinning (Hebrews 7:25).

When sin occurs in a believer's life, however, the Bible prescribes a divinely provided cure for the effects of sin. This cure is suggested in Jesus' washing the disciples' feet (John 13:11).[203] Though Peter had bathed before coming to the Passover feast, an action that typifies salvation, he needed to have his feet washed; that is, his conduct before the Lord needed cleaning. This cleansing is through the Word, as Christ reminded the disciples in John 15:3.

The familiar story of the Prodigal Son in Luke 15:11-32[204] is another illustration of how confession leads to restoration. When the Prodigal Son became thoroughly convinced of his sin, he went back to his father with confession, and his father eagerly welcomed him back.

After a Christian has sinned against God restoration is possible because the precious blood of Christ shed on Calvary has fully provided not only for salvation but also for restoration of saints who confess, and turn from their sins. As long as one is grieving the Holy Spirit by unconfessed sin, he cannot expect the filling of the full work of the Spirit in his heart and life.

Though strangely slighted, neglected, and unrecognized, the Spirit is the adorable, majestic, ever-glorious, equal Member of the Godhead. Disregard for the Holy Spirit is not due to any failure on the part of the Bible to declare His person or to set forth the boundless character and infinite importance of His work. Naturally human thought begins with the first Person and extends to the second Person, and it is highly probable that, having contemplated these, the point of saturation is so nearly reached that there is little ability left for responding to the proper claims of the third Person in the Godhead. However, the solemn duty of every serious student of God's Word is to correct, insofar as possible, every tendency to ignore the truth concerning the Spirit, and by prayer and meditation to come into a deeper realization of His person and presence. In view of the Spirit's ministry to glorify Christ, there is no warrant from the Word of God for the indignity that a common disregard for the Spirit imposes on Him.

GENERAL FACTS ABOUT ANGELS

From ancient to modern times man has become increasingly aware of the vastness of the universe. Though the Scriptures make it plain that man inhabits only the earth and after death goes to heaven (those that are born again), speculation continues whether planets and stars in the universe are inhabited. All evidence to the present has revealed no support for such habitation.

Because angels are spiritual beings who are not visible to man and are not confined to material things as man is, it is entirely possible that angels have access to the entire universe even though man has no means of determining this fact. It is clear from Colossians 1:16 that God created things both visible and invisible. Angels and men are equally subject to God's power (1 Peter 3:22).[205] The holy angels are sometimes referred to as dwelling in heaven and sometimes on earth.

Some fallen angels are said to have "abandoned their own home" and are "kept in darkness, bound with everlasting chains for the judgment on the great Day" (Jude 6; 2 Peter 2:4).[206] The location of fallen angels who are bound is not revealed in Scripture. It is possible that angels who were created long before man could have inhabited the earth before the time of the formless earth of Genesis 1. The Scriptures indicate that the scope of angel activity and power is vast, and is true of both holy angels and fallen angels. For this reason the Apostle Paul spoke of struggle with unseen powers (Eph. 6:12). Elisha reassured his servant that God could take care of Israel by opening the servant's eyes to see "the hills full of horses and chariots of fire all around Elisha" (2 Kings 6:17). This refers to angelic forces rather than human armies. Though holy angels have great power and often represent God, they are not to be worshipped (Col. 2:18; Rev. 22:8-9).[207]

As a created being, man is somewhat inferior to angels as indicated in Psalm 8:1-5 and Hebrews 2:-7,[208] which state that in His humanity Christ was lower than the angels. In some respects, however, man is clearly superior to angels in that the human race is made in the image of God, which is never said of angels (Gen. 1:27).[209] Each human being possessing a material body has capacity for experiences foreign to angels. In their ultimate destiny in salvation believers will be elevated above angels and will be their judges (1 Cor. 6:3).[210] Though man in some ways in his sinful state is lower than angels, in his ultimate exaltation he will be far above them.

Some people tend to regard angels as beings somewhat less than real persons, but the Scriptures reveal that angels have personality and have a quality of morality similar to that of man. Their functions as messengers of God indicate that they are individual beings, that they can render intelligent worship, that holy angels behold the glory of God (Matt. 18:10), and that they know their limitations (24:36).[211] They know they are inferior to Jesus Christ as the Son of God (Heb. 1:4-14). The fact that they have intellect, possess capacity for moral choice, and can render intelligent worship (Ps. 148:2) indicates that angels have personalities similar though somewhat different from that of man. Holy angels having elected to serve God in eternity past are rendered secure in that choice just as fallen angels having elected to sin against God are hopeless in their fallen estate and are not subject to salvation.

It may be assumed according to Colossians 1:16 that angels were created simultaneously and are innumerable. They are not subject to death or extinction. Like the human race, they are subject to God's judgment and reward. Angels are without sex and do not have capacity to procreate (Matt, 22:28-30).[215] Apart from the human race angels are God's highest form of creation. Holy angels continue to serve God in many capacities including that of constant worship. Sometimes they are used as instruments of judgment (Matt. 13:41-42). They may assume bodies similar to those of the human race but they do not have these permanently. On occasion they can reflect the glory of God and appear in dazzling, brilliant light (Matt. 28:2-4). Pictorial representations of angels need to be compared to precise scriptural revelation. Because they fly (Dan. 9:21) it is assumed they have wings. Some specifically are described as having wings (Isa.6:1-6). Angels, however, are characteristically described as spirits, and their bodily form may be temporarily assumed in appearances on earth.

According to Mark 13:32 angels live in heaven but they are sent on errands or special assignments, as fulfilled by the Angel Gabriel (Dan. 9:21). Paul also spoke of "an angel from heaven" as though that would be the normal origination of an angel sent as a messenger (Gal. 1:8). Though fallen angels seem to have an abode other than heaven, no specific location is given except that Satan will be bound in the "Abyss" for the thousand years after the Second Coming before he is released (Rev. 20:3). Likewise the plague which seems to be demonic is spoken of as coming from the Abyss (Rev. 9:1-3). Fallen angels also have a king who is referred to as "the angel of the Abyss" Rev. 9:11). The destiny of fallen angels is the lake of fire (Matt. 25:41). The holy angels will dwell in the new heavens and new earth described in Revelation 21-22.[216]

The numberless multitudes mentioned in Daniel 7:10 are apparently angels. The heavenly hosts greeting the birth of Christ also were angels (Luke 2:13-14). The heavenly hosts in Revelation 5:11 seem similar to those mentioned in Daniel 7:10. Hosts of angels in the heavenly city are mentioned in Hebrews 12:22.[217]

Like all created beings, angels derive their power from God but are not able to do things that only God can do such as create and do other tasks that require omnipotence or omniscience. Angels are not all- powerful and sometimes they require assistance from other angels in their conflict with evil (Jude 9).[218] Though their strength exceeds that of men, angels fall far short of the power God has.

The angel who destroyed 70,000 persons in David's kingdom in three days (2 Sam. 24:15-16)[219] may have been the Angel of *Yahweh*. It is also probable that the Angel of *Yahweh* who is a theophany of Christ, also destroyed the firstborn of Egypt (Ex. 12:29-30) since in this instance the Lord Himself brought on the judgment. The destruction of the hosts of the Assyrians (2 Chron. 32:21) was a similar act by an angel. Any power angels have is derived from the power of God.

Angel's are sometimes described as governmental rulers. Five major representations of governmental supremacy among angels are indicated; thrones, powers, rulers, authorities, "heavenly bodies", "miracles", (Col.1:16; Luke 21:26; 2 Thes. 2:9; 1 Peter 3:22.[220] Thrones may refer to those who sit in them, powers to those who exercise dominion, rulers to those who rule, authorities to those who exercise supremacy by virtue of their power. Whether referring to individual functions or not, these terms describe the various types of demonic power in the world.

The elect angels (1 Tim. 5:21)[221] refer to holy angels who are included in the elect purpose of God. Little more is revealed about them in Scripture except that they apparently correspond to those among men who are elected to salvation.

In the life of Christ angels had a ministry in announcing His birth, caring for Him after His temptation, and being immediately available at His command if He chose to use their power which He did not do.

A summary of their activity with regard to the saints is given in Hebrews 1:14.[222] Angels are described as "ministering spirits sent to serve those who will inherit salvation."

Angels are involved in many important events and situations in Scripture.[223] In the Old Testament angels are sometimes called sons of God. In the New Testament this is reversed as angels are servants and Christians are called the sons of God.

As has been previously observed, angels are watching to see the unfolding of God's redemptive plan. There must have been tremendous reaction on the part of the angels when they saw Christ born, live on earth,[224] and die on the cross. They also observe God's joy when a sinner repents.[225] They are said to observe the judgment of God on those who worship the beast and his image. Though believers in Christ will not judge each other, they will judge angels.[226] The fact that angels were present in important events in biblical history indicates their large share in what is accomplished. Among these items are their observation of Creation (Job 38:7), the giving of the Law (Gal. 3:19; Acts 7:53) delivery of messages from God (Heb. 2:2), the birth of Christ (Luke 2:13), the temptation of Christ (Matt. 4:11), the resurrection of Christ (28:2), the ascension of Christ (Acts 1:10), and His second coming (Matt, 13:37-39; 24:31; 2 Thes. 1:7).[227]

ANGELIC PARTICIPATION IN THE MORAL PROBLEM

The problem of evil is one of the major questions in both philosophy and theology. People of great intellect have wrestled with the problem as to how God who is good could permit evil, especially if He is omnipotent and omniscient. Some philosophers have attempted to solve the problem by postulating that God is good but is not omnipotent and therefore is unable to stem the tide of evil. This is contrary to Scripture which affirms His omnipotence. Generally speaking, however, human philosophy has never solved the problem of evil either in its origin or in its continuance and has never offered a solution such as biblical salvation.

Only the Bible explains how evil originated and gives some hints as to why a good God would permit an evil world. The moral problem in the Bible is related to three major events: (1) the fall of angels into sin (2) the fall of man into sin, and (3) the death of Christ as the Sin-Bearer.

The ultimate question as to why God created angels and the human race is probably best answered by the fact that God desired creatures who could fellowship with Him in moral issues and would be able to exercise moral choice. In such a situation there is always the possibility of one choosing what is wrong, and this is what eventuated.

In contrast to the human race, however, angels were created in a perfect environment where holiness reigned supreme. There was no evil influence within or without that might cause an angel to sin, and the environment they were created in would tend to help them preserve their holy estate. Angels, however, did commit sin against God, and many of them became fallen angels or demons in contrast to holy angels who resisted this temptation. Because of their decision to serve God, holy angels were rendered forever secure.

The fallen angels give rise to two important theological questions: (1) How could a holy God permit any creature to sin: (2) How could an uninfluenced, unfallen angel sin? Though the answer may not be completely given in Scripture, it may be assumed that God permitted angels to sin for holy and wise reasons even though these were entirely different than the reason for permitting man to sin. The question of how an unfallen angel could sin can only be explained by the fact that in moral choice there is obviously the capacity to do evil as well as to do good.

In creating angels God knew in His omniscience that they would sin, and this would introduce the whole sin problem into the universe and ultimately influence men to sin as well. This can be explained by the fact that God desired to manifest His grace in the redemption of man. About the only explanation that can be given to the fall of angels is that this was antecedent to man's sinfulness.

The nature of sin in an unfallen angel is best explained as being self-seeking. This is supported by scriptural revelation concerning the reasons for Satan's departure from God, which at the time seemed to be because of his self-interest.

In the providence of God the sin of angels as well as the sin of man was not immediately dealt with, and sin was allowed to mature to its ultimate course. Nations were allowed to manifest their full capacity for evil as in the case of the Amorites (Gen. 15:16). Even in the present age good and evil grow together until the harvest (Matt. 13:39). Even the man of lawlessness (2 Thes. 2:6-8) is allowed to manifest his full sinfulness before divine judgment commits him to the lake of fire.[228]

Though the problem of evil is one that baffles the human mind and can only be partially solved even by scriptural revelation, only the Bible gives a reasonable explanation as to the cause, course, and ultimate destiny of evil and helps explain how a good and omnipotent

God would endure widespread sinfulness in the world through human history.

INTRODUCTION TO SATANOLOGY

In the Bible, spirit beings, whether holy or unholy, are called angels (Rev. 12:7). Unholy angels are frequently referred to as demons or devils, (1 Cor. 10:20-21; 1 Tim. 4:1; James 2:19; Rev:20).[229] As such they are distinguished from the devil himself who is referred to more than 30 times in the New Testament. In Matthew 4:1-11 the devil is seen tempting Christ and in Revelation 20:19 he is cast into the lake of fire.

In view of the many references in the Bible to Satan and his activities, it is a serious error to deny his personality or power. The concept that he is only a personification of evil hardly fits the many evil deeds he does such as possessing pigs and causing their destruction (Matt. 8:28-32). The fact that men are possessed by demons and that Satan could tempt Christ certainly exceeds the limits of a personification of evil. The personality of Satan is just as clear as the personality of angels, men, or God Himself.

According to one survey, 45 percent of Americans don't believe in Satan. But Jesus did. Jesus believed in Satan because he saw him and talked to him. There's a fascinating account of their conversation in Matthew 4:1-11.[230]

Though the Bible is the only accurate source of information on the character of Satan and the demon world, belief in evil spirits penetrated heathen religions long before the Bible was written. The evidence for the devil and demons is so pervasive that it is commonly believed in heathen religions. Objections to the doctrine of Satan on the ground that it had its origin in mythology, that it conforms to the dualism of Zoroastrianism, or that it destroys the unity of God are false and misleading. The doctrine of Satan is thoroughly scriptural and is based on divine revelation.

THE CAREER OF SATAN

The extended career of Satan from eternity past to eternity future is a major area of biblical revelation which is most revealing as to the character of evil and the character of satanic temptation today.

In a prophecy given against the King of Tyre (Ezek. 28:1-19),[231] the prophecy is not only a description of the King of Tyre and his pride against God but beyond the King of Trye to the one whom he personifies, Satan himself. The King of Tyre declared that he was God and sat on the throne of God (vv. 1-2). In verses 7-10 his downfall is predicted because of his pride and opposition to the true God. In verses 11-19, however, statements are made that obviously go beyond the King of Tyre to Satan Himself.

Additional information is revealed concerning Satan's fall in Isaiah 14:12-17.[232] In this passage Satan is described as having "fallen from heaven" and being "cast down to earth" (v. 12). The nature of his sin is indicated as ambition in verses 13-14, "You said in your heart, 'I will ascend to heaven; I will raise my throne above the stars of God; I will sit enthroned on the mount of assembly, on the utmost heights of the sacred mountain. I will ascend above the tops of the clouds; I will make myself like the Most High.'"

Dr. Charles Ryrie states this well in his book- Balancing the Christian Life:

"From the time of his first sin until his final defeat, Satan's plan and purpose have been, are, and always will be to seek to establish a rival rule to God's kingdom. He is promoting a system of which he is the head and which stands in opposition to God and His rule in the universe".[233]

Though Satan was cast out of heaven, no longer to hold his position as a major angelic servant of God, he still has access to heaven. This is seen in Job 1-2 and in the fact that he is destined in the future to be cast out of heaven (Rev. 12:7-9).[234]

The fall of Satan for the sin of pride is also referred to in 1 Timothy 3:6. Satan's sin was his desire to secure (1) the highest heavenly position, (2) regal rights both in heaven and on earth, (3) messianic recognition, (4) glory which belongs to God alone, and (5) a likeness to the Most High, the "Creator of heaven and earth" (Gen. 14:19).[235] It is apparent from Scripture that the angels, who joined with him in his defection, shared his fate and now form the demonic world.

More than 100 references to Satan, the devil, and demons are found in the New Testament. These references portray the demonic worlds much as Satan was in the Old Testament. In both Testaments he is seen as the accuser of the saints and he and his cohorts oppose the work of God. The first reference in the New Testament, Matthew 4:1, refers to the temptation of Christ by the devil. In addition to being the tempter of Christ, Satan is accused of sowing weeds (Matt. 13:39), which represents false profession within the kingdom of heaven. Christ accused the Jewish religious leaders of belonging to "your father, the devil" (John 8:44). In Mark 4:15 Satan is accused of snatching the Word of God from the hearts of hearers so that they may not believe and be saved. In John 6:70-71 Judas Iscariot is called a devil, that is, though a man, he was doing the work of Satan. In John 13:2 the plan of Judas to betray Christ is said to have been implanted in his heart by the devil and later Satan entered into him.[236]

In Halley's Bible Handbook Satan is described; "The Dragon is identified as the Devil, Satan, the Old Serpent (Rev. 12:9). He had already been mentioned as Persecuting the Churches in Smyrna and Pergamum (2;10, 13); and he, or one of the angels, from the abyss, as king of the army of Demon Locusts (9:11), and murderer of the Two Witnesses (11:7). "Red" (12:3), may symbolize his murderous nature".[237]

Christ's temptation by Satan reveals much of Satan's character and purpose. Being led by the Spirit into the wilderness, Jesus there underwent a testing that continued 40 days and nights. Climaxing this testing, Satan presented a threefold suggestion. The first involved the breaking down of that separation which Christ faithfully preserved between His deity and His humanity (Matt. 4:3-4). If the common demands of food and drink were supernaturally supplied by His deity, He would not have been tempted in all points as are His followers in this world.

In all three testings Christ met Satan's proposal with the Word of God, and demonstrated the fact that the actions Satan suggested were not the will of God. The first Adam was overcome by Satan; the last Adam drove him away. As Son of God with His deity in view, the outcome could not be otherwise; as a man with His humanity in view, the victory formed a pattern for all saints.

When Jesus Christ was crucified, it would seem that Satan had achieved a master stroke in putting to death the Son of God. What appeared to be a sad ending to the ministry of the Messiah of Israel became instead the cause of Satan's downfall. Besides removing the grounds of accusation against the saints of God concerning their sins, the Cross was also the basis on which Satan himself is to be judged. The death of Christ on the cross was accepted by God the Father as a suitable sacrifice for the sins of the whole world. In coming to earth it was God's purpose that Christ should fulfill the sacrifice by which was the necessary basis for the acceptance of sinners by a righteous God.

More was accomplished by the death of Christ than being a sacrifice for sin. As brought out in two major passages, Colossians 1:15-22 and 2:14-15,[238] the death of Christ was actually a massive victory over the forces of evil in the universe. In Colossians 1:15-18 Christ is referred to as the Creator, the One who has preeminence above all creation, and the Head of the church, His body. In verses 19-22 the reconciling work of Christ on the cross is described as a supreme achievement: "For God was pleased to have all His fullness dwell in Him, and through Him to reconcile to Himself all things, weather things on earth or things in heaven, by making peace through His blood, shed on the cross. Once you were alienated from God and were enemies on your minds because of your evil behavior. But now He has reconciled you by Christ's physical body through death to present you holy in His sight, without blemish and free from accusation."

The death of Christ also triumphed over His opponents and disarmed demonic power. Because of this triumph, Satan now stands judged. Christ anticipated the ultimate judgment of Satan in John 12:31, "Now is the time for judgment on this world; now the prince of this world will be driven out" "The prince of this world now stands condemned" (16:11).[239] Because of the Cross Satan is already defeated, doomed, and judged. Yet God has allowed him freedom in this present age to carry out his program of opposition to the works of God. In his ultimate destiny, however, Satan will be cast into the lake of fire (Rev. 20:10).[240] An analogy to this is seen in the fact that Saul was dismissed from being king over Israel, and David was anointed to replace him. Yet years went on while Saul continued his reign until his death before David was able to assume the throne. Since Samuel told Saul he was a failure, David's ultimate possession of the throne was a certainty. Similarly though Satan is allowed some freedom in the present world, God is fulfilling His plan in calling out His church. He will give Satan one last fling at the end of the Millennium. Yet he is already defeated by the fact that Christ triumphed in His death on the cross.

Though the future execution of Satan's judgment is still pending, he has already suffered three major judgments: (1) the moral degradation and corresponding loss of standing because of his fall, (2) the sentence pronounced against him in the Garden of Eden, and (3) the judgment on the cross. Since Satan's original sin was striving to be like God, it is inevitable that Satan would ultimately be completely judged.

Satan will be loosed after the 1,000 years, after the Millennium has been completed. He immediately will rally those who paid only lip service to Christ and will assemble them to battle surrounding Jerusalem the capital city. The satanic army gathered against Christ will not be permitted a triumph, however, and so the devil will be "thrown into the lake of burning sulfur" and will be "tormented day and night forever and ever". Satan, who began his career as a holy angel with a high place of authority in heaven, at long last will be brought to his everlasting doom. Rev.12:7-20:10.[241]

SATAN'S EVIL CHARACTER

Sins that are possible for men are impossible for angels. Angels are not tempted by sins that are expressed through the human body such as immoral relations, gluttony, or the perversion of normal bodily functions. Angelic sin is along two closely related evils – ambitious pride and untruth. Satan's major sin was to assume the position of anti-God.

Ambitious pride characterizes the entire career of Satan. Scripture passages directly indict Satan with respect to this sin. Instructing Timothy concerning the characteristics of an overseer or elder, Paul wrote, "He must not be a recent convert, or he may become conceited and fall under the same judgment as the devil. He must also have a good reputation with outsiders, so that he will not fall into disgrace and into the devil's trap" (1 Tim. 3:6-7).[242] This passage also speaks of the reproach of the "slanderous accusation" of the devil (2 Peter 2:11; Jude 9), and "the trap of the devil" (2 Tim. 2:26). This pride has been the characteristic sin of Satan though it can also be the besetting sin of mankind.[243]

Untruth or lies is the second characteristic sin of Satan. Arguing with the Pharisees, Christ said, "You belong to your father, the devil, and you want to carry out your father's desire. He was a murderer from the beginning, not holding to the truth, for there is no truth in him. When he lies, he speaks his native language, for he is a liar and the father of lies, (John 8:44). John wrote in 1 John 3:8, He who does what is sinful is of the devil, because the devil has been sinning from the beginning".[244] Those who lend themselves to preaching a lie as the Pharisees did are guilty of the same sin as Satan, that of being the mouthpiece for lies.

The force of the man of lawlessness will be revealed in the end time just before the second coming of Christ. The man who is so designated is Satan's last and most misleading deception, a person who will head the ten-nation confederacy, the revival of the Roman Empire, in the period before the Second Coming. He will be the ultimate in satanic deception and will be a counterfeit of Christ; therefore he is designated by some as the Antichrist.

The force of the One holding back the man of lawlessness until the proper time for his revelation is the Holy Spirit who contends with human sin and attempts to restrain it's manifestation (Gen. 6:3). Restraint has been going on through human history and will continue until the Rapture of the church. When the church indwelt by the Holy Spirit is raptured, the restraining power will be partially taken away and the ultimate in wickedness will then be revealed (2 Thes. 2:7). This lawless man will not be identifiable while the church is here, but once the church is raptured it will be possible for him to begin his evil work beginning with the conquering of three of the ten countries.[245]

The force of Christ will be revealed when He will judge the wicked world at His second coming (Rev. 19:11-21). This climax to human history makes possible the 1,000-year kingdom of Christ, which will end in one more brief rebellion against God, led by Satan, before he is cast into the lake of fire (Rev. 20; 7-9).[246] The evil character of Satan is revealed in his influence on the world throughout his career and will reach its ultimate in the future Great Tribulation.

Satan holds the revealing title of chief of all sinners. He is the original sinner. He has brought on the most injury. He has practiced sin longer than any other. He sinned against the greatest light. Only God can compare the extent and hideous character of Satan's sinfulness. Yet Satan's sin is of such nature that man in his depravity will embrace it. The unregenerate will claim it to be their personal right to live in independence of God.

The power of Satan and his fallen angels is limited. They are only finite creatures who can do nothing outside the permissive will of

God. Satan was able to do nothing against Job until he was divinely permitted to do so. Satan and his angels possess great knowledge, but they are not omniscient; they have vast power when permitted to employ it, but they are not omnipotent; they can suggest evil, but they are not able to coerce the will of another creature. They may spread snares and traps to ruin the children of God, but they can create nothing, nor can they use God's creation other than as He decrees. They will never defeat God. In fact God uses Satan as an instrument to chasten and correct erring saints, (Luke 22:31-32; 1 Cor. 5:5; 1 Tim. 1:20).[247] The knowledge of those limitations can be a comfort to Christians who take seriously their conflict with the powers of darkness.

THE SATANIC COSMOS

Because the world is evil and is dominated by Satan, the Scriptures speak of the darkness of the cosmos. Christ came to bring light to the world (John 12:46; cf. 1:6-11). The Spirit of God was sent by Christ to convict the world of its sinfulness and to reveal the righteousness and judgment of God (16:8-11). Christ declared that His disciples were not of this world (17:14). Christ also asserted, "My kingdom is not of this world" in (18:3). The world does not know God by its own wisdom (1 Cor. 1:21). Christians are exhorted not to be contaminated by the world. (James 1"27; 2 Peter 1:4; 2:20).[248]

The cosmos is a vast order or system that Satan has promoted and that conforms to his ideals, aims, and methods. The cosmos embraces the world's godless governments, conflicts, armaments, intelligences, education, culture, and its false religions of morality and pride. The world can be considered a satanic system.

It is into this world that God sent His Son (1 John 4:9). In spite of its being sinful, God so loved the world that He gave His Son (John 3:16). A friend of the world is an enemy of God (James 4:4). Satan has been permitted to assume authority over it and to misdirect it. Christ employed the Greek term *kosmos* more often than *aion* and *oikoumena* combined, and it especially appears in the Gospel of John and the First Epistle of John.[249] The world as the cosmos appears more than 40 times in the Upper Room Discourse (John 13-17). He was very aware of the fact that He was a contradiction to the evil of the world and was bringing light to bear on its satanic character.[250]

In tempting Christ Satan asserted that the world was delivered to him and that he had the power to deliver it to whomever he wished (Luke 4:5-7). Though Scripture is clear in maintaining the omnipotence of God, Satan has been given much power, and with the permission of God, the rulers of this world have been appointed by Satan.

Christ frequently referred to Satan as the prince or ruler of the cosmos (John 12:31; 14:30; 1:11). Paul also wrote of Satan as "the ruler of the kingdom of the air" (2 Cor. 4:4). Paul also asserted, "Our struggle is not against flesh and blood, but against the rulers, against the authorities, against the powers of this dark world and against spiritual forces of evil in the heavenly realms" (Eph. 6:12). He also spoke of "the shield of faith, with which you can extinguish all the flaming arrows of the evil one" (v. 16). The unseen warfare between the forces of God, whether human or angelic and Satan are very real. First John 5:19 states that "the whole world is under the control of the evil one."[251]

Had not Christ become an atoning Sacrifice for the sins of the world (1 John 2:2), were not He the Savior of the whole world (2 Cor. 5:19),[252] none could ever come out of the world and believe on Him. But as it is, they who do believe on Him come out and are separated from the world. In contemplating the evil character of the world, the indictments against Satan recorded in Isaiah 14:12, 1-17 and the record of Satan's influence on Job (Job 1:13-19; 2:7) must be viewed as power which God has permitted Satan to exercise. All these manifestations of power anticipate the future power of Satan which will be revealed through the lawless one (2 Thes 2:9-10) and the two beasts of Revelation 13:1-17.[253]

The root of evil in the cosmos is that its all-comprehensive order or system has been organized on the basis of complete independence of God. As such it is Satan's supreme effort to perpetuate the lie that he is good. The world as Satan has structured it includes many humanitarian ideals, morals, and aspects of culture designed to appeal to the natural man. Essentially, however, it is Christ-rejecting. "The rulers of this age" are the ones who "have crucified the Lord of glory" (1 Cor. 2:8). If Satan were completely free, he would destroy Christ again and any who follow Him. The sinfulness of the world is described in Romans 3:10-12, "As it is written: 'There is no one righteous, not even one; there is no one who understands, no one who seeks God. All have turned away, they have together become worthless; there is no one who does good, not even one." The evil character of the cosmos is revealed in many Scriptures.[254]

The things of the world, though of the satanic order, may be used by a believer but not abused. As stated in 1 John 3:17, "If anyone has material possessions and sees his brother in need but has no pity on him, how can the love of God be in him?" Christ described the evil character of the world in these words: "But the worries of this life, the deceitfulness of wealth, and the desires for other things come in and choke the Word, making it unfruitful" (Mark 4:19). The Scriptures refer to the proper use of worldly possessions (1 Cor. 7:29-31); James 2:5).[255] Poverty in the things of this world is not dishonorable, and Christians should not count possessions as their real wealth.

The Scriptures are clear that the evil cosmos will be judged by God. Christ in His second coming will destroy the power of this world. In Psalm 2 mankind is urged to worship the Son before the time of the world's destruction. In revelation given to Daniel on the course and final end of Gentile power, God indicated that eventually the evil world will be reduced to chaff on a threshing floor, swept away by the wind (Dan. 2:35). God's judgment of the nations will take place after His second coming (Matt. 25:31-4). The sheep, representing the righteous, will be allowed to enter Christ's millennial kingdom while the goats, representing the unsaved, will be consigned to everlasting fire. The ultimate power of evil embodied in the man of lawlessness ruling in the period before the Second Coming will be destroyed at the second coming of Christ (2 Thes. 2:8). The extensive coming judgments of God in the Great Tribulation are revealed in Revelation 6-8. The present power of this evil cosmos will ultimately be destroyed (1 Cor. 7:31; 2 Peter 3:10; 1 John 2:17).[256]

SATAN'S MOTIVE

Satan's motive in beginning his long career must be seen in contrast to the divine motive in which God permitted evil to be present. In light of God's omnipotence it is obvious that He could have avoided creating both men and angels. Having created the angels, He could have prevented Satan and the demon world from manifesting their power. What was God's motive in bringing the world into existence as it is?

Traditionally the explanation has been given that God created the world to manifest His own glory. For man to seek self-recognition is evil, but for God in His infinite perfections to manifest His glory is obviously good. Though the Bible only partially draws aside the veil of the divine motives in Creation, human history as well as the earlier facts concerning Satan's career all point to the conclusion that God's wisdom is demonstrated by permitting Satan and man to display every form of wickedness and independence of God only to have these claims confounded, refuted, and destroyed.

Four milestones mark the way of Satan's course in his willful sin against God.

(1) "I will make myself like the Most High" (Isaiah 14:14).

(2) In his tempting of Adam and Eve he offered them the possibility of being "like God, knowing good and evil" (Gen. 3:5). Here he transferred his own goal to the human race. The whole program of Satan in the cosmos is to make men feel that they are independent of God, and by taking this action to recognize Satan instead. His suggestion that Adam and Eve could be like God was a lie because he did not explain that they would know good and evil but would not have the power to accomplish the good or to avoid the evil apart from divine grace.

(3) In tempting Christ, the last Adam, Satan did not offer to Him

the possibility of being like God because he knew Christ already is God. Instead he attempted to have Christ worship him. In offering Christ the kingdoms of the world Satan's motive was to tempt Christ with the role of becoming the King of kings without going to the cross. It was audacious beyond measure for Satan to suggest that God the Creator should be a worshiper at his feet.

(4) The final manifestation of Satan's lie will be to exalt the man of lawlessness as a world ruler who will oppose God and attempt to exalt himself above God. The prophesied destruction of the world ruler at the second coming of Christ is anticipated in the words addressed to the prince of Tyre in Ezekiel 28:2-9.[257] The destruction of the prince of Tyre will have its ultimate fulfillment not only in the destruction of the prince of Tyre but in the destruction of Satan and the man whom he foists on the world as their god and supreme ruler. Though the lawless one is given great power (Rev. 13:3-8), his destruction is certain and with it the ultimate judgment on Satan. Until that day Satan will continue to deceive the world and will substitute anything except true faith in Christ. Cold formality, heartless arrogance, proud self-complacence, highly esteemed external respectability, and other deceptive symbols of human morality will be shown to be deceptions coming from Satan himself. Though religious, respectable, and decent, unsaved man because of his sin will end in death (Romans 6:21).

SATAN'S METHOD

Satan's method of operation must be seen in keeping with his transcendent objective to be like the Most High rather than being unlike the Most High (Isaiah 14:14). To accomplish this goal Satan's method of deception is to use subterfuge, treachery, and fraud. Satan's objective in the present age is to deceive mankind in the inhabited earth (Rev. 12:9), and in the Tribulation he will seek to trick "the inhabitants of the earth" (Rev. 13:14). After the Millennium he will attempt to reach the entire earth in his deceptive practices (20:3, 8, 10).[258]

Satan has the twofold objective of exalting himself and opposing God. Therefore he has enmity toward all who put their trust in God. Satan wages no warfare against the unregenerate; by contrast new believers in Christ soon learn that they have an enemy who opposes their Christian faith. For this reason Christ predicted tribulation for His followers (John 16:33; 2 Tim. 3:12; 1 John 3:13).[259] Paul also warned the Ephesians that their battle was against the devil and his schemes. He exhorted the Ephesians, "Put on the full armor of God so that you can take your stand against the devil's schemes. For our struggle is not against flesh and blood, but against the rulers, against the authorities, against the powers of this dark world and against the spiritual forces of evil in the heavenly realms" (Eph. 6:11-12). In keeping with this concept Christ prayed for His disciples, "My prayer is not that You take them out of the world but that You protect them from the evil one" (John 17:15).[260]

Being particularly active in opposing the Gospel, Satan may promote physical health, morality, and religious forms, to divert individuals from the truth of God's way of salvation. Satan also has great power and is able to do supernatural things as will be evident in the Great Tribulation (Rev. 13:13-15). The history of the church reveals that all too often Satan is successful in diverting those who should be preachers of the truth to preach error. In all his deceptive practices Satan's motive is to divert worship and obedience from the true God to himself.[261]

In creation Satan was the highest of all the angels. He fell into sin and became deceived by the distortion which pride engenders. His sin took the form of acting independently of the Creator and becoming the promoter of untruth (lies) in contrasts to the truth. In the wisdom of God, Satan is allowed to carry out his schemes and demonstrates in history the lies of his claims. In pursuing his diabolical goals Satan is allied with humanity insofar as humanity serves his end. In the final judgment those who share Satan's doctrine will share his fate of being cast into the lake of fire. By contrast how matchless is the grace of God toward fallen humanity (Rom. 5:10). How wonderful are the words of Christ that those who believe in Him "shall not perish but have eternal life" (John 3:16).[262]

DEMONOLOGY

Though Scripture places emphasis on Satan and his work, mention is made of "his angels" (Matt. 25:41; Rev. 12:9). When Satan sinned and departed from his early holy estate he took with him many angels who joined in this rebellion against God. This resulted in ceaseless warfare between Michael and his holy angels against Satan and the fallen angels. This will come to a climax when Satan and his angels will be cast out of heaven at the beginning of the Great Tribulation (Rev. 12:9). At the Second Coming, Satan will be bound for 1,000 years, and all the fallen angels will similarly be rendered inactive. Their brief freedom at the end of the Millennium will end in their being cast into the lake of fire prepared "for the devil and his angels" (Matt. 25:41). Demons, who possess some individuals (Matt. 12:22-29), are fallen angels.[263]

Satan has power not only over fallen angels who joined him in rebelling against God but also over the cosmos itself. Satan is called "the god of this age" (2 Cor. 4:4), "the prince of demons" (Matt. 9:34; 12:24; Mark 3:22), "prince of this world" (John 12:31; 14:30; 1:11), and the "ruler of the kingdom of the air" (Eph. 2:2).[264]

In contrast to fallen angels who operate freely as demons in the cosmos, some fallen angels were confined after they rebelled against God. According to 2 Peter 2:4 some of them were confined immediately, "God did not spare angels when they sinned, but sent them to hell, putting them into gloomy dungeons to be held for judgment." According to Jude, "The angels who did not keep their positions of authority but abandoned their own home – these He has kept in darkness bound with everlasting chains for judgment on the great Day." Through demons who are not confined, Satan is able to exert his power in the entire cosmos. However, he is not omnipotent or omnipresent. He also is not omniscient even though he is far wiser than mankind.[265]

Idol worship is a sacrifice to demons and so Christians should have nothing to do with it. As the Apostle Paul expressed it, "No, but the sacrifices of pagans are offered to demons, not to God, and I do not want you to be participants with demons. You cannot drink the cup of the Lord and the cup of demons too; you cannot have part in both the Lord's table and the table of demons" (1 Cor. 10:20-21).[266]

One of the characteristics of demons is that they seek embodiment. In Christ's healing ministry He healed many who were possessed with demons (Matt. 8:16). An illustration of this is seen in 9:32-33. In this instance, "A man who was demon-possessed and could not talk was brought to Jesus. And when the demon was driven out, the man who had been dumb spoke." Casting out demons was also practiced in the early church (Acts 8:6-7). The young woman mentioned in Acts 16:16 who was possessed by a demon was healed and the demon cast out. According to Mark 5:1-13, Christ cast out demons from a man who had been insane, and the demons begged Christ not to disembody them. So He cast them into a herd of pigs who were feeding. This caused the heard to run wildly into the Sea of Galilee where they were drowned.

Another factor in considering demons is that they are wicked, unclean, and vicious. This is evident in references to demonic power in the Gospels.[267]

Considered as a whole, demon influence is prompted by two motives; to hinder the purpose of God for humanity, and to extend the authority of Satan. Demons as such are at the command of Satan, and they are ceaselessly active in promoting his power and opposing the things of God.

Demons have power to cause dumbness (Matt. 9:32-33), blindness 12:22), insanity (Luke 8:26-35), personal injury (Matt. 17:15), great physical strength (Luke 8:29), and to inflict suffering and deformities (13:11-17). The Scriptures are clear that Satan and the demons have great power, but a Christian takes refuge in the fact that God has greater power and can protect him from demonic oppression and influence.[268]

INTRODUCTION TO ANTHROPOLOGY

Anthropology, the science of man, is approached from two widely different perspectives, namely, that of secular human philosophy and that of the Bible. Secular anthropology is extra-biblical and avoids scriptural revelation.

Anthropology from a biblical point of view confines its studies to the Word of God. Biblical anthropology is based on revelation from God which presents the record of man's creation, sin, and subsequent experiences. Biblical anthropology enters into the deeper realms of things moral, spiritual, and eternal.

The true nature of man can never be learned by secular anthropology. This is because the necessary elements that are given only by revelation are often omitted or are given an inadequate definition. Biblical anthropology is essential to understanding the biblical philosophy of history, the plan of God for salvation of fallen man, and the explanation of the origin of sin. While human understanding of anthropology from a secular position may continue to change and its conclusions may be debated, the Word of God continues as an unchanging final record of how God regards man and what His plans are for man's salvation. The study of anthropology from a biblical standpoint is indispensable to a complete theology.

THE ORIGIN OF MAN

The answer to the problem of the origin of man is of immeasurable importance, for the whole structure of anthropology depends on it. Man's nature, responsibility, and destiny are affected by whether he was created or evolved. The Bible reveals that man was created by an act of God which contradicts the naturalistic evolutionary theory that man descended from earlier evolution stand absolutely opposed as two different explanations for man's origin.

Organic evolution is an attempt to explain the origin of man and all other organic things whether animal or vegetable in a way that contracts with what the Bible reveals about them as objects created by God. The evolutionary process is advanced as the method by which God developed man from earlier forms of life, which some evolutionists admit were created. Though organic evolution is held almost universally by the scientific world, it defies scientific proof and remains to this day a theory which is contradicted by scientific facts. The objectives of organic evolution are to-eliminate God from the natural world and to ignore the creation of man. Destitute of divine activity, evolution attempts to eliminate man's moral responsibility to a personal God.

There may be room for debate on the date of the origin of the inorganic world since the Bible does not date the original Creation of Genesis 1:1. On the other hand Scripture is clear, if taken in its natural meaning, that the human race is relatively recent.

Most so-called proofs for organic evolution are based on an argument that first structures geology on the basis of evolutionary theory, dates fossils according to their evolutionary assumptions, and then prove on the basis of geological records or recovered fossils that there is any evolutionary connection between man and other organic beings. To this day no scientist has been able to reproduce the tremendous change between animal life and human life. As the Bible makes clear, man, having been created in the image and likeness of God, has a moral character and an ability to commune with God which is lacking in all other creatures. Organic evolution is the greatest hoax ever advanced in the name of science and requires more faith on less evidence than the biblical faith of Christians.

The first account of man's creation (Gen. 1:27) records with sublime simplicity a most different theme that man has physical life and yet in a special sense is made in the likeness of God. As the Triune *Elohim*, God is the Creator. In the second account (Gen. 2:20-23) further revelation is given that man and woman are alike in nature and yet as man was created from the earth, and woman was created as a part of man, both were created by God and were created to complement each other. God's dealings with man, as seen throughout Scripture, are built on the concept that Adam and Eve were products of divine creation.[269]

For those who accept the Bible as the Word of God, the time of man's origin is not entirely clear though it is obvious the record teaches that man is the final creative act of God. Irish Archbishop James Ussher (1581-1656), on the basis of his study of Old Testament genealogies, dated the creation of Adam as 4004 B.C.[270] The early church fathers, as well as theologians ever since, have questioned whether the method he used can be sustained by Scripture. A comparison of genealogies of the Old Testament and the New Testament shows that there are gaps in the genealogies and, therefore, the dates mentioned cannot be added up to give a final answer.

On the other hand, it is not feasible to argue that these gaps in the generations embrace thousands of years as there is no biblical proof for this. While Ussher's dates may be questionable, the Bible clearly intimates that man is recent and was the last act of God's creation. At best the creation of man can only be dated a few thousand years before Ussher's dates.

A further complication is the question of the date of the flood in Noah's day, which Ussher dates 2349 B.C. As in the case of Egyptian history, written history is dated from as early as 3,000 B.C., but civilization was not wiped out and there is no place in it for a universal flood. Most conservative scholars agree with Unger, who wrote, "The Flood occurred sometime long before 4,000 B.C."[271] Early traditions speak of a flood, but assigning a date is impossible. Without being able to determine a specific date for the Flood and Adam's creation, the divine creation of animal and human life is recent, compared to the possible longevity of the inorganic world. Most evolutionary scientist refer to vast ages when they discuss the problem of life on earth, but their assumptions of antiquity are based on unproved theories.

THE MATERIAL PART OF MAN

The truth regarding man's being may be divided into seven main parts: (1) the material part of man, (2) the immaterial part of man, (3) the environment of the first man, (4) the responsibility of the first man, (5) the moral qualities of the first man, (6) the tempter of the first man, and (7) the temptation of the first man.

The human physical body is combined with the immaterial, a soul and a spirit. Though animals have a similar twofold nature of material and immaterial, their immaterial part is but a form of created life and does not have existence after death. Only man is made in the image and likeness of God. The human body provides a medium for sensation, ecstasy, and pain in contrast to the less exalted requirements of animal life. The bodies of human and animals exhibit the thought and design of the Creator, but the body of man, being more delicate and refined, is an imposing and impressive manifestation of the divine image.

The Word of God declares that God formed man's body from the dust of the ground (Gen. 2:7). The elements of the soil are said to be present in the human body; calcium, carbon, chlorine, fluorine, hydrogen, iodine, iron, magnesium, manganese, nitrogen, oxygen, phosphorus, potassium, silicon, sodium, and sulfur.[272] These minerals compose nearly 6 percent of the body, the remainder being water and carbon. These facts demonstrate that the biblical disclosure of the human body as being "of the earth" (1 Cor. 15:47-49) is accurate. In the process of normal growth a person is sustained by unceasing appropriation of new materials which come directly or indirectly from the dust of the earth. At death man's body returns to the dust from which it was originally derived (Gen. 3:19).[273] The Bible is clear in its revelation that the body, soul, and spirit can be separated. James spoke of this, "As the body without the spirit is dead, so faith without deeds is dead" (James 2:26). In discussing the human body the Apostle Paul stated, "Therefore we are always confident and know that as long as we are at home in the body we are away from the Lord. We live by faith, not by sight. We are confident, I say, and would prefer to be away from the body and at home with the Lord" (2 Cor. 5:8). In like manner the Apostle Paul referred to the outward body as "wasting away" while the inward is "renewed day by day" (4:16). Peter mentioned a similar contrast between the body and the soul: "I think it is right to refresh your memory as long as I live in the tent of this body, because I know that I will soon put it aside, as our Lord Jesus Christ has made clear to me. And I will make every effort to see that after my departure you will always be able to remember these things" (2 Peter 1:13-15). Christ also warned against those who could kill the body but not kill the soul (Matt. 10:28). The human body was affected by Adam's fall into sin for the seeds of death were planted in his body which eventually caused its death. As Hebrews 9:27 states, "Man is destined to die once, and after that to face judgment".[274]

The Scriptures are clear that there is a future for the human body, for both the saved and the unsaved. Christ stated, "For as the Father has life in Himself, so He has granted the Son to have life in Himself. And He has given Him authority to judge because He is the Son of Man. Do not be amazed at this, for a time is coming when all who are in their graves will hear His voice and come out – those who have done good will rise to live, and those who have done evil will rise to be condemned" (John 5:26-29). According to Daniel 12:2, the righteous dead of Israel will awake to everlasting life in contrast to others who will later be resurrected to shame and everlasting contempt (Rev. 20:12). Many passages indicate that there is an order of resurrections beginning with the resurrection of Christ and closing with the resurrection of the wicked. In the end all who die will be resurrected (1 Cor. 15:22-26).

A grand exception to the normal rule of death and resurrection is the translation of Christians at the time of the rapture. Paul bore witness to this: "Listen, I tell you a mystery: We will not all sleep, but we will all be changed – in a flash, in the twinkling of an eye, at the last trumpet. For the trumpet will sound, the dead will be raised imperishable, and we will be changed" (1 Cor. 15:51-52). The resurrection of the righteous and the unrighteous is also mentioned in Acts 24:15.[275]

Paul described the process of resurrection as an exchange of the believer's earthly body for a body like the Lord's glorious body (Phil. 3:20-21). The unsaved after the resurrection will stand before the Great White Throne to be condemned (Rev. 20:12).[276]

The contrast between the earthly body and the resurrection body are seen in 1 Corinthians 15:42-44, "So will it be with the resurrection of the dead. The body that is sown is perishable, it is raised imperishable; it is sown in dishonor, it is raised in glory; it is sown in weakness, it is raised in power; it is sown a natural body, it is raised a spiritual body." The fact that the word "sown" is used rather than the word "bury" indicates that in burial there is expectation of the resurrection.

Biblically the word "immortality" refers to the resurrection body, not to the endless existence of the soul. The human body is mortal and subject to death, but in resurrection, believers' bodies become immortal. "The perishable must clothe itself with imperishable, and the mortal with immortality" (v. 53). Though Christ died, He did not see corruption, and in His resurrection His body became immortal. Psalm 16:10 predicted Christ's death and stated that He would not see decay. The Apostle Peter referred to this in his sermon on the Day of Pentecost (Acts 2:25-31). Christ in His resurrection became "the firstfruits" of the human race which is subject to both death and resurrection.

The Old Testament alludes to resurrection frequently (Gen. 22:5; Job 19:25-27; Isa. 26:19; Dan. 12:2, 13; Hosea 13:14). The resurrection of Jesus Christ is a clear testimony to resurrection which

Jesus Himself predicted (Luke 24:1-8; John 1:18). At the time of Christ's resurrection a token resurrection (Matt. 27:52-53) fulfilled the typology of the Feast of Weeks in which a sheaf of grain was brought to the Lord as a token of the coming harvest (Lev. 23:15). The universality of resurrection is witnessed in John 5:28; Rev. 20:4; John 5:25-29; 1 Cor. 15:22-23; 1 Thes. 4:14-17; Rev. 20:11-13. The resurrection of the unsaved will occur a thousand years after the resurrection of the righteous (Rev. 20:5). A special resurrection is provided for the martyrs of the Tribulation (Rev. 20:4). In the resurrection of believers their bodies will be completely transformed into new bodies (1 Cor. 15:50-53; Phil. 3:20-21) even though they will have continued identity. The resurrection body of the wicked will prepare them for eternal punishment (Rev.20:7-15).[277]

The expression "the body of Christ" is used in a twofold way in Scripture. It may refer to His own human body or it may refer to the mystical body composed of those who are saved, over which He is the Head.

Christ was given a body (Heb. 10:5) so that He might be the antitype of Old Testament sacrifices and might shed His blood as the ground for our redemption. His body, which was always sinless, has now in resurrection put on immortality by which it became a body of unsurpassing glory (Rev. 1:13-18; 5:6; 19:12).

When the mystical body is referred to as the church, it indicates the unusual relationship that exists between Christ and the church. That relationship is similar to the head and the body of a human being. As the head directs the body, so Christ directs the church, and the response of the body to the direction of the head makes possible one's service for God. As the body of Christ, the church magnifies Him in this world and is His medium of activity through the Spirit.

By creation the human body is a product of the dust of the earth. It is sustained by elements derived from the dust, and it returns to dust when it dies. Physical death comes because of Adam's fall into sin.

Because of Christ's death and resurrection, the body will continue on eternally, as will also the soul and the spirit of man.[278]

THE IMMATERIAL PART OF MAN

In contrast to the material part of man which was created out of the dust of the earth, the immaterial part of man is not created at all, but was breathed out by God, "The Lord formed man from the dust of the ground and breathed into his nostrils the breath of life, and man became a living being" (Gen. 2:7). On the other hand, angels, who are immaterial beings without material bodies, were created and not made from any preexisting entity (Ezek. 28:15).[279]

The fact that man's immaterial nature was not created seems to imply that God imparted something of His own nature into man. This is indicated in Genesis 1:27, "So God created man in His own image, in the image of God He created him; male and female He created them." As God Himself is immaterial and since creating man in His own image and likeness referred to the immaterial aspect of God, the immaterial part of man seems to have the character of transmission from God rather than immediate creation. The "living being" which man became by divine inbreathing is more uncreated than created. It is an impartation from the Eternal One.

In this contrast in the origination of angels and men, men are intended for a higher level of ultimate existence than the angels even though in their human existence on earth they may be lower than the angels (Heb. 2:7). Even Jesus in His earthly life was "a little lower than the angels" (v. 9). Though angels never rise above the level of their creation, man is destined to be like Christ in heaven (1 John 3:2). The implications of divine inbreathing point to man's prominence and permanence as originated in the outbreathing of God as *Elohim*, implying that all three Persons of the Godhead shared in the creation of man.

All that God created was said to be "very good" (Gen. 1:31). In creating man, God made a creature with whom He could have fellowship, and who could share the moral quality of holiness. However, man became marred by the fall into sin. In the eternal purpose of God, however, man, though in a fallen state, could be redeemed and reconciled to God and restored to a spiritual state in which he would reflect the righteousness and holiness of God (Eph. 4:24). Man, in his present state when saved by faith in Christ, immediately achieves a position of holiness in Christ. His spiritual state, however, awaits perfection until the resurrection when he will receive a new sinless body and be rendered secure from any subsequent sin.

It is apparent that in creating Adam and Eve God gave them knowledge, language, and capacity to reason. In their state of innocence they were free from all sin and were able to commune with God without hindrance.

In creating man, God designed a creature who would display the glory of God and His moral perfections throughout eternity. This is accomplished by the grace of God through the sacrifice of Christ, and man is in contrast to angels who knew neither salvation nor grace experientially (Eph. 2:4-7).[280]

Though man was created innocent before he sinned, man in redemption becomes a new creation; he is more than what Adam was before sinning. Standing before God positioned in His holiness, a redeemed person is an illustration of the grace of God in a sense that Adam in his innocence could never have been. In the eternal plan of God, man in salvation is destined to be conformed to the likeness of God's Son (Rom. 8:29), which is more than was achieved in the original Creation. This conformity to Christ is evident even in the resurrection or translated body that believers will receive and is indicated in the fact that God "will transform our lowly bodies so that they will be like His glorious body" (Phil. 3:21; 1 John 3:2).[281]

In defining what is meant by the image of God one can affirm that it distinguishes man from animals and that man has facilities and moral capacity which apparently animals do not have. Man has an intellect or rationality different from that of animals in that man can think God thoughts, especially in his redeemed state. Man has an element also of self-consciousness made more acute in his redemptive estate (Roman 8:16). In general man can be compared to God in that he has personality, including in intellect, sensibility, and will. These characteristics are what identify man as being somewhat like God and which make it possible for man to fellowship with God.

The immaterial part of man is difficult to comprehend. One reason is that the Scriptures use many different terms for that part of man. Apart from the immaterial the human body does not continue to exist; it decays into the dust it came out of. The principle of life is necessary for the continuance of the human being in the body.

Terms such as soul, spirit, heart, flesh, and mind all refer to different aspects of man's immaterial part. Yet some of these terms represent the entire person. Soul and spirit are given special prominence in Scripture in relation to the theology of the immaterial part of man.

Three texts distinguish between soul and spirit. "it is sown a natural body, it is raised a spiritual body" (1 Cor. 15:44). "May God Himself, the God of peace, sanctify you through and through. May your whole spirit, soul, and body be kept blameless at the coming of our Lord Jesus Christ" (1 Thes. 5:23). "The Word of God is living and active. Sharper than any double-edged sword, it penetrates even to dividing soul and spirit, joints and marrow; it judges the thoughts and attitudes of the heart" (Heb. 4:12).[282]

Some works of the flesh are wholly unrelated to the body such as those included in the acts of the sinful nature in Galatians 5:19-21, "The acts of the sinful nature are obvious: sexual immorality, impurity, and debauchery; idolatry, and witchcraft; hatred, discord, jealousy, fits of rage, selfish ambition, dissension factions, and envy; drunkenness, orgies, and the like." While such things as "drunkenness, orgies, and the like" as well as "debauchery" may be related to the body, such sinful acts as hatred, discord, and jealously are manifestations of the flesh or the sin nature but are not related directly to the body.

In some passages of Scripture the flesh is contrasted to the Holy Spirit. Victory over the flesh is possible only by the power of the Holy Spirit (Rom. 8:2-4). A major passage is Galatians 5:15-17, "So I say, live by the Spirit, and you will not gratify the desires of the sinful nature. For the sinful nature desires what is contrary to the Spirit, and the Spirit what is contrary to the sinful nature. They are in conflict with each other, so that you do not do what you want." Other pertinent Scriptures add additional light on the subject (Rom. 8:13; Gal. 5:24-25; 6:8; Col. 2:11; Jude 20-23).[284]

The mind *nous* (gr.) is another reference to the immaterial part of man, which is closely related to the Holy Spirit and the flesh. The mind of the sinful man leads to death, but the mind controlled by the Spirit leads to life and peace (Rom. 8:6). Paul also contrasted the mind and the sinful nature with these words, "So then, I myself in my mind am a slave to God's Law, but in the sinful nature a slave to the law of sin" (Rom. 7:25). Paul also stated, "The sinful mind is hostile to God. It does not submit to God's Law, nor can it do so" (Rom. 8:7). The minds and conscience of the unsaved are corrupted (Titus 1:15).

The "spirit," "soul," and "heart" may each be related to the evil flesh or the sin nature, or each of these may be related to the new nature and the indwelling Holy Spirit. The challenge is to let God's provision for the holy life have its corresponding effect on the whole immaterial part of man.[285]

In discussing the immaterial part of man, consideration should be given not only to the elements that comprise the aspect of man's personality, but also the activities or functions of an individual, including the intellect, sensibility, and will.

The elements of immaterial man (soul, spirit, heart, flesh, and mind) and the modes of expression of the immaterial nature (intellect, sensibility, and will) form the major aspects of human experience. The mind may originate thoughts, the memory may retain thoughts, the spirit may discern the value of thoughts, and the soul respond to the thoughts, but the conscience judges thoughts in respect to their moral worth.

THE STATE OF INNOCENCE

When God planted the Garden of Eden, the prospect was as pleasing as could be secured by material things. The attractiveness of the Garden was in harmony with all else that God had created and concerning which He had said, "It is very good" (Gen. 1:31). Streams watered the ground (2:6), and trees in the Garden were "pleasing to the eye and good for food" (v. 9). A poor environment might encourage one to evil, but that is not likely. The situation in which the first man and woman were placed could not have contributed at all to their failure. The Garden reflected the power, goodness, and omniscience of the infinite God.

The obligation resting on the first man was a norm or pattern for all human life on earth. He was responsible to do the will of God. In the Garden of Eden Adam lived in unbroken fellowship with God and received daily counsel and direction from God. Only one prohibition was imposed on him (Gen. 2:17), which was a small part of God's gracious instructions. Too often the negative side of God's will is stretched out of all proportion. Though some things are evil and not convenient and are things which Christians should abstain, the will of God is positive. There is much that a Christian may do in joyous fellowship with the Father and with His Son (1 John 1:3-4). A Christian may walk and talk with God, enjoy the guiding and teaching ministries of the Holy Spirit, and receive His enabling power to realize God's perfect will. This illustrates the high privilege and responsibility of the first man when no cloud intervened between his Creator and himself.

As holiness may be either active or passive, the moral qualities of the first man were passive; he was innocent of any wrongdoing. No opportunity had been given him to develop a tested moral character, but the Bible implies that having been endowed with a conscience, he understood the difference between right and wrong. Adam was wholly accountable to God, and this fact alone certifies the moral development he sustained. Adam was created a mature man, with age built in to his creation. Though he had no past history to recall nor did he have the value of accumulated experience, no higher attestation of full-grown human excellence could be found than is exhibited in the truth that as created was well pleasing to God and thus was received into divine companionship.

According to Genesis 3, Satan approached Eve in the form of a beautiful serpent. Satan is identified as a "serpent" in Revelation 12:9 also. The earlier history of Satan, including his creation and fall into sin and his motivation to be like God, has already been discussed. The record is clear that Satan is the one who tempted Adam and Eve (2 Cor. 11:3; 1 Tim. 2:14).

In instructing Adam and Eve about their service for the Lord, He "commended the man, 'You are free to eat from any tree in the garden; but you must not eat from the tree of the knowledge of good and evil, for when you eat of it you will surely die' " (Gen. 2:1-17). In the conversation between Eve and the serpent, Eve reported that God had said, "You must not eat fruit from the tree that is in the middle of the garden, and you must not even touch it, or you will die" (3:3). In restating God's command Eve made it more severe than it actually was for she told Satan that she could not even touch the fruit. Satan replied by denying what God had said, "You will not surely die,' the serpent said to the woman. 'For God knows that when you eat of it your eyes will be opened, and you will be like God, knowing good from evil'" (vv. 4:5). Satan's deception is typical of his way of temptation. Satan questioned the accuracy of the word of God and the certainty of punishment for sin. And he also said that God was withholding what was good for man- which Satan would give them if they obeyed him. The temptation appealed to natural human desires in that the tree seemed to be good for food and beautiful, "pleasing to the eye" (v. ; 2:9). Also it appealed to man's desire to achieve by making the fruit "desirable for gaining wisdom" (3:6).[286]

Three avenues of temptation are mentioned in 1 John 2:16, "For everything in the world – cravings of sinful man, the lust of his eyes, and the boasting of what he has and does- comes not from the Father but from the world." What Eve did know was that what was good for food was not necessarily good for her, that what was beautiful was not necessarily wise to posses and that while she would have increased knowledge of good and evil, she would not have the power in herself to resist the evil or to do the good. Being deceived she partook of the fruit. Adam was not deceived (1 Tim. 2:14) but chose to follow the example of his wife, and thus Adam sinned. The results are revealed in history. Through Adam's sin, the human race was plunged into sin and made liable to physical and spiritual death to the whole human race.[287]

Though there has been considerable speculation as to the moral nature of Adam in his innocence, it is obvious in tempting Eve, Satan was desiring to gain control of both Adam and Eve, and to divert them from worshiping and serving God.

The penalty that fell on Adam, both physical death and spiritual death, has often been considered too severe by those who do not recognize the infinite holiness of God and the infinite depth of any sin against God. The question of whether Adam would ever have suffered physical death if he had not sinned is not answered in the Bible. But it is possible that if he and Eve had resisted their first temptation, they would have been rendered impeccable or unable to sin as the holy angels were after their test. This, however, is pure speculation on my part, and the fact is that God knew from eternity past that man would sin and would need His redemptive program. Genesis 2-3 are the theological basis on which the whole system of biblical theology rests. Recognition of its accuracy and historicity is indispensable to an accurate theology.[288]

THE FALL

The fall of the first man must be seen in the light of what preceded it- Adam's innocence, the tempter, the temptation, and what followed the temptation, namely, spiritual death and depravity for the whole human race including physical death.

The extended doctrine concerning death is a fulfillment of the warning that God gave Adam and Eve, "When you eat of it you will surely die" (Gen. 2:17). This penalty was executed, and death in three forms was imposed on them. (1) Spiritual death, the separation of the soul and spirit from God, fell on them the moment they sinned. (2) Physical death began at once its process of disintegration and eventual separation of the soul and spirit from the body. (3) Adam and Eve became subject to the second death, which is the lake of fire, the eternal separation of the soul and spirit from God in hell. Though the lake of fire (hell) was prepared for the devil and his fallen angels (Matt. 25:41), men are now liable to its eternal punishment promised Satan if they follow Satan and forsake God.[289]

Though spiritual death and physical death differ, they both originated as a result of the first sin of man. Spiritually dead persons may be physically alive as illustrated in the Ephesian believers before they were saved (Eph. 2:1-2).

In performing his first sin Adam became degenerated and depraved, with a fallen nature contrary to God and prone to evil. His constitution was altered fundamentally. A similar fall into degeneracy had been experienced by Satan and the angels who fell from their first estate. But those who are descended from Adam do not become sinners by sinning but are born sinners as a result of their sinful parentage. They receive the sin nature that Adam passed on to his posterity.

Physical death, though originating from the same sin, is not comparable to spiritual death. Man may be spiritually dead and physically alive or physically dead and spiritually alive. Spiritual death merges into the second death, which is eternal separation from God (Rev. 20:14). Ultimately physical death will be destroyed, but spiritual death will be the lot of all who are not saved by the grace of God.

INTRODUCTION TO HAMARTIOLOGY

The doctrine of man's nature and fall form the background
for the whole doctrine of hamartiology as well as the ultimate
plan of God for redemption on Christ.

The sin of man and the holiness of God are both infinite in proportion. Under satanic influence people have often tended to minimize the sinfulness of man, and in so doing, they also minimize the redemptive plan of God. Sin and redemption are to be as sharply contrasted as hell and heaven. Interpreters faithful to the Scriptures recognize the infinite extent of both.

The problem that sin creates is more than a conflict between good and evil in human conduct. It involves conflict between that holiness which is true of God, and all that is opposed to it. The subject includes more than the loss or injury sustained by the one who sins. It intrudes into God's role as Creator. The ultimate triumph of righteousness over unrighteousness is assured and secured by the very nature of God and by God's unqualified promise of the new heaven and the new earth in which righteousness shall dwell. The Bible frequently anticipates the time when evil will be banished from the created world and remain only in the lake of fire.

The holy character of God is the final and the only standard by which moral values may be accurately judged. The influence of the standards of social customs over the dictates of an unsure and perverted conscience are not sufficient to identify sin. Sin is sinful because it is unlike God. Though disobedience to God's Law is sin, it does not follow that sin is restricted to disobedience of the Law. Selfishness is sin, but sin is not always selfishness. The "love of money is a root of all kinds of evil" (1 Tim. 6:10), but not all evil is represented in the love of money. So also unbelief is sin, but sin is more than unbelief.

Sin still draws its essential character of sinfulness from the fact that it is unlike God.

The term "evil" and "sin" represent somewhat different ideas. Evil refers to what, though latent and not expressed, is conceivable as the opposite of what is good. Sin is what is concrete and actively opposed to the character of God. The human mind does not have the capacity to depict the time when there was not an opposite to good even though at the time no one was sinning. Since God Himself could not err, sin could not come into existence until other beings were created such as the angels and then men.

The Bible reveals little concerning the derivation of evil. Scripture does record the sin of Satan and the angels who fell with him from their previous holy estate. Scripture also records the sin of Adam and Eve. In both cases the guilt of those who sinned is attributed to them. Because of God's perfect holiness He could not create evil, and evil had to be a departure from God by disobedience.

The presence of sin in the universe is due to the fact that God permits it. Obviously God would not have permitted it if it had not been for a justifiable purpose. In view of the perfection of God it may be assumed that such permission of sin was done for a justifiable cause.

In permitting sin God was not overtaken by a disaster He did not foresee. If the imagination of men could penetrate the past and picture God confronted with 10,000 possible blueprints of the plan adopted for the present universe with its triumphs and tragedies, its satisfactions and sufferings, it gains and losses, man can only by faith conclude that the best plan and purpose that could be devised by the infinite love of God.

Though it is impossible for mankind to understand fully why a holy God would permit sin, it is evident that God's purpose required this permission. God, who could have hindered sin, did permit it. Believers recognize that they have profited by God's redemptive plan while at the same time realizing that God is not implicated in sin's guilt and wickedness.

PERSONAL SIN

The term "personal sin" refers to the form of sin that originates with or is committed by individuals. This includes the sins of angels as well as the sins of human beings. Personal sin is an important ground for divine condemnation. In man personal sin is the fruit of the sin nature, and yet dealing with personal sin does not solve the entire sin problem.

The personal sin of Adam and Eve plunged the human race into sin which resulted in (1) passing the sin nature from parents to children and (2) imputing sin to all people in that Adam represented the human race.

In the final analysis there are only two philosophies of life. One is to be conformed to the will of God, which is the original divine arrangement. The other is to forsake the Creator and renounce His authority. Satan's purpose in enticing Adam and Eve to sin was to create a vast world system in which he would become the object of man's worship and obedience. Satan realized that his goal of world domination was at stake in the Garden of Eden. He must gain supremacy over man or fail completely. Adam and Eve did not realize that they were becoming bondslaves to sin and Satan.

Sin is essentially a restless unwillingness on the part of the creature to abide in the sphere and limitation in which the all-wise Creator placed him. In general, sin is lack of conformity to the character of God. In the case of Adam his personal sin resulted in his nature becoming sinful. In the case of Adam's descendants they are born with a sinful nature which manifests itself in personal sin.

Sin can be measured by its contrast to the infinite holy character of God. Fallen man does not understand the depths of human sin. Only by accepting the revelation of what sin is as revealed in the Word of God can man in his limitation partially understand the infinite character of sin against God.

The scripture distinguished between sin as a state of heart or mind and sin as an act. The sinful nature of man is contrasted to the fruit of that sinful nature.

Jesus expressed this in these words, "What comes out of a man is what makes him 'unclean.' For from within, out of man's heart, come evil thoughts, sexual immorality, theft, murder, adultery, greed, malice, deceit, lewdness, envy, slander, arrogance, and folly. All these evils come from inside and make a man 'unclean'" (Mark 7:20-23).[290]

Personal sin includes two aspects: sin against God, and sin against law.   Sins against God's person are suggested by such terms as "godlessness," "defilement," and "selfhood," and sins against God's moral government are indicated by such terms as "transgression," "rebellion," and "lawlessness."

Because of its immoral nature sin outrages and insults the holy person of God, who is infinitely pure and righteous. As Habakuk expressed it, "Your eyes are too pure to look on evil; You cannot tolerate wrong" (Hab. 1:13). John stated, "This is the message we have heard from Him and declare to you: God is light; and in Him there is no darkness at all" (1 John 1:5). In regard to temptation James wrote, "When tempted, no one should say, 'God is tempting me.' For God cannot be tempted by evil, nor does He tempt anyone" (James 1:13).[291]

The theory sometimes is conveyed that sin is essentially selfishness. This view is advanced by Julius Muller and Augustus H. Strong.[292] Though it is true that selfishness is sin, it is an inadequate definition to say that all sin is selfishness. Opposition of God and exaltation of self do spring from the same self-motive. Jesus stated the contrast to selfishness: "Love the Lord your God with all your heart and with all your soul and with all your mind.' This is the first and greatest commandment. And the second is like it: 'Love your neighbor as yourself.' All the Law and Prophets hang on these two commandments" (Matt. 22:37-40). Self-interest is not necessarily present in malice, enmity toward God, or unbelief. As unselfishness in Christ did not exhaust His virtues, selfishness in Satan does not exhaust his iniquity. If it were theoretically possible for a lost soul to love God it would not relieve his essential condemnation. It is true that God is love, but He is more than love. He is also truth, faithfulness, and righteousness. Selfishness, though a large factor in man's sin, does not completely apply to every act, attitude, or the sin nature.[293]

The Bible makes clear that personal sin is the result of an individual having a sin nature (Gal. 5:1-21). Being born with a sin nature (Ps. 51:5) is not the same as committing personal sin though it does involve condemnation, that is, being unlike the character of God. In addition to being born a sinner, each individual faces guilt and condemnation because of personal sin. The divine cure for personal sin is forgiveness and justification.[29]

Christ's outcry at the cross, "My God, My God, why have You forsaken Me?" (Mark 15:35) a quotation of Psalm 22:1, indicates the fact that Christ was the sin offering from which God had to turn away. Because Christ has assumed the burden of all the sins of the world, until His atonement was complete, God the Father had to turn away from His Son, something that had never happened before. This fulfilled the typological meaning of the nonsweet savor offering.

The sweet savor offering represented Christ's righteous acts which God accepted and which are imputed to the believer in his justification. Justification then is not mere removal of personal sins by forgiveness but is a divine decree which declares the believer to be eternally clothed with the righteousness of God. This act of God is based on the death of Christ on the cross. His death made divine justification possible by a righteous God who must condemn sin. Because the believer is justified he cannot be condemned (Rom. 8:31-35). As justified individuals, believers will demonstrate the grace of God throughout eternity to come (Eph. 2:7), and those who are unsaved will disclose the wrath of God (Rom. 9:22).[295]

The term "original sin" carries with it two implications: (1) the first sin of the race and (2) the state of man in all subsequent generations as a result of sin. Though theology is primarily concerned with the result of the sin, in considering personal sin, attention must be paid to the first sin of Adam which brought about nature as Adam's original sin; if placed in the position of Adam as the creation of God and as the federal, unfallen head of the race, anyone who would have sinned would experience the same results. The first sin serves as one of the best measurements of the evil character of all sin.

In popular usage guilt refers to the consciences of sin. From the theological point of view, however, such a definition is defective. Sin draws its evil character from the fact that it is unlike God, and the sin is evil whether the sinner realizes it or not. A distinction also has to be observed between being worthy of blame and being guilty. The Apostle Paul admitted his sin in persecuting the church even though he did it ignorantly (1 Tim. 1:13). Guilt on the other hand though blameworthy belongs to the individual where his own estimation concerning himself might not coincide with God's point of view. Christ made even the glance of an eye equivalent to adultery (Matt. 5:27-28).[296]

Apart from the work of Christ on behalf of believers in His death on the cross, no sinner could ever remove the guilt of his sin. Christ did not bear man's guilt in the sense that the sin of man became the obligation of a divine justice. Accordingly He was made our sin offering, dying as the righteous One for the unrighteous (2 Cor. 5:21). In a sense the basis of a sinner's guilt remains forever, and it is only possible to escape its just penalty by receiving the righteousness of Christ.

The universality of sin is indicated in the statement, "God was reconciling the world to Himself in Christ, not counting men's sins against them" (2 Cor. 5:19). The universality of sin is also the argument in Romans, "For all have sinned and fall short of the glory of God" (Rom. 3:23; Gal. 3:22; 1 John 1:10).[297]

Personal sin is traced in the Scriptures to the fact that everyone possesses a sin nature inherited from his or her parents. Though some attempt to deny the sin nature in Christians, who are new creations in Christ, full attention to Scripture reveals that all sins are traceable to the sin nature, which all men possess.

THE TRANSMITTED SIN NATURE

As every effect must have a cause, there is a cause for the fact that personal sin is universal. That cause is the sin nature, the inborn sin, or the lesser self. The effect of the first sin on unfallen Adam was degeneration. Because of his sin, Adam became a different kind of being from what God had created. Each descendent of Adam has reproduced his fallen nature, following the law that each person produces according to his kind (Gen. 1:25).[298]

Adam's experience was unique in that he became a sinner by sinning. Every other member of the human race except Christ sins because he is a sinner by birth. In Adam's case a personal sin caused the sin nature; in the case of all other human beings except Christ the sin nature causes personal sin.

The sin of Adam merited the penalty of death as God had warned. That penalty is evident in three forms. One of these is physical death, which, as God had warned, would be the result of disobedience (Gen 2:17). In addition to physical death Adam died spiritually, which is a separation of the soul and spirit from God just as physical death is called "the second death" (Rev. 20:14), which is eternal separation from God.[299]

Though theologians have differed on the subject, spiritual death and the sin nature are transmitted mediately from parent to child in all generations. The last child to be born into the race will bear spiritual death and a sin nature just as Cain received these from his father Adam.

In becoming a sinner with a sin nature, Adam, while retaining some aspect of the original creation, was in an injured or disabled state in which he could know to do good but not have the power to do it. W.G.T. Shedd's writes with force on the question of the fallen nature and its guilt, an issue which has divided Calvinists and Arminians. Shedd states:

"Original sin, considered as corruption of nature, is sin in the sense of guilt…'Every sin, both original and actual, being a transgression of the righteous law of God doth in its own nature bring guilt upon the sinner, whereby he is bound over to the wrath of God, and made subject to death, temporal and eternal." Westminster Confession, VI. vi. "Corruption of nature doth remain in those that are regenerated, and although it be through Christ pardoned and mortified, yet both itself and all the motions thereof are truly and properly sin". Westminster Confession, VI. v. The Semi-Pelagian, Papal, and Arminian anthropologies differ from the Augustinian and Reformed, by denying that corruption of nature is guilt. It is physical and mental disorder leading to sin, but it is not sin itself."[300]

The fact that man has a sin nature is the reason he is considered totally depraved. Such a statement does not mean that man is as sinful as he can be, but rather that every aspect of his character has been affected by his sin nature. Many Scriptures support the concept of depravity (Gen. 8:21; Ps. 14:23; 51:5; Jer. 17:5, 9l John 3:6; Rom. 1:18-8:13; 1 Cor. 7:14; Gal. 5:17-21; Eph. 2:3.[301]

The word "flesh" (Gr., sarx) often means the human nature in its corruption. The works of the flesh are in contrast to the fruit of the Spirit. As Jeremiah states, "The heart is deceitful above all things, and desperately wicked; who can know it?" (Jer. 17:9, KJV) The NIV reads this way: "The heart is deceitful above all things and beyond cure." The sinfulness of man is a consistent theme of Scripture.[302]

The remedy for man's sin nature is found in the divine revelation of God's plan of salvation. The problem of the sin nature in the Christian's daily life relates to the subject of the spiritual life and God's provisions for the Christian's victory over sin. As the sin nature demonstrates the need of salvation in the unsaved, it is a misrepresentation of the Gospel to assure people that they are lost because of their personal sins. Man is lost by nature because he was born a lost soul with no hope of redemption apart from the redeeming blood of Christ. The twofold remedy for the sin nature is (1) the judgment for believers of the sin nature by Christ on the cross and (2) the gift of the indwelling Spirit as One who is able to give victory over every evil disposition. Though a redeemed person still has a sin nature, he is not condemned because "There is now no condemnation for those who are in Christ Jesus" Rom. 8:1).[303]

The fact that a fallen nature was received immediately from Adam is supported by the following facts: (1) The fact of the fallen nature is established by Scripture. (2) The fallen nature is observed in all of human history. (3) The fallen nature is witnessed to by the conciseness of man.

IMPUTED SIN

The word *impute* means "to attribute something to a person that usually is derived from another".[304] An illustration is found in Paul's word to Philemon concerning Onesimus, "So if you consider me a partner, welcome him as you would welcome me. If he has done you any wrong or owes you anything, charge it to me" (Phile. 17-19). The word "charge" (Gr., *ellogeo*) is also found in Romans 5:13, "For before the Law was given, sin was in the world. But sin is not taken into account [Gr., *ellogeo*] when there is no Law".[305] In the KJV, Romans 5:13 is translated, "For until the Law sin was in the world; but sin is not imputed when there is no Law." The thought in both translations is that of imputation or rendering or not rendering something to the account of another.

The more common word used in the New Testament for imputation is found in 4:6 and relates to imputation of righteousness, "David says the same thing when he speaks of the blessedness of the man to whom God credits [Gr., *logizomai*] righteousness apart from works." In verse 8 the same word is used of imputation of sin, "Blessed is the man whose sin the Lord will never count against him." This word for imputation is found 41 times in the New Testament with occurrences in Roman 4.

In connection with man's relation to God, the Bible presents three major imputations: (1) imputation of Adamic sin to the human race, (2) imputation of the sin of man to the Substitute Christ, and (3) imputation of the righteousness of God to the believer.

Imputation may be either real or judicial. When it is used in a real sense it is reckoning to one what is antecedently his, while judicial imputation is the reckoning to one what is not antecedently his. If the trespass mentioned in 2 Corinthians 5:19 were imputed to those mentioned, it would have been a real imputation. The trespasses were their own and the reckoning of those trespasses to them would have been no more than the official declaration of their accountability. In contrast to this when the apostle said in Philemon 18, "Charge it to me," he spoke of a dept which was not antecedently his own.

By contrast, human sin was imputed to Christ. This is a clear instance of judicial imputation. Likewise the imputation of the righteousness of God to the believer is said to be just on the part of God because He justifies those who believe in Christ, bestowing on them something which is not antecedently their own. This imputation is also judicial in character.

The subject of imputation of sin may be discussed under three headings: (1) the scope of the doctrine of imputation, (2) theories of imputation, and (3) the divine remedy for imputed sin.

The actual imputation of Adamic sin to all men is clearly indicated in the text by Charles Hodge, he states pretty clearly:

"The doctrine of imputation is clearly taught in this passage. This doctrine does not include the idea of a mysterious identity of Adam and his race; nor that of a transfer of the moral turpitude of his sin to his descendants. It does not teach that his offense was personally or properly the sin of all men or that his act was, in any mysterious sense, the act of his posterity. Neither does it imply, in reference to the righteousness of Christ, that His righteousness becomes personally and inherently ours, or that His moral excellence is in any way transferred from Him to believers. The sin of Adam, therefore, is no ground of self-complacency in those to whom it is imputed. This doctrine merely teaches, that in virtue of the union, representative and natural, between Adam and his posterity, his sin is the ground of their condemnation, that is, of their subjection to penal evils; and that, in virtue of the union between Christ and His people, His righteousness is the ground of their justification. This doctrine is taught almost in so many words in vs. 12, 15-19" (Romans) "It is so clearly stated, that very few commentators of any class fail to acknowledge, in one form or another, that it is the doctrine of the apostle.[306]

Many have difficulty with the concept of federal headship, the relationship between Adam and the race, because this is not true of any other man apart from Christ. However, Christ is the Head of the new creation, the church. As Adam's sin is reckoned to all men, the righteousness of Christ is reckoned to all who are in Him.

Another illustration is Hebrews 7:9-10, which speaks of Levi paying tithes to Melchizedek. But Levi did so representatively because he was not yet born. The same idea of representation is found in 1 Corinthians 15:22, "For as in Adam all die, so in Christ all will be made alive." Divine reckoning of the whole human race is seen as being in Adam, and every believer is seen as being in Christ. Further evidence is seen in Romans 5:13-14, and points out that death, which was experienced by the human race between Adam and Moses, is traceable to the fact that they were in Adam. Undoubtedly some people were saved in the period between Adam and Moses, and yet death was all-inclusive with one exception of Enoch. In verses 15-19 the contrast of the imputation of Adam's sin to the race is seen in Christ's giving justification to believers. Condemnation came through one sin, whereas justification came in spite of many offences. In verse 20 sin because of the Law is contrasted to the righteous reign of grace, which was secured by Jesus Christ when He died on the cross. The triumphant conclusion is stated in verse 21, "So that, just as sin reigned in death, so also grace might reign through righteousness to bring eternal life through Jesus Christ our Lord.[307]

In summary, the theological fact of imputed sin means that the initial sin of Adam converges on every member of the human race. A crucial distention must be maintained between the transmitted sin nature which is received mediately, and imputed sin which is received immediately. Both the sin nature and imputed sin are distinct from personal sin. The sin nature is not an act of sin. In contract to this, though men are held individually responsible, the penalty of physical death for their sin was a personal sin in Adam's experience. Imputed sin is held in the Scriptures to be unlike personal sin, and this unlikeness is demonstrated with extended argument.

MAN'S ESTATE UNDER SIN
AND HIS RELATION TO SATAN

The phrase "under sin" occurs three times in the New Testament in the KJV: "We have before proved both Jews and Gentiles, that they are under sin" (Rom. 3:9); "But I am carnal, sold under sin" (7:17); and "But the Scripture hath concluded all under sin" (Gal. 3:22). The NIV translates Romans 7:14, "Sold as a slave to sin." The important meaning of the phrase may be seen when compared with similar expressions "under Law" and "under grace." The word "under" as used in these passages implies more than a system of sin, Law, or grace. "Under sin" suggest that an inherent dominion is over the individual.

The concept of being "under sin" is true for both unregenerate Jews and Gentiles. Both Jews and Gentiles can be saved by the same Gospel of divine grace offered to them all. Paul stated in regard to this, "As the Scripture says, 'Everyone who trusts in Him will never be put to shame.' For there is no difference between Jew and Gentile – the same Lord is Lord of all and richly blesses all who call on Him, for, 'Everyone who calls on the name of the Lord will be saved," (10:11-13; Acts 15:9; Rom. 3:22).[308]

Paul spoke of the Israelites who had a special relationship to God before the Church Age: "For I could wish that I myself were cursed and cut off from Christ for the sake of my brothers, those of my own race, the people of Israel. Theirs is the adoption as sons; theirs the worship, and the promises. Theirs are the patriarchs, and from them is traced the human ancestry of Christ, who is God over all, forever praised! Amen".

The position of all people in the present age as being under sin is due to divine decree. According to Galatians 3:22, "But the Scripture declares that the whole world is a prisoner of sin, so that what was promised, being given through faith in Jesus Christ, might be given to those who believe." Also Romans 11:32 states, "For God has bound all men over to disobedience so that He may have mercy on them all." These declarations remove any obscurity as to whether Jews and Gentiles are the same before God in the present age.

The remedy for this meritless and therefore hopeless estate is the saving grace of God through Christ in all its magnitudes and perfections. In the present age an individual is either under sin or under grace and all that grace secures. Besides having his sins forgiven, the person under grace is also justified freely (Rom. 3:24) and stands in all the perfection of Christ (Eph. 1:6; Col. 2:10). These Scriptures also reveal the supreme objective in the death of Christ, to demonstrate His love for lost men and the desire of all three Persons of the Trinity to redeem man. The Father's love is manifested in the giving of His Son (John 3:16). Christ after His suffering was satisfied by the salvation He provided (Isa. 53:11), and the Holy Spirit is satisfied as were the other two Persons of the Trinity, "in bringing many sons to glory" (Heb. 2:10). Though people may be satisfied with the fact of their salvation, God is also infinitely satisfied that in love He can redeem those who were formerly lost. The full extent of this salvation will be revealed when Christians are presented to God in heaven fully conformed to His holiness (Rom. 8:29; Eph.2:7; 1 John 3:2).[309]

The fact that a man is saved without respect to any human merit is an important truth emphasized in the New Testament. Salvation does not include anything good in man but is based entirely on God's grace and Christ's death on the cross. The result is that saved mankind is a new creation (2 Cor. 5:17). Though salvation is not based on any human works or merit, when one is saved he is "God's workmanship, created in Christ Jesus to do good works, which God prepared in advance for us to do" (Eph. 2:10). The fact that this great salvation is not based on human works is brought out clearly in Romans 4:4-5 and 11:16.[310]

The estate of unregenerate people may be summarized as follows: (1) They are subject to death in all its forms because of participation in Adam's sin. (2) They are born in depravity or spiritual death and are forever separated from God unless regenerated by the saving power of God. (3) They are guilty of personal sins, each of which is as sinful in the sight of God as the first sin of Satan or the first sin of Adam. (4) They are under sin, in which estate every human merit is disregarded. (5) They are under the influence of Satan who is in authority over them, who energizes them. The only relief from this sad situation is for an individual to be saved by faith in Jesus Christ.

THE CHRISTIAN'S SIN AND ITS REMEDY

A believer cannot be effective in reaching others unless he has attained by God's grace a victory in his own life and is walking in fellowship with Him as stated in 1 John 1:7, "But if we walk in the light, as He is in the light, we have fellowship with one another, and the blood of Jesus, His Son, purifies us from all sin." Walking in the light does not infer that it is possible for an individual to be sinless; it means that his life should correspond to the revelation of the written Word as taught by the Spirit of God.

Though human failure is inevitable, God has provided for restoration, "If we confess our sins, He is faithful and just and will forgive us our sins and purify us from all unrighteousness".   A Christian, by confessing his sin to God and seeking God's help for victory, can attain by God's grace a life that is pleasing to the Lord.

The Christian walk is supernatural and is made possible by the grace of God. Because of his unique position in Christ a Christian will have conflicts with the world and the devil as well as with the sin nature he still retains. A Christian's conflict is threefold: (1) against the world, (2) against the flesh or the sin nature, and (3) against the devil.

The world (Gr., *kosmos*) is the sphere of the Christian's conflict. As revealed in the New Testament the world is seen in its order, system, and regulation. Because of satanic influence it is opposed to God. Its characteristics are planned by Satan himself who seeks to promote himself as the world's prince and god. The modern world illustrates this with low ideals and sordid entrainment. Some aspects of the world are close counterfeits of the things of God and the believer should seek divine guidance regarding where to draw the line of separation between the things of God and the things of Satan's world.

Though some aspects of the world are clearly of Satan and not of God, often borderline issues become confusing. In regard to this the Spirit of God can give guidance and discernment to the believer to enable him to overcome the world as stated in 1 John 5:4, "For everyone born of God overcomes the world. This victory that has overcome the world, even our faith: The apostle continued in verse 5 with, "Who is it that overcomes the world? Only he who believes that Jesus is the Son of God".

Though "the flesh" (Gr., *sarx*) sometimes refers to human physical bodies, more often it refers to man's sinful nature which includes the desires of the body. The flesh in its moral significance is incurably evil in the sight of God. From it comes evil victory over these things through the larger and restraining power of the Holy Spirit.

Paul recognized the nature of this spiritual conflict when he wrote, "I know that nothing good lives in me, that is, in my sinful nature. For I have the desire to do good, but cannot carry it out. For what I do is not the good I want to do; no, the evil I do not want to do- this I keep on doing. Now if I do what I do not want to do, it is no longer I who do it, but it is sin living in me that does it" (Rom. 7:18-20).[312]

Closely related to a Christian's two enemies, the world system and the flesh or sin nature, is another enemy, Satan. Satan uses means such as his control of the world and its standards in his conflict with Christians. Though the world and the sinful nature are influenced by Satan, the conflict between the regenerate and Satan is a personal conflict. Just as the world is energized by Satan (Eph. 2:2), so the Christian is enabled by the Holy Spirit to have victory, as Paul indicated in Romans 7:7-25. In Ephesians 6:10-18 the conflict between Satan and the Christian is spoken of as warfare in which the Christian must use the available means of the power of God, His armor, His truth, His shield of faith, His helmet of salvation, and the sword of the Spirit in order to gain victory. The power of Satan should not be underestimated, but it is possible for a Christian enabled by the grace of God to resist Satan (James 4:7; John 15:5; 2 Cor. 10:3-5; Phil. 2:13; 4:13; 1 Peter 5:9).[313] Though the conflict with Satan is real, God has provided for victory.

The Word of God is one of the believer's principal means for contending against Satan. The psalmist declared, "I have hidden Your Word in my heart that I might not sin against You" (Ps. 119:11). The Word of God is also used to provide spiritual achievement (John 15:7). Paul summarized the importance of Scripture in contending against Satan, "All Scripture is God-breathed and is useful for teaching, rebuking, correcting, and training in righteousness, so that the man of God may be thoroughly equipped for every good work" (2 Tim. 3:16-17). The sanctifying power of the Word of God is also mentioned in John 17:17.[314]

As Christians are forgiven by God, they should also forgive their fellow Christians (Eph. 4:32; Col. 3:13). As Christ pointed out to His disciples, one cannot expect God to forgive and restore if he does not in turn forgive others (Matt. 6:14-15). This refers not to the forgiveness at the time of salvation but to the restoration of a sinning Christian.

It should also be noted that forgiveness is promised if Christians confess their sins. So it is not necessary to ask God for forgiveness because He has already promised to do so. It is necessary constantly to distinguish between the once-for-all forgiveness a Christian secures at the time of salvation and the restoration to fellowship which occurs experientially later in the Christian's life.[315]

Further illustration is given in John 13:1-17 where Christ distinguished between bathing feet and taking a whole bath. In His discourse with Peter, Christ pointed out that he did not need a bath, but he did need to have his feet washed. The important point which should not be lost is that God intends for a Christian to undergo continuous cleaning from the filth and defilement of the world and from any act of disobedience which may arise. This cleansing is available to the Christian on confession of his sins.

The reference to Jesus Christ as "the Righteous One" indicates the ground on which forgiveness is secured. It is not simply His own character as righteous but also the righteous basis on which He is requesting forgiveness for the sinning Christian. Christ presents His own death as evidence that He bore that sin on the cross. So the penalty for sin in the life of a believer is withheld.

While the justice of God has been fully met by Christ as one's Advocate, the effect of Christ's intercession is such that a sinning Christian can have his sin forgiven on the basis of confession. On the other hand if a Christian persists in his sin, he is subject to the discipline of God to bring him back to a place of fellowship (1 Cor. 11:31-32).[316]

The death of Christ does not provide any automatic victory for the believer, and in his own strength a Christian cannot command and control the old nature. Though he has a new nature, this fact in itself cannot gain him victory over the old nature. This is illustrated in Paul's struggle as stated in Romans 7:7-25. Paul confessed that the struggle between the old and the new natures is not one that he could resolve himself but must be accomplished by divine power, "through Jesus Christ our Lord".[317]

In Romans 8 Paul stated the fact that in Christ one can be free from the Law of sin and death and delivered from the domination of the sin nature. Not only was Paul free from condemnation because he is in Christ, but also "through Christ Jesus the law of the Spirit of life set me free from the Law of sin and death (Rom. 8:2). The secret of victory is to live not according to the sin nature but by the guidance and direction of the Holy Spirit (v. 4).[318]

These truths make clear that victory over sin is not accomplished by eradicating the sin nature but rather by depending on the superior power of the Holy Spirit. The Christian never reaches the point where he is not able to sin, but by the grace of God he can achieve being able not to sin. A believer's consciousness of sin and of his tendency to sin can lead to his coming into closer fellowship with

God, and having drawn nearer to God, to abhor his sinful nature.

Paul concluded, "Therefore, Brothers, we have an obligation – but it is not to the sinful nature, to live according to it. For if you live according to the sinful nature, you will die; but if by the Spirit you put to death the misdeeds of the body, you will live, because those who are led by the Spirit of God are sons of God.[319]

Physical death is the penalty for imputed sin (Rom. 6:13). Though Christians have entered into a righteous relationship with God, they are still subject to physical death until the return of Christ. No longer can they receive condemnation for their sin because now they are in Christ (Rom. 8:1). Other Scripture passages confirm the wonderful change that is wrought when a believer puts his trust in Christ and condemnation is removed (John 3:18l Rom. 8:38-39; 1 Cor. 11:32). Though physical death is still with him, the sting of death has been removed. Paul stated, "Where, O death, is your victory? Where, O death, is your sting? The sting of death is sin, and the power of sin is the Law. But thanks be to God! He gives us victory through our Lord Jesus Christ" (1 Cor. 15:55-57). Even if physical death overtakes a Christian, he has eternal life which brings him into the presence of God forever (Rom. 6:23).[320]

This relationship is only a memory as Paul stated in Ephesians 2:11. What was once a complete condemnation is exchanged for the infinite righteousness of Christ. A place in the world has been exchanged for a place in the Kingdom of God. The doom of sin's judgment has been exchanged for an immutable position in the sovereign grace of God that never ceases. Those under sin are said to be without Christ, having no hope and being without God (v. 12). Those under grace are described as having an unchanging righteous standing before God. "Praise be the God and Father of our Lord Jesus Christ, who has blessed us in the heavenly realms with every spiritual blessing in Christ" (Eph. 1:3).

PUNISHMENT

In the Bible punishment is referred to in three ways: chastisement, scourging, and retribution. The first two relate to God's way of dealing with impenitent Christians and the last to God's final dealing with the unsaved. I want to elaborate on these three, but only in brief outline in this section.

Chastisement is suffering brought into the life of a believer who is not living in the will of God for the purpose of correcting him. Though suffering is natural for a Christian, all suffering is not chastisement. Chastisement only refers to those trials God uses to being a Christian back into His will.

David spoke of this: "I will instruct you and teach you in the way you should go; I will counsel you and watch over you. Do not be like the horse or the mule, which have no understanding but must be controlled by a bit and bridle or they will not come to you. Many are the woes of the wicked, but the Lord's unfailing love surrounds the man who trusts in Him" (Ps. 32:8-10). In the same psalm David spoke of the suffering which led to his confession and restoration (vv. 3:6).[321]

The experience of scourging is closely related to chastisement and seems to refer to the conquering of the will and to result in a surrendered life to the Lord. Mentioned only once in Scripture (Heb. 12:6) it seem to be a crisis experience in the life of a Christian which does not reoccur, in contrast to chastisement which may be repeated.[322]

The universe God has created is clearly the product of an infinite mind and infinite power and wisdom. If all the unsaved knew was only what is clear from their observation of the physical world, they ought to worship God on the basis of this natural revelation. However, in practical experience they are never saved by such revelation; instead that revelation remains the ground of their condemnation.

The unsaved are utterly lost until they receive the Gospel and believe in Christ.

THE FINAL TRIUMPH OVER ALL SIN

Revelation and reason unite in one testimony that unjudged evil is temporary in the universe of God. Reason declares that God is infinitely holy and the Designer and Creator of the universe. Evil must have begun it's manifestation after Creation by His permission and will serve a purpose compatible with His righteousness. Reason also anticipates that when that purpose is accomplished, evil will be dismissed. God will complete His task in the perfection that characterizes all His works. The Bible is clear that God's ultimate victory is sure and judgment on sin and reward for righteousness will characterize eternity to come.

The ultimate victory of God is stated in 1 Corinthians 15:24-28. "Then the end will come, when He stands over the kingdom of God the Father after He has destroyed all dominion, authority, and power. For He must reign until He has put all His enemies under His feet. The last enemy to be destroyed is death. For He 'has put everything under His feet.' Now when it says that 'everything' has been put under Him, it is clear that this does not include God Himself, who put everything under Christ. When He has done this, then the Son Himself will be made subject to Him who put everything under Him, so that God may be all in all." (v.20). Christians will follow and be resurrected when Christ returns for His church. Before human history has run its course and merged into eternity, all human beings will be resurrected. All the righteous will be raised in a series of resurrections before the thousand years of Christ's reign. But the unsaved will not be raised until the climax at the end of the Millennium when they will be judged before the Great White Throne (Rev. 20:11-15).

The final triumph over sin and rebellion against God in the millennium reign of Christ will occur. God's triumph over sin will climax in the judgment of the wicked. The enemies of God must be put down and the last enemy, death, will be "swallowed up in victory" (1Cor 15:54).[323]

When Christ said in the Upper Room, "In My Father's house are many rooms" (John 14:2), He was indicating the various abodes in the universe which are related to the work of God. Four such dwelling places can be distinguished: (1) heaven, the abode of God; (2) the celestial city, the New Jerusalem which will come down from heaven to the earth (Rev. 21:2,19; (3) the new earth which will be inhabited by the saints who dwell in the celestial city; and (4) the abode of the unsaved who will not be allowed in the city (v.8). No revelation is given concerning the new heaven in the eternal state except that it does not have a sun or the moon (v.23). If the new earth corresponds to the heavenly bodies existing today it is apparently round as suggested by the directions of north, south, east, and west (vv. 12-14). The other possibility is to postulate a flat earth, which creates many problems.

A high wall will surround the celestial city with three gates on each of its four sides carrying the names of the 12 tribes Israel. The foundation of the city will be made of precious jewels of all colors of the rainbow. The inhabitants of the city will include God Himself, the holy angels, the church, the saved of Israel, and all righteous men (Heb. 12:22-24). The New Jerusalem is described as aglow with the glory of God. Its material will be translucent, thus allowing the glory of God to penetrate every place in the celestial city. The city will be of great size, some 1,500 miles square and 1,500 miles high. This will be the dwelling place of saints of all ages for all eternity to come.[324]

The new earth apparently will be not an old earth renovated but an entirely new creation. According to 2 Peter 3:7-13, the present heaven and earth will be dissolved and consumed with fire as confirmed by Hebrews 1:10-12. The heavenly city will be a place of joy, righteousness, peace, and adoration of God. Forever gone will be tears, death, sorrow, suffering, and pain (Rev. 21:3-4). In the celestial city men will marvel at the glory of God and will worship and serve Him for all eternity, Amen.

The triumph of God will be perfect and eternal. In the words of the Apostle Paul, "Oh, the depth of the riches of the wisdom and knowledge of God! How unreachable His judgments, and His paths beyond tracing out! 'Who has known the mind of the Lord? Or who has been His counselor? Who has ever given to God, that God should repay him? For from Him and through Him and to Him are all things. To Him be the glory forever! Amen" Rom. 11:33-36.[325]

SOTERIOLOGY

Soteriology is that division of theology which deals with the doctrine of salvation. The word "salvation" is the translation of the Greek word *soteria* which is taken from the word *soter* meaning "savior".[326] The word "salvation" communicates the thought of deliverance, safety, preservation, soundness, restoration, and healing. In theology, however, its major use is to denote a work of God on behalf of men, and as such it is a major doctrine of the Bible which includes redemption, reconciliation, propitiation, conviction, repentance, faith, regeneration, forgiveness, justification, sanctification, preservation, and glorification. On the one hand salvation is described as a work of God rescuing man from his lost estate. On the other hand salvation describes the estate of a man who has been saved and who is vitally renewed and made a partaker of the inheritance of the saints. Accordingly Gospel preaching may on the one hand warn the wicked to flee from the wrath to come, or it may attempt to win them by contemplation of those benefits which God's infinite grace provides.

The need of salvation has already been considered regarding man's fallen estate. According to Scripture man is doomed because of his fallen nature and because of his participation in Adam's original sin. Salvation therefore gives freedom from the curse of the Law (Gal. 3:13), from wrath (John 3:36; 1 Thes 5:9), from death (2 Cor. 7:10), and from destruction (2 Thes. 1:9).[327]

In the Old Testament the doctrine of salvation is taught but not with the same clarity as in the New Testament. According to John 1:17, "The Law was given through Moses; grace and truth came through Jesus Christ." The fact that God can provide salvation, however, is clearly taught in the Old Testament as stated in Jonah 2:9, "Salvation comes from the LORD," which may be considered the theme of the entire Bible.

God's promise of a redeemer is said to come first through Isaac, not Ishmael (Genesis 26:2-5), and then through Jacob, not Esau (28:13-15). The promise of salvation through the Messiah does not assure that every individual Israelite will be saved, for this is promised only to a remnant (Rom. 9:27). The statement that "all Israel will be saved" (11:26) refers to their physical deliverance at the second coming of Christ in which saved Israelites will be allowed to enter the millennial kingdom, and unsaved Israelites will be purged out (Ezek. 20:33-38) Similarly only saved Gentiles will be allowed to enter the millennial kingdom (Matt. 25:31-46).

The study of soteriology may be pursued under the following main divisions: (1) the Savior, (2) divine election including the question of for whom Christ died, (3) the saving work of the Triune God, (4) eternal security of the believer including deliverance from the reigning power of sin, and (5) the terms of salvation.

THE PERSON OF THE SAVIOR

In relating the total revelation of Scripture concerning the Savior, in addition to what has already been considered under Trinitarianism, four important aspects of Christ's person are revealed: (1) Christ's seven positions, (2) His office, (3) His sonships, and (4) the hypostatic union.

The spiritual progress of a Christian may be measured by the growth he makes in "the grace and knowledge of our Lord and Savior Jesus Christ" (2 Peter 3:18). In John 16:14, it is declared that the Holy Spirit will be sent to "bring glory to Me by taking from what is Mine and making it known to you". This includes knowledge of Christ's seven positions.[328]

The preincarnate Christ possessed all the glory and attributes of God. This is revealed in many passages of the Bible.[329]

In John 1:1-2 it is revealed, "In the beginning was the Word, and the Word was with God, and the Word was God. He was with God in the beginning." In verse 15 it is added, "The Word became flesh and lived for a while among us. We have seen His glory, the glory of the One and only Son, who came from the Father, full of grace and truth." Though Christ never referred to Himself as the *Logos*, in using this expression the Holy Spirit referred to Christ not only as a rational Person but also as the "Word" or declaration of what God is. Though the Old Testament revealed God in many ways, Christ in His person and work revealed God in a way that could never have been revealed otherwise. Though the attributes of God in themselves are unreachable and beyond comprehension, Christ has revealed those attributes in ways that mankind can understand. Through Christ one can know the character of God and the infinite attributes He possesses.

Three important truths are revealed by John in his Gospel

concerning the *Logos*: (1) Jesus Christ was with God, and as God He is from eternity (vv. 1-2); (2) Christ became flesh (v.14); and (3) He ever manifests the attributes of the first Person (v. 18). As such, Christ in His person is revealed to be the adorable, almighty, all-wise, eternal Person who came into the world to be the Savior of men.

The incarnate Christ, combining in His person undiminished Deity and perfect humanity, is a revelation of the infinite attributes of God as well as humanity in perfection. Though Christ possessed all the attributes of Deity, He added the quality of being man which He, as the second Person of the Godhead, possesses in contrast to the Father and the Spirit. Christ as incarnate continuously reveals both the characteristics of the infinite God and of the perfect Man.

Christ in His death revealed God as He could not be revealed by any other means. The death of Christ revealed the love of God, the righteousness of God, the wisdom of God, and God's method of making possible the redemption of mankind.

The resurrected Christ also revealed the power of God's plan for the glorification of humanity. Christ in His resurrection achieved a state of revelation beyond anything man could have contemplated about God. In His second coming, Christ will reveal God as "the blessed and only Ruler, the King of kings and Lord of lords, who alone is immortal and who lives in unapproachable light, whom no one has seen or can see. To Him be honor and might forever" (1 Tim. 6:15-16). The resurrection of Christ was His stepping-stone to returning to glory and being exalted above all.

Christ has ascended to heaven and is seated on His Father's throne, ministering as Head over all things to the church, and serving as the believer's High Priest, Advocate, and Intercessor (Heb. 7:25). Though Christ is bodily in heaven carrying on His present work, in His deity He is omnipresent, indwelling every believer and present with Christians in every situation. In heaven Christ is glorified as illustrated in His appearance to the Apostle John in Revelation 1:13-

18. John fell at the glorified Savior's feet as one who was dead. In contemplating Christ in His present work Christians should realize that Christ is now the glorified One whom they will see when He returns.[330]

Christ's return is anticipated in many Scripture passages as a glorious appearing. To the church He will appear at the Rapture of the church when Christians will see Him as He is (Titus 2:13; 1 John 3:2). To the world He will appear at His second coming to the earth to set up His kingdom, a frequent subject of prophecy in both the Old Testament and the New Testament (Isa. 63:1-6; Dan. 7:13-14; Matt. 24:27-31; Acts 15:16-18; 2 Thes. 1:7-10; Rev. 19:11-16). His return as King of kings is in sharp contrast to His lowly birth in Bethlehem.[331]

Beginning with His second coming Christ will reign forever. He will be King over the earth during the millennial kingdom and then will continue to be in authority in the new heaven and the new earth. In the sense of His political reign during the millennium He will turn over the kingdom to God the Father once He has destroyed all opposing forces (1 Cor. 15:24-28). In other passages His reign is pictured as everlasting on the throne of His father David (Isa 9:6-7; Ezek. 37:21-25; Dan. 7:13-14; Luke 1:31-33; Rev. 11:15). A Christian by faith accepts all that Jesus Christ is in time and eternity.[332]

The title "Christ" in the New Testament as well as the title "Messiah" in the Old Testament imply a threefold official responsibility, that of Prophet, Priest, and King. Each of these offices is involved in the extensive ministry of Christ.

In Scripture Christ is presented as having four sonships while He was on earth. Christ is presented in Scripture as the Son of God. The meaning of this title has been debated in theology, and various attempts have been made to explain it.

Some believe that He became the Son of God by virtue of His incarnation in which Deity and humanity were united in one Person. This implies that He was not the Son of God before the Incarnation.

Another view is that He became the Son of God by baptism, because at His baptism the Father declared, "This is My Son, whom I love; with Him I am well pleased" (Matt. 3:17). This point of view, however, has no support in Scripture.

The doctrine of Christ as the Son of God is supported by statements that refer to Christ as the Firstborn (Rom. 8:29; Col 1:15, 18; Heb. 1:6; Rev. 1:5),[333] that is, as the Heir of all creation because of His resurrection.

Christ is also called the Son of man about 80 times in the New Testament (Matt. 8:20; 9:6; 11:19; 12:8). In other instances He is called the Son of David (9:27; 12:23). Another title given to Jesus is the Son of Mary (13:55). Of great significance is the fact that even a Canaanite would apply the term "Son of David" to Him (15:22).[335]

As the Son of David, Christ is the One prophesied to reign on the throne of David forever (2 Sam. 7:11-13; Matt. 1:1, 6, 20; 9:27; 12:23; 15:22; 20:30-31; 21:9). In a similar way the title occurs in the other Gospels and throughout the New Testament. Christ is seen as the Descendant of David in Revelation 3:7; 5:5; and 22:16. The fact that Christ is called the Son of David shows that part of God's purpose was for Christ to fulfill the promise to David that a Descendant of his would sit on his throne forever.

The Son of Abraham is another title given to Christ. Just as the term Son of David links Christ to the promise given to David, so the term Son of Abraham relates Christ to the promises given to Abraham extending to the whole human race (Gen. 12:3) indicates the wide extent of Christ's ministry as the Son of Abraham and forms the basis for the Gospel going throughout the entire earth (Matt. 28:18-20).[335]

The uniqueness of the person of Christ, including all that is God and all that is man apart from sin, is at the heart of all of His work as the Incarnate Son of God. In understanding the Scriptures relating to the Incarnate Christ the interpreter must be constantly diligent on the one hand not to neglect the essential character of His humanity. It is difficult in some of the acts of Christ to detect how the two natures combine in their activity. The two natures constitute the one and only theanthropic Person, and no one before of after Christ will ever have these characteristics. In attempting to understand what Christ accomplished in His incarnation, knowledge of the person of Christ and the hypostatic union of the two natures is essential to all that He did in His life, death, and resurrection.

INTRODUCTION TO THE SUFFERINGS OF CHRIST

Probably no other subject is as essential to the theology and revelation of biblical truth as the fact that Christ suffered and died for the sins of the world. In His sufferings Christ supremely revealed the infinite love of God, the commitment of God to infinite righteousness, and the desire of God to make fallen humanity savable. It was not only a man who suffered, but God was in Christ when the blood of Christ was shed on the cross (Acts 20:28).[336]

In studying this subject one can't help but marvel not only at the love of God but also at His omniscience in which He knew fully what would eventuate if God created the world and man in it. If there had been any other way to accomplish God's purpose He would not have required His Son to die on the cross. The fact that He was motivated to offer Christ, and that it was absolutely necessary to accomplish salvation reveals God's attributes of love, righteousness, omnipotence, and divine goodness.

The sufferings of Christ may be considered to be under two headings: (1) the sufferings of Christ in life, and (2) His sufferings in His death. The theological importance of His sufferings in death out weighs the sufferings in His life.

The sufferings of Christ in His life are in keeping with the requirement that the Passover lambs be without blemish, being kept for four days to demonstrate their perfection. In His sufferings in life Christ manifested all the perfection of God's holiness.

The life sufferings of Christ can be classified, (2) sufferings due to His character, (2) sufferings due to His compassion, and (3) sufferings due to His anticipation of the supreme ordeal of His sacrificial death. His sufferings in life were the proper background for the finished work, which He accomplished in dying on the cross.

The centrality of the Cross is acknowledged by all who accept the Bible as the inspired Word of God. To the world the Cross is foolishness (1 Cor. 1:18-19). If in fact Christ did not accomplish redemption for the entire race and did not bear the sins of the whole world, the death of Christ was indeed useless and without result. If the death of Christ accomplished what the Bible said it did, namely, to permit God to be just and at the same time to justify the ungodly who believe, then the Cross is of infinite worth (Rom. 3:26; 4:5; 1 Cor. 1:23-24). To Paul the Cross was supreme, not only in salvation but in his whole relationship to God in contrast to his relationship to the world. Paul stated at the close of his Epistle to the Galatians, "May I never boast except in the cross of our Lord Jesus Christ, through which the world has been crucified to me, and I to the world" (Gal. 6:14). The Cross demonstrated the enormity of the sin of the world and at the same time should stand between the world and its charms and the Christian and his commitment to God. The significance of Christ's suffering in death is essential to the integrity of Christian theology. If the meaning of the Cross as revealed in Scripture is rejected, the whole structure of Christian doctrine falls.[337]

In Scripture both human and divine responsibility were involved in Christ's death. In all, eight individuals or groups are accountable. Four of these are named in Acts 4:27-28, "Indeed Herod and Pontius Pilate met together with the Gentiles and the people of Israel in this city to conspire against Your Servant Jesus, whom You anointed. They did what Your power and will had decided beforehand should happen." The fifth responsible individual was Satan, which is brought out in the prediction that Christ would bruise the serpent's head, but in turn His heel would be bruised (Gen. 3:15). The Cross was the ultimate in the mighty conflict waged between Christ and the power of darkness (John 12:31; 14:30; 16:11; Col. 2:14-15).[338]

The remaining three who are said to be accountable for Christ's death are the Father, the Son, and the Holy Spirit. In the death of Christ God Himself provided the Lamb (Gen. 22:8). As Christ indicated on the cross, there is a sense in which God the Father forsook Christ the Son as He became a sin offering (Ps. 22:1; Matt. 27:4; Mark 15:34). Many other Scriptures indicate that the death of Christ was at the hands of God the Father.[339]

On the cross Christ provided for all men, but the application of what He accomplished is only to those who will believe. The unsaved are asked to believe that God has graciously provided a sacrifice in Christ, which is sufficient for a holy God to receive a sinful soul. God has been propitiated, that is, His justice has been completely satisfied, and He is now able to receive the sinner who trusts in Christ to restore in him a measure of holiness even in this world, and ultimately to him perfect in heaven.

THINGS ACCOMPLISHED BY CHRIST IN HIS SUFFERING AND DEATH

The theme of the sufferings of Christ in death is the ground of all right doctrine and cannot be overestimated as an important central fact in biblical theology. His sufferings and death were a major purpose of His becoming incarnate. When Pilate said, "You are a King, then!" Jesus replied, "You are right in saying I am a King. In fact, for this reason I was born, and for this I came into the world, to testify to the truth. Everyone on the side of truth listens to Me" (John 18:37). Earlier Christ had said, "For the Son of man came to seek and to save what was lost" (Luke 19:10).[340]

Christ's sacrifice for sinners involves the doctrine of substitution, that is, Christ's dying for sinners and in their place. The doctrine of substitution may be considered under five aspects: (1) the words that imply substitution, (2) vicarious suffering in general, (3) mediation, (4) substitution with respect to the judgment of sin, and (5) substitution in the realm of divine perfection.

Many passages referring to Christ's death seem to indicate that His main purpose for coming was to be a sacrifice for sinners. Some claim that leaving heaven, deprivation, and hardship of life were vicarious in character. No doubt others were benefited, but His life as such was not a sacrifice for sin. Only by dying on the cross did Christ provide a sacrifice sufficient to satisfy both the love and righteousness of God.

All objections to the scriptural doctrine of substitution in Christ's death try to escape the difficulty that if Christ did not die for the sins of all, then His death was unjust, because He Himself was sinless. The fact that Christ could not avoid the cross, even though this was His prayer, supports the conclusion that the death of the Christ on the cross was the only way by which He could die for the sins of the whole race. His death was forensic in that His sacrifice was infinite in value and sufficient for the sins of the entire race. The tragedy continues that mankind apart from salvation goes into eternal punishment not because it is inevitable, but because unbelievers have rejected what God in His love has provided.

It may be observed that Christ in His sufferings and death bore more than the penalty of sin. As the many Scriptures already indicate, Christ identified with the sinner for man's sin, however, Christ did not injure His own holy character; He had to be a perfect sacrifice in order to take the sinner's place. Though the death of Christ remains, to limited human minds, an inscrutable mystery as to what was consummated when the infinite God accomplished His greatest undertaking. It is possible for man in his limitation, to accept by faith what God has provided in the death of Christ.

In the Old Testament the Mosaic Law was not intended as a way of salvation. Those who were saved were obligated to keep the Law as a basis for fellowship with God. The Mosaic Law was a meritorious system in which God promised blessing for those who kept the Law and punishment for those who broke it. As such, the Law of Moses was the rule for an Israelite's conduct for almost 1,500 years beginning with the giving of the Law at Mount Sinai. Its force ended at the Cross of Christ, which introduced and made possible the present age of grace.

The Law was a schoolmaster or "child governor" which was designed to point Israelites to Christ. This is revealed especially in Galatians 3:21-25, "Is the Law, therefore, opposed to the promises of God? Absolutely not! For if the Law had been given that could impart life, then righteousness would certainly have come by the Law. But the Scriptures declare that the whole world is a prisoner of sin, so that what was promised, being given, through faith in Jesus Christ, might be given to those who believe. Before this faith came, we were held prisoners by the Law, locked up until faith should be revealed.

So the Law was put in charge to lead us to Christ that we might be justified by faith. Now that faith has come, we are no longer under the supervision of the Law." [341]

The Law in itself did not offer or promise salvation for those who observed the Law. It was designed to make clear that salvation is only by grace in every dispensation, and that man is hopelessly sinful and can be saved only by the grace of God. As such, the Mosaic Law was a preparation for the people of Israel to make them understand that when Jesus Christ came He introduced additional revelation that made clear that salvation is not by the Law but by grace.

One of the major reasons for giving the law is keeping the Nation of Israel free from apostasy; this is explained very well by Renold E. Showers; What on earth is God doing?[342] "Because Israel was to be the nation which the Redeemer would come, it was essential that she be kept free from apostasy and perverted life style of other nations. In order to insure this freedom, God placed Israel under the Law. The Law was to be an external restraint upon the sinful, apostate tendencies until the Redeemer would come (al. 3:15-4:5). In order to exercise such restraint, the Law required that those guilty of apostasy and perversion be put to death immediately (Exodus 21:12-17; 22:18-20). The coming of the Redeemer was more crucial for the benefit of mankind than was the life of an individual rebel or pervert."

The New Testament clearly teaches that Christ is the end of the Law of righteousness. "Christ is the end of the Law so that there may be righteousness for everyone who believes (Rom. 10:4). Paul stated that Christian Gentiles, who had not followed the Mosaic Law, obtained righteousness by faith, while Israel, following the righteousness provided in the Mosaic Law, did not obtain righteousness because of their complete obedience (Rom. 2). Abraham, to whom God promised he would be the source of blessing to the one whole world (Gen. 12:3), was counted righteous because he believed in God (15:6; Rom 12:3,9). It was possible even under the Law for one who trusted

God to have righteousness imputed to him. As David was quoted in verse 7-8, "Blessed are they whose transgressions are forgiven, whose sins are covered. Blessed is the man whose sin the Lord will not count against him".[343]

In summary it can be restated that in the three sweet savor offerings, Christ established the righteous ground on which God can freely justify even the ungodly who believe. In the nonsweet savor offerings, there is ground in the death of Christ for justifying the sinner by declaring him righteous in the presence of the Holy God.

Three great doctrinal words need to be considered in connection with the death of Christ, namely, redemption, reconciliation, and propitiation. These doctrines define Christ's death as it relates to forgiveness, regeneration, justification, and sanctification with each of these doctrines contributing an important aspect to the doctrine as a whole.

In redemption the work of Christ on the cross paid in full the price of releasing the sinner from the bondage and judgment of his sins. When on the cross Jesus said, "It is finished" John 19:30), He referred to the fact that His death had fully paid all that God demanded for the forgiveness of sinners.

Redemption is the sinward aspect of Christ's work on the cross and has to do with the payment of the price of the sins of the whole world. Redemption is an act of God by which He Himself pays as a ransom the price of human sin, which price the outraged holiness and government of God requires. This contrasts with reconciliation, which pertains to the solution of the problem of the sinful state of the sinner, and with propitiation, which relates to the fact that God has been offended by sin. Redemption offers sinners release from sin and from the situation of being a bondservant to sin. Redemption results in liberation because the price has been paid to free the sinner from his sin.

In the New Testament various Greek words are translated

"redeemed" or "redemption".³⁴⁴ The Greek word is *agorazo*, which means to purchase in the market *(agora)*. The concept here is that an unsaved person is a bondslave to sin because he was "sold as a slave to sin" (Rom. 7:14). Before being saved a person is dominated by Satan (1Cor. 12:2; Eph 2:2); and is "condemned" (John 3:18; Gal. 3:10). Christ in His death paid the ransom price for the sinner's redemption (Matt. 20:28).

A second Greek word used for redemption is *exagorazo*, which means to purchase "out" of the market (the preposition ek means "out of"). This has the added thought of not only being redeemed but also removing the one from the marketplace and not leaving him up for sale (Gal. 3:13; 4:5).

A third word *lytroo*, means to loose or set free from bondage (Luke 24:21; Titus 2:14; 1 Peter 1:18). The noun *apolytrosis* is derived from *lytroo*. This is translated "redemption" (Luke 21:28; Rom. 3:24; 8:23; 1 Cor. 1:30; Eph. 1:7, 14; 4:30; Col. 1:14; Heb. 9:15, "ransom").

Christ in His death on the cross went into the marketplace and bought the unsaved who are regarded as slaves. His death made it possible for Him to take them out of the marketplace and not subject them to further resale, and to set them free from the bondage and judgment of sin.³⁴⁵

The doctrine of redemption depicts the full payment for all sin accomplished by the death of Christ so that one who formerly was a slave to sin and subject to the righteous judgment of God is set free to serve the Lord voluntarily in a gracious relationship.

In Scripture, reconciliation is the manward aspect of Christ's work on the cross. It is strictly a New Testament doctrine. In ordinary human relations, reconciliation is usually viewed as each of two parties conceding something to bring about harmony in their relationship. In the Bible reconciliation is the work of Christ on the cross, which completely changes man in his relationship to God by removing all grounds for condemnation. The central idea is that man is completely changed. In the Old Testament, though some English translations are "making an atonement for sin" (Lev. 6:30; 8:15; 16:20; 1 Sam. 29:4; 2 Chron. 29:24; Ezek. 45:15, 17, 20; Dan. 9:24). Though different Hebrew words are used, none of them connotes precisely the doctrine of reconciliation as taught in the New Testament. They view sin as being covered or they refer to that which atonement has been made.

In the New Testament, reconciliation of members of the human race is mentioned in Matt. 5:24 which uses the Greek word *diallassomai*. This word is used only here of human relations and is never used of reconciliation of man to God.[346]

Propitiation refers to the value of Christ's death as a satisfaction of God's righteousness and a vindication of His righteousness in saving sinners. Propitiation in the New Testament is revealed in various words that stem from the same Greek word (*hilasmos*, 1 John 2:2; 4:10); the place of propitiation (*hilasterion*, Rom. 3:25, KJV; Heb. 9:5, "atonement cover," or "mercy seat," KJV); to be merciful or forgiving (*hileos*, 8:12, "forgive," "merciful," KJV); and to be merciful or propitiated (*hilaskomai*, Luke 18:13, "have mercy," "be merciful," KJV).[347, 348]

In each case propitiation has in view the effect of the death of Christ on a righteous God, and the truth that the death of Christ satisfied God completely as far as His righteous demands are concerned. In 1 John 2:2, Christ "is the atoning sacrifice {propitiation} for our sins, not only for ours but also for the sins of the whole world." The same thought is embodied in 4:10. "This is love: not that we loved God, but that He loved us and sent His Son as an atoning sacrifice {a propitiation} for our sins."

The Scriptures are clear, however, that though God has been propitiated, a person who does not receive Christ by faith as his Savior, and God as just, is lost as if Christ had not died. The tragedy of eternal punishment is that the finished work of Christ on the cross was sufficient for all but is applied only to those who believe.

The Scriptures distinguish individual or personal sins from sin as a nature. In 1 John 1:18 the statement is made, "If we claim to be without sin, we deceive ourselves and the truth is not in us." Here sin, used in the singular, refers to the sin nature. In verses 9-10, however, the acts of sin are mentioned, as indicated by the plural, "If we confess our sins, He is faithful and just and will forgive us our sins and purify us from all unrighteousness. If we claim we have not sinned, we make Him out to be a liar and His Word has no place in our lives." Christians sin because they have a sin nature. The death of Christ, just as it deals with personal sins, also is God's remedy for the sin nature. For instance 1 Corinthians 15:3 states, "Christ died for our sins according to the Scriptures," but Romans 6:10 (KJV) states that He died unto sin once." The same verse in the NIV reads, "The death He died, He died to sin once for all; but the life He lives, He lives to God." He died for the sins of the world, but He also died in respect to the sin nature.

The relationship of the death of Christ to the sin nature, however, does not eradicate or change the sin nature as such. It transforms a believer into a new creation, which includes a divine nature that longs to obey God.

The secret of victory over the sin nature is not its eradication but the presence of the indwelling Holy Spirit who can enable the divine nature to fulfill its longing to walk in the will of God. The Christian remains in a sinful world, possesses a sin nature or "the flesh," and contends with the devil. These problems are not removed, but there is added to the Christian's experience the possibility of being filled with the Spirit and not fulfilling the lusts of the sin nature.

This is confirmed by the fact that when Christ died, He gained victory over Satan. According to John 16:11, "The prince of this world now stands condemned." Though Satan has been condemned, his final disposition awaits a future judgment from God. In like manner a Christian retains his sin nature that awaits a future removal at the time of his death or the rapture.

In God's plan for the sanctification of the believer, provision has been made for a sinner to conquer the desires of the flesh (the sin nature) and live a holy life in the will of God.

The central passage bearing on the judgment of the sin nature is Romans 6:1-8;13. In contrast to the earlier chapters of Romans which relate to sin and salvation, these chapters discuss the Christian's sanctification and victory over sin. The problem is what the Christian is able to do about the sin nature. In the opening verses of this passage, Paul stated, "What shall we say, then? Shall we go on sinning so that grace may increase? By no means! We died to sin; how can we live in it any longer?" (6:1-2) As Paul then explained, whatever Christ did becomes true of the Christian as well because he has been baptized into Christ. In Christ the Christian dies, in Christ the Christian is buried, and in Christ the Christian is raised from the dead. This is a picture of new life in Christ, made possible because the believer is identified with Christ in His death and resurrection.

Since this is true, there should be a corresponding change in the life of a Christian as Paul stated, "If we have been united with Him in His death, we will certainly also be united with Him in His resurrection. For we know that our old self was crucified with Him so that the body of sin might be rendered powerless, that we should no longer be slaves to sin- because anyone who has died has been freed from sin. Now if we died with Christ, we believe that we will also live with Him. For we know that since Christ was raised from the dead, He cannot die again; death no longer has mastery over Him. The death He died, He died to sin once for all; but the life He lives, He lives to God" (vv. 5-10). Because Christ died once for all and believers died in Him, Paul exhorted them, "In the same way, count yourselves dead to sin but alive to God in Christ Jesus. Therefore do not let sin reign in your mortal body so that you obey its evil desires" (vv.11-12).

Paul then affirmed that through the death of Christ a believer, who once a slave to sin and living in accord with the desires of the sin nature, is now made new in Christ. He has died with Christ and was raised again and is able now by the power of the Spirit to refuse to let the sin nature to reign. Paul concluded, "For sin shall not be your master, because you are not under Law, but grace."

Sin can be cured only by the blood of Christ. In the case of the unsaved, they are forgiven judicially and are justified by faith. After justification, when a Christian sins, restoration is needed between himself as a child of God and his Heavenly Father. This restoration is obtained only by confession of sin. All forgiveness and justification depends on the blood of Christ and the act of Christ in dying for the sinner on the cross of Calvary.

A sinning Christian who claims to be without sin may deceive himself, but he does not deceive others. In addition he must disregard God and the plain revelation of Scripture concerning sin. A life of fellowship with God requires constant confession of known sin and walking in the will of God as far as the individual knows God's perfect will.

Jesus Christ presents His righteous work of dying on the cross as an atoning sacrifice for the Christian's sins. This should encourage a Christian both to walk in the light of God's will and also to confess any sins that occur, being assured that Christ is already interceding for him at the right hand of God and is pleading the sufficiency of His finished work on the cross. This is the work of Christ in propitiation, making the Christian fully confident.

In the Old Testament those who were saved were temporarily covered by offering the sacrifices in anticipation of the complete sacrifice for sin which Christ would offer on the cross. The Hebrew word *kaphar* is frequently used in the Old Testament in regard to the atonement for sin and related doctrines. The Old Testament sacrifices were temporary covering for sin as implied in *kaphar*, with all such sacrifices being temporary in value and looking forward to the final act of Christ on the cross which would provide a sacrifice for sin forever.

The Scriptures reveal that individual Israelites need to be saved from sin and delivered from condemnation just as unsaved Gentiles need salvation. This was true in the Old Testament and also in the present age (Rom. 3:9). In the present age God is calling both Jews and Gentiles to put their trust in Christ.[349]

In the light of God's present work of salvation for Israel the question is raised whether the covenants of God with Israel in the Old Testament are abrogated. The answer is clearly given in Romans 11, that their covenants (except for the Mosaic Covenant) are irrevocable. The question is posed whether God has rejected His people (v.1). As Paul pointed out, God has not rejected His people Israel; in the present age He is saving individual Israelites such as Paul. In every age godly Israelites have been saved, even in the time of Elijah (vv. 2-4) when Israel as a whole was apostate. Most Israelites, however, in the present age have not come to Christ and are to a limited extent blind to the truth of the Gospel (v.25). In the present age Gentiles have been grafted unto the olive tree, which represents the place of God's blessing and grace (v.17). He predicts, however, that in the future Israel will be grafted in again and become a primary recipient of the grace of God.

When the Rapture occurs, Israel's present blindness will be lifted and many will come to the Lord. Then "all Israel" will be "saved". That is, she will be delivered from her persecutors for "the Deliverer will come from Zion. He will turn godlessness away from Jacob. And this is My covenant with them when I take away their sins" (Rom. 11:26-27).[350]

The grace of God made possible by the death of Christ is sufficient not only for Jews but also for Gentiles. Some Gentiles are saved in the present age, but even in the millennial kingdom where Israel is in prominence, Gentiles will share the millennial earth with Israel.

The godly remnant of Gentiles at the Second Coming are "the sheep" who will have eternal life and enter the kingdom (Matt. 25:31-46). References to the blessings of Gentiles are revealed in many passages (Isa. 60:3; 62:2). The saved among the Gentiles are also seen in the new earth in eternity (Rev. 21:24). Eternal mercies to Gentiles as well as to Israel stem from the sacrifice of Christ on the cross.[351]

Because Satan is referred to as the prince of this world who has power over the political rulers (Matt. 9:34; 12:24; John 12:31; 14:30; Eph. 2:2), both political governments on earth and the powers of Satan in the demon world are sometimes commingled and are both regarded as evil. On the other hand, Christians are urged to abide by the government of civil rules (Rom. 13:1; Titus 3:1) unless this requires them to transgress the law of God. In contrast to both political powers on earth and extramundane powers in heaven, Christ is supreme with all things under His authority (Col. 2:10-15). This indicates that Christ is the final power over both political rulers and the demon world. Though some fallen angels were immediately bound after their transgression (Jude 6) the Scriptures indicates that Satan and the demon world have great power.

The combat between Christ and Satan, which was waged on Calvary's hill when Christ died, is beyond comprehension by finite minds. The Scriptures reveal that Satan exercised his utmost power which led to the death of Christ. The striking of the heel of the Savior also resulted in Satan's head being crushed, that is, Satan's power was destroyed (Gen. 3:15). On the divine side, the death of Christ was determined by His Father (John 3:16; Rom. 3:26; 8:32), by Christ Himself as a sacrifice (John 10:18; Gal. 2:20), and through the work of the eternal Spirit (Heb. 9:14).[352]

Because of the death of Christ, it is possible for the sinner through faith in Christ to have peace with God as is stated in Romans 5:1, "Therefore, since we have been justified through faith, we have peace with God through our Lord Jesus Christ.

In the present age it is also true that there is peace between Jews and Gentiles who have been brought together in the body of Christ. It is also possible for Christians to experience the peace of God.[353]

In the future Millennium, peace will be brought to the nations of the world (Col. 1:20). This peace will follow the judgments of God at the Second Coming (Isa. 63:1-6; Ps. 2:1-3, 8-9; Matt. 25:31-46). Ultimately, having established peace, Christ will deliver the kingdom up to the Father (1 Cor. 15:27-28).[354]

Because of the original sin of Satan and the fallen angels and the added pollution of the world resulting from the human race falling into sin, it is necessary for things both in heaven and earth to be purified. Sin has brought the entire creation into bondage (Rom. 8:20-23). Heavenly things also have to be purified with sacrifices, but only Christ was able to do this cleansing of heaven (Heb. 9:23-28). The same thought is expressed in verses 11-12. Inasmuch as Satan has been permitted to accuse brethren in heaven, it follows that in a sense heaven itself has been introduced to sin (Rev. 12:10). Christ, having shed His own blood on earth, is prepared to enter into heaven as a holy place and by His sacrifice bring sinners who are saved with Him. In extending the purification of things on earth to things in heaven through the cleansing blood of Christ, the Bible does not teach universalism, or that all men will be saved. The Scriptures are clear that those who reject Christ do not receive the benefits of His death on the cross.[355]

THE SUFFERING AND DEATH
OF CHRIST IN TYPES

In systematic theologies typology is a neglected subject and is rarely mentioned. The Scriptures are clear, however, that God intended some events, objects, and persons to be types in the sense that a type is a divinely purposed anticipation which illustrates its antitype. Though some have gone to extremes by trying to find types in every situation, the Scriptures are relatively conservative, but those designated as types in the New Testament indicate that all types are not expressly mentioned.

Three major factors exhibit the unity between the two Testaments: type and antitype, prophecy and fulfillment, and continuity in the progress of narration and doctrine. These factors run from one text to the other and are like woven threads combining them into one fabric.

Two Greek words are used to represent types in the New Testament, *typo* and *hypodeigma*.[356] *Typos* is variously translated in the KJV and other English translations, but the thought is that of an example (1 Cor. 10:11; Phil.3:17; 1 Peter 5:3) or a model (1 Thes. 1:7; 2 Thes. 3:9). The word *deigma* means a specimen, and when combined with *typo* it means "example" (John 13:15; Heb. 4:11; James 5:10).[357] Both words clearly illustrate that types are an example or model for truth.

Types can be classified as persons (Rom. 5:14; Adam, Melchizedek, Abraham, Sarah, Ishmael, Isaac, Moses, Joshua, David, Solomon, etc.); events (1 Cor. 10:11; the preservation of Noah and his sons in the ark, redemption from Egypt, the Passover memorial, the water drawn from the rock, the serpent lifted up, and many sacrifices); things (Heb. 10:20; cf. the tabernacle, the laver, the sacrificial lamb, the Jordan River); a city (Rev. 11:8); and institutions (Heb. 9:11; the Sabbath, the sacrifices, the priesthood); and ceremonials (1 Cor. 5:7).

It is important to distinguish types from allegories or analogies. Obviously any type identified in the New Testament should be considered a biblical type, but there are other types not specifically mentioned. In referring to the many historical acts of Israel when they committed sin, Paul stated, "These things happened to them as examples and were written down as warnings for us, on whom the culmination of the ages has come" (1 Cor. 10:11). The events he itemized are considered examples though they are not formally identified or defined. For example Joseph is no doubt a type of Christ, even though he is not directly so specified in the New Testament. A true type in a prophecy of its antitype and has been designed by God to have an antitype. Of all the antitypes Christ is the outstanding One and the supreme Object of both Old and New Testament typology.

Abel's offering (Gen. 4:4) indicates that divine instruction on the importance and value of blood sacrifices had been given to the first of the human race as they emerged in the Garden of Eden. By his sacrifice Abel obtained witness that he was righteous (Heb. 11:4; 9:22).

Noah's alter and sacrifice (Gen. 8:20-22) also indicates that the revelation had been given about the necessity of blood sacrifice. As Exodus 20:24-26 makes clear, it is not the altar which is important, but the sacrifice on the altar, even though specific instructions are given on the construction of the altar. All sacrifices of the Old Testament which anticipate the death of Christ are types.

The five offerings in Leviticus 1:1-7; 38 are types of Christ. The sweet savor offerings – the burnt offerings, the meal offering, and the peace offering – speak of Christ and His death on the cross as representing obedience to God. The sin offering and the trespass offering, referred to as nonsweet savor sacrifices, represent Christ bearing the sin of the whole world as a substitute for mankind. In the sweet savor offerings the obedience of Christ is considered as righteousness, and on this basis God can justify sinners. In the nonsweet savor offerings the death of Christ is anticipated as judgment on sin.

THEORIES TRUE AND FALSE ON THE VALUE OF CHRIST'S DEATH

No doctrine is more essential to Christian theology than the fact of Christ's death and its value to God, man, and angels.

General facts about the value of Christ's death are revealed in Scripture. Before man sinned, he was in harmony with God; Adam and Eve had unbroken communion with God. When Adam and Eve sinned, however, God was compelled to drive them from the Garden and to deal with them and all mankind on the basis of forgiveness which can be provided only through the shedding of blood. The value of Christ's death therefore becomes an essential factor of Christian faith and hope.

The history of the church provides a record of the struggle of theologians to understand the death of Christ properly. Various views of the value of Christ's death may be divided into three time periods: (1) from the beginning of Christian theology to Anselm ((c. 1100); (2) Anselm to Grotius (c. 1600); and (3) from Grotius to the present time.[358]

The first thousand years of Christian theology were built on the early church accepting in simplicity that Christ died for the sins of the world. The comprehension of the early church, however, was not entirely accurate as some taught that Christ paid the ransom to Satan when He died on the cross. Though it is true that Christ in His death on the cross accomplished the judgment of Satan (John 12:31; 16:11; Col. 2:14-15), Satan, rather than receiving a ransom for sin, was defeated at the cross. Satan had no right to such a payment, and it is far better to consider the doctrine of propitiation as teaching that when Christ died He was satisfying not an obligation to Satan but the requirements of the righteousness of God. Some godly men did oppose the concept of a payment to Satan and accepted the scriptural view that God accepted the value of Christ's death because in was in keeping with His moral government of the universe and because it made possible man's salvation and sanctification.

In the 500 years from Anselm to Grotius the writing of Anselm in his *Cur Deus Homo*, "Why the God Man," helped to teach the doctrine of divine propitiation. But some failed to comprehend the full-orbed work of Christ on the cross as it related to other aspects of the plan of God for salvation and there was diversity in doctrine as it related to the death of Christ.

In this period there also was discussion on the question of whether Christ actually bore the total penalty of sin on the cross, or whether He died in a forensic sense, that is, His death was universal in its value and was applicable to all men even though some would be unsaved. The concept that Christ became actually the one who sinned when He died on the cross was inaccurate, because if Christ were actually the sinner, then His death was forensic, that is, sufficient for all even though it was not applied to all.

From Grotius (1583-1645) to the present time there has been little advance of his so-called governmental theory of the value of Christ's death. Like many other theories it is short of what the Bible actually teaches and is not superior to the view of Anselm that the death of Christ satisfied God's view which has become the predominant view of orthodoxy since the Protestant Reformation.[359]

The problem with all views on the value of Christ's death except the view of satisfaction is that they have a weak view of sin, a limited comprehension of the extent of salvation provided in Christ, and in one sense or another suggest that Christ's death was not an actual substitution. To deny the satisfaction theory is in effect to deny that man is as desperately sinful as the Bible presents.[360]

THE FACT OF ELECTION

In the study of the Scriptures, we find it difficult in accepting the doctrine of divine election. This is because divine election and the human experience of choice are difficult to harmonize.

In the universe there are things which God obviously determines, such as Creation, one star differing from another, men being born in various races with differing advantages, great variety in human civilizations, and differences in natural gifts. Though divine election seems to be an arbitrary work of God, it must be considered in light of the fact of God's universal love revealed in sending His Son (John 3:16). Much that cannot be entirely understood by human intelligence can nonetheless be accepted by faith. The ultimate question is, what does the Bible teach? Obviously the Bible does not teach what would contradict divine justice, divine love, or divine goodness. Christians have little difficulty in seeing the infinite blessing of measureless possessions and positions in Christ and the wonder of their being the objects of His Grace. Difficulties do arise when contemptlating God in His relationship to the unsaved world which never avails itself of the grace of God.

Obviously God chose the saved before they chose Him (John 15:16). One who is saved can to some extent understand sovereign grace, election, God's calling, His redemption, and His regeneration. Christians can also experience God's divine preservation and the hope of being presented faultless before the glory of God in the future. To attain these ends God has employed means such as the sacrifice of His only begotten Son. It is not enough that sin should be declared sinful. Its curse must be borne by the Lamb of God, the will of man must be moved to take the step of faith, regeneration must be wrought by the Spirit, and every spiritual heavenly blessing must be secured by union with Christ. In human experience, man is conscious only of his power to choose or reject salvation in Christ with the realization that he is saved or lost according to his belief or disbelief in Christ as Savior.

Much in the doctrine of divine election transcends the limitations of finite understanding, but it is obvious that both God and man have power of choice and that God's will is infinitely greater than human will. Accordingly in the study of the doctrine of divine election, the human mind must submit to divine revelation which should be accepted by faith even though it may not be entirely understood.

In biblical usage the word "election" designates a sovereign, divine purpose so formulated as to be independent of human merit, consent, or cooperation. This entire doctrine is in harmony with the truth of God's sovereignty observed in His creation in which both variety and selection are everywhere present. The term is used of Israel (Isa. 65:9, 22), of the church (Rom. 8:33; Col. 3:12; 2 Tim. 2:10; 1 Thes. 1:4; 1 Peter 5:13), and of Christ (Isa. 42:1; 1 Peter 2:6).[361]

Though the facts of divine election may be difficult to understand, the doctrine stands on specific revelation of Scripture. This is not to say it is free from complexity or that it is capable of complete human comprehension.

Though it is difficult for man to conceive of divine election as being other than an arbitrary act of God, it should be clear from Scripture that God in eternity past chose a perfect plan. He is omniscient and knew all possible plans. Because He is infinitely good, He must choose the best of all possible plans. Giving man choices, God knew that he would choose the wrong path. God knew not only the ones who would respond to the revelation of God but also those who would not respond. In adopting any plan that involved freedom of choice, God automatically chose the results even though to some extent people are free to choose one way or the other so far as their own experience is concerned. It was impossible for God to give angels or men choices without the certainty that some would choose the wrong way. In choosing that plan, God knew who these would be and yet they are entirely responsible for their choices. Election is that aspect of the divine degree that relates to those who are chosen.

FOR WHOM DID CHRIST DIE?

The question of the purpose of Christ's death is often related to the so-called five points of Calvinism: (1) total depravity, (2) unconditional election, (3) limited atonement, (4) irresistible grace, (5) perseverance or eternal security of the saved.

These five points are often referred to as TULIP, which is an acronym based on the initial letter of each of the five points (limited atonement), whereas moderate Calvinists hold that Christ died for the whole world (unlimited atonement). Since capable orthodox theologians hold each view, it is not a question of orthodoxy versus nonorthodoxy. Ultimately the question is what the Bible teaches.

The so-called TULIP was an outgrowth of the Synod of Dort (1618-19)[362] which affirmed limited atonement in opposition to the teachings of Joacob Arminus (1560-1609). The Synod of Dort took the position that when an unsaved man, who was elect, comes to faith in Christ, he experiences irresistible grace which causes him to be regenerated. Then, because he is regenerated, he comes to faith in Christ. Moderate Calvinists feel that this position is in error because it confuses what is called prevenient grace with regeneration. The proper order should be that an unsaved person is graciously enabled by God to believe, and then, as a result of believing, he is regenerated. The Synod of Dort changed that order and viewed regeneration as preceding faith. This reduced the human response to the Gospel to a minimum and affirmed that salvation even to the point of a person's willingness to believe is all the work of God. The Scriptures, however, do not use the adjectives irresistible or efficacious, in relation to grace, nor do they use the word "sufficient," which is often used by Armenians. Though it is true as Christ stated, "No one can come to Me unless the Father who sent Me draws him" (John 6:44), The Scriptures constantly refer to salvation as involving man's faith.

On the cross Christ secured not only forgiveness through His death but also the right to bestow eternal life, justification, and a believer's position in Christ. Also some aspects of sanctification are made possible by Christ's death.

Because Christ died for the lost, God is free to express divine benevolence toward those who are saved by not only giving them forgiveness but also a place in the family and household of God, adoption, heavenly citizenship, access to God, and freedom under grace from the merit system of the Law.

Clarity is given to the situation when it is realized that the elect before they believe are just as lost as the nonelect. Any view on the extent of Christ's death must respect the doctrine of election which indicates that all who are predestined for salvation are ultimately glorified (Rom. 8:30).[363]

Because the dispensations in Scripture deal with rules of life rather than ways of salvation, dispensationalism has only an oblique relationship to the question of unlimited atonement.

In dispensationalism Israel is regarded as an elect nation and is therefore subject to future restoration as a nation. The elect in Israel and the church will be saved and glorified (Rom. 8:30).

National election should not be confused with individual election (9:4-13). Individual Israelites were not saved by the fact that they were part of the elect nation. They needed individual salvation just as any Gentile did. Even in the prophetic future many Israelites will be rejected (Ezk. 20:33-44; Dan. 12:1-3).[364] It is true, however, that God is gracious in recognizing that a remnant of Israel will be saved and will have a part in His eschatological purpose (Rom. 11:5, 27). Israel's national salvation will ultimately be realized when the godly Israelite remnant will have her sins taken away (Jer. 31:34). Even in the present age individual Israelites can be saved by faith in Christ though Gentiles are predominantly being blessed in this present age (Acts 15:14). Israel's future restoration is promised (Amos 9:11-15;

Acts 15:16-17).[365] In the Mosaic dispensation the Law was not a way of salvation, though it is probable that those who were saved sought to keep the Law. Salvation is always by faith and through grace.

As has been considered, redemption, reconciliation, and propitiation summarize the work of the death of Christ. These great realities, redemption from sin, reconciliation of God, and the death of Christ as a propitiation or satisfaction to God, apply to all who believe. Other great words are used in regard to salvation such as forgiveness, regeneration, justification, and sanctification, and all who experience one experience the other.

Though some oppose unlimited redemption on the ground that if Christ died for all then all are saved, the Scriptures are clear that salvation was provided for all but is applied to those who believe when they believe. So even an elect person before he comes to faith may manifest all the depravity of an unsaved person. An elect person is not saved or regenerated until the moment of faith. In their spiritual condition before salvation the elect are not saved until they believe, it should be clear that the death of Christ is provisional for all but effective only in those who believe.

In preaching the Gospel should those who believe in the doctrine of election avoid offering salvation to all? In Scripture God discloses nothing whereby the elect can be distinguished from the nonelect as both classes are unregenerate. Since a preacher of the Gospel cannot know who in his audience is elect, he is free to offer salvation to all without creating a problem for the nonelect. Even some elect persons may resist the claim of the Gospel until the day of their death. Because the Bible affirms that Christ died for all, all can be offered the Gospel without anyone attempting to determine whether they are elect or nonelect.

The question may be asked, "is God defeated if men are lost?" This question relates to a much larger question, that is, whether any sin or defiance of God means that God is defeated. Actually the total process of people being saved or unsaved brings glory to God because it manifests His infinite attributes. There is no defeat for God because His purposes are being perfectly fulfilled even by the judgment on the lost in which His holiness and righteousness are revealed. Rejecting Christ and His redemption, as every unbeliever does, is anticipated in the plan of God, though at the same time it is not according to the wishes of God who is benevolent in His relationship to all mankind. As stated in 2 Peter 3:9, "The Lord is not slow in keeping His promise, as some understand slowness. He is patient with you, not wanting anyone to perish, but everyone to come to repentance".

THE CONVICTING WORK OF THE SPIRIT

In accomplishing the salvation of an individual two factors are involved: (1) a righteous dealing with the problem of sin which Christ accomplished as the Lamb of God who takes away the sin of the world; (2) faith in the heart of man in what God has promised and provided in Christ in His plan of salvation. The inner work of God in the heart of one who comes to faith in Christ is inscrutable, but Scripture portrays it as including both the action of man who wills to believe and the action of God who by grace enables the person to believe.

When Christ's death is considered an unlimited redemption, it enables the person who is attempting to lead souls to Christ to offer salvation to everyone, even though he knows that only the elect will respond. There must be a corresponding work of God as He calls, draws, and enlightens the unsaved person, making possible his intelligent reception of Christ.

In connection with the convicting work of the Spirit it is necessary to examine three areas: (1) the need of the Spirit's work, (2) the fact of the Spirit's work, and (3) the result of the Spirits work.

In order for an unsaved man to come to faith in Christ it is necessary that he be the object of the convicting work of the Holy Spirit. Man in his natural mind cannot comprehend the mystery of the death of Christ for the sins of the whole world and how this truth applies to him personally. In the Upper Room Discourse of Christ[366] it is recorded in John 16:8-11 that the Spirit of God would reveal to the unsaved their need of salvation and God's remedy for it.

In the Upper Room where Christ was speaking of the present age, He gave a new revelation concerning the work of the Holy Spirit in the hearts of unregenerate men. This is not equivalent to regeneration but relates to the general field of common grace. It is the enlightenment of an unsaved man by the Spirit which enables him to know the facts concerning the way of salvation.

Christ said, "but I tell you the truth: It is for your good that I am going away. Unless I go away, the Counselor will not come to you; but if I go, I will send Him to you. When He comes, He will convict the world of guilt in regard to sin and righteousness and judgment: in regard to sin, because men do not believe in Me; in regard to righteousness, because I am going to the Father, where you can see Me no longer, and in regard to judgment, because the prince of this world now stands condemned".[367]

The Spirit of God also convicts the unsaved person of the fact that the righteousness of God has been demonstrated by Christ on earth. Now with His departure to the Father the Holy Spirit takes up this revelation. Judgment is also revealed by the fact that "the prince of this world now stands condemned". Though Satan is allowed freedom in the present world, the truth is that he stands condemned, and it is only a matter of time until he is judged along with all others who do not trust in Christ. An unbeliever may not completely understand all of this, but these are the three areas which he needs illumination: Of his Guilt; the Righteousness of God; the judgment to come.

Before an unbelieving individual can be saved the supernatural work of the Spirit is required to enlighten him and make clear to him the terms of the Gospel which are stated emphatically in Ephesians 2:8, "For it is by grace you have been saved, through faith – and this not from yourselves, it is the gift of God."[368] This verse is interpreted by those who hold to limited atonement as indicating that faith is a gift of God, but this is an inaccurate exegesis of this verse. The point in the verse is that salvation is by grace in its totality. The use of "this" (*touto*, neuter gender) makes it plain that it is not related to faith (*pisteo*), which is in the feminine gender. The word "this" refers to the whole work of salvation as coming from God, not any particular part of it. Though it is true that faith on the part of an unsaved person would be impossible apart from divine help, it nevertheless is a human decision, however difficult it may be to separate the human work from the divine work. The problem with making faith a particular gift from God is that it removes from man any responsibility to believe and leaves it entirely in the hands of God. If this were true it would be useless to exhort men to believe inasmuch as they could not do so.

The difficult question of the relationship of the supernatural to the natural in men's faith is not unlocked in Scripture and remains a paradox, but both are true. God works and man believes. The convicting work of the Spirit in itself does not assure salvation. All of these truths emphasize the truth that it is important to preach the Bible. "Consequently, faith comes from hearing the message, and the message is heard through the word of Christ" (Rom. 10:17).

THE RICHES OF DIVINE GRACE

A distinction needs to be observed between the work of God in the immediate salvation of an individual and those responsibilities and activities that belong to the Christian life and service. A Christian's works that follow salvation (Eph. 2:10) should not be confused with the conditions of salvation. It is in this regard that Arminianism falls short because on the one hand it makes salvation entirely a decision of man and on the other hand it views salvation as conditional and something that can be lost because it depends on the works of man.

No one would deny that a holy life is proper for a Christian in view of the fact that he is a child of God and a member of Christ's body. In Hebrews 6:9 mention is made of "things that accompany salvation." A Christian who is born again may be expected to have a change in life, and from human observation unless there is some change there is grounds for question of his salvation. On the part of God, however, no confirming works are needed, as He knows the heart and can distinguish between what is true and what is not true about a believer's standing with Himself.

Because salvation is by grace, no one is partly saved and partly lost. An individual may be cultured, refined, educated, moral, and religious but still be lacking salvation as was the case of Nicodemus in John 3. A believer must be born again by the grace of God in order to qualify for God's eternal salvation.

In preaching to the public, distinction must be made between what is addressed to the unsaved and what is addressed to the saved. To the unsaved God makes no appeal in regard to his manner of life, nor is improvement or reformation required. What God requires of an unsaved person is to hear and believe the Gospel. After he believes and becomes a Christian, then the exhortations of Scripture for a God-honoring life are to be heeded.

In the later discussion of "the riches of grace" the infinite care of God for the sinner in his salvation prompted by God's infinite love will be considered. The extent of the riches of the grace of God make it plain that only by God's saving of souls can His infinite love for the world be satisfied. Though salvation is wonderful in its effect and expectation on the part of man, it is also a matter of infinite satisfaction to God.

The Scriptures reveal that as a Christian, we now posses every spiritual blessing as stated in Ephesians 1:3, "Praise be to the God and Father of our Lord Jesus Christ, who has blessed us in the heavenly realms with every spiritual blessing in Christ." The riches of grace contemplated in the "every spiritual blessing" which a believer has in Christ the moment of salvation. All the possessions which together measure the riches of divine grace are traced to the believer's place in Christ.

As all these blessings indicate, salvation is a work of God for man, not a work of man for God. What a Christian experiences is what God's love has prompted Him to do for those who had no merit before Him but who are now recognized in the merit of His Son because of their faith in Christ. The truth of the riches of divine grace are almost overwhelming, and it is difficult to express a proper understanding of this divine grace. Those of us who preach the Gospel, however, must make clear how abundant are the riches all believers have in Christ when they place their faith in Him and how blessed is their eternal estate.

INTRODUCTION TO THE
DOCTRINE OF SECURITY

The doctrine of security is one of the five points commonly related to the Calvinistic system of theology, but its proof rests on a scriptural foundation. It is true that some Christians who claim to have salvation do not bear the fruit or evidence of it. Under superficial examination some Scriptures seem to contradict the concept of eternal security. On the other hand many Scriptures that affirm the believer's eternal security are so clear that their testimony out weighs any objections that may be raised. Generally speaking those who hold to a Calvinistic system of theology hold to eternal security or perseverance of the saints, and those who hold to an Armenian system of theology generally affirm that a saved person can be lost.

No doubt some who profess salvation have never been saved. That such people should fall away is to be expected. On the other hand the extensive character of the salvation of a believer in Christ is such that it is an irreversible work of God which cannot be changed by human decision or failure.

The concept of eternal security builds on other doctrines such as the doctrine of depravity. Because man is depraved, he cannot be saved except by divine grace. Only God makes salvation possible and actual. The fact of sovereign and eternal election makes it impossible for an elect person once saved to lose his salvation.

If salvation is something that man does for himself, obviously it could be lost. If salvation is an act of God, then it is a work that man cannot undo. This is brought out in passages such as Romans 8:30, "And those He predestined, He also called; those He called, He also justified; those He justified, He also glorified." All who are predestined to salvation will be justified, and all who are justified will be glorified. Their salvation is thus secure.

In the history of the church[369] some have accepted the doctrine of eternal security while others have accepted the possibility that some believers may fall from salvation. In the Lutheran Church, for example, some believe that a saved person can be lost while others believe in eternal security. Historically Lutherans define regeneration as something that happens when an infant is baptized. At the same time they hold that regeneration is not equal to salvation. Ultimately the question has to be decided as to what the Scriptures teach, and obviously the Scriptures do not teach both views.

In the following, it will be pointed out that the truth of eternal security is inherent in the nature of salvation itself. If salvation is no more than a detached coin which one holds in his hand and which he has only by virtue of a feeble human grasp, it might be easily lost. On the other hand if salvation is the creation of a new being composed of unchangeable and imperishable elements that depend on the perfect and immutable merit of the Son of God, then there can be no failure.

Actually there is no proper ground for drawing a distinction between salvation and safekeeping though for practical purposes such a distinction may be established. The fact is that God's salvation is eternal by its very nature. Even though human experience can vacillate, eternal security means that no soul once saved had ever been lost. Doubts about security can be traced to failure to comprehend the reality that God accomplishes salvation by His sovereign grace.

Three major systems of theology have characterized the history of the doctrine of salvation: Socinianism, Arminianism, and Calvinism. Socinianism is usually attributed to those who are liberal in theology and who pay little attention to what the Scriptures teach. It is the forerunner of modern liberalism. Arminianism is more biblical and orthodox in its treatment of Scripture. It avoids the rationalism of Scocinianism but falls short of the declaration of Calvinism.

In using the terms Arminianism and Calvinism, there is no intent to magnify human points of view but rather simply to give titles to two approaches to the doctrine of salvation. From a practical as well as a theological standpoint it is most important to establish whether the salvation of a believer continues forever or whether the saving work of Christ on the cross includes the safekeeping of the ones who have put their trust in Him or whether it does not. The question is whether a Christian can be condemned. According to Romans 8:1, "There is now no condemnation for those who are in Christ Jesus."

The importance of determining the truth in this doctrine is evident. If there is no sufficient ground for the removal of condemnation and no sufficient ground for the impartation of eternal life and imputing of the merit of Christ, then salvation is nullified. Accordingly while godly men hold differences of opinion on this subject, the importance of the conclusions cannot be overestimated. NOTE! There is no record in the Bible of a person who was born again being lost. If this were possible there would be no way for such an individual to be restored. This is because the Bible is silent on how a person once saved and then lost could be saved again. Salvation by its very nature is a work of grace which God accomplished for those who are being saved and not a work by which a Christian can elevate himself spiritually into experiencing salvation.

THE CALVINISTIC DOCTRINE OF SECURITY

The terms "Arminian" or "Calvinistic" are unsatisfactory because they relate to human interpreters who obviously are not infallible. Because Arminianism generally exalts human responsibility in one's decision to receive Christ as opposed to Calvinism which exalts God's sovereignty and grace, the two views tend to be set over against each other on the question of the Christian's eternal security. Ultimately the question is not who holds the doctrine, but what do the Scriptures actually state?

Though the discussion could consider many Scriptures, 12 reasons, each one complete and conclusive in itself, are given as evidence for eternal security. In general, the New Testament presents the Father as purposing, calling, justifying, and glorying those who believe on Christ; the Kinsman-Redeemer, as dying a substitutionary and efficacious death, as rising from the dead to be the living Savior as Advocate, Intercessor, and as Head over all things to the church; and the Holy Spirit is presented as administering and executing the purpose of the Father and the redemption the Son has provided. It is reasonable then that all three Persons of the Godhead should have Their individual share in bringing to fruition what God has determined for the Christian's salvation.

Four reasons for security which are accomplished by God the Father are (1) the sovereign purpose of God, (2) the Father's infinite power, (3) the infinite love of God, and (4) the influence on the Father of the prayer of His Son. (1) The sovereign purpose of God is to provide eternal salvation for those who believe, Romans 8:28-30; Ephesians 1:11-12. (2) The Father's infinite Power; This power is set free in grace by the death of Christ. Because of this, God, who is infinitely righteous, can offer eternal salvation to one who sinned and who will continue to be imperfect. (3) God's Infinite Love supports the doctrine of eternal security. According to Ephesians 1:4-5, "In love He predestined us to be adopted as His sons through Jesus Christ, in accordance with His pleasure and will." (4) The prayer as recorded in John 17 supports the concept of eternal salvation.[370] Just as the Trinity cannot be severed, so believers cannot be severed from God.

The four reasons for a Christian's security which depends on God the Son are summarized in Romans 8:33-34, "Who will bring any charge against those whom God has chosen? It is God who justifies. Who is he that condemns? Christ Jesus, who died – more than that, who was raised to life – is at the right hand of God and is also interceding for us".[371]

THE CONSUMMATING SCRIPTURE

The Epistle of Paul to the Romans is a summary of the theology of the New Testament and is especially appropriate in its revelation of God's complete plan of salvation which includes the concept of eternal security. The Epistle to the Romans may be divided into three parts, (1) salvation, chapters 1-8; (2) dispensational truth, chapters 9-11; and (3) exhortation, chapters 12-16.

The first section, chapters 1-8, may also be subdivided into three parts. In the introduction the Apostle Paul declared that man was lost and under the universal condemnation of sin. In presenting God's remedy, salvation, three aspects are discussed: (1) salvation for the unregenerate person which is consummated in justification (2:21-5-21); (2) salvation for the believer from the power over sin unto sanctification (6:1-7:25); and (3) security for those who are saved (8:1-39).[372] In Romans 8 the doctrine of the believer's security is presented in a clear and convincing statement. The extensive treatment of the doctrine of salvation in the Epistle to the Romans is brought to its completion in chapter 8, which answers questions concerning the extent of salvation and the security of that salvation.

The chapter begins with the broad statement, "Therefore, there is now no condemnation for those who are in Christ Jesus" (v. 1). Pail affirmed that God "condemned sin in sinful man, in order that the righteous requirements of the Law might be fully met in us, who do not live according to the sinful nature but according to the Spirit" (vv. 3-4). It should be obvious that a Christian's life is never perfect and cannot meet the requirements of the Law. Christians are characterized by their testimony as those "who do not live according to the sinful nature but according to the Spirit" (v.4). The cause-and-effect relationship should be clearly established. A Christian's walk in the will of God is possible because of the fact that he is already justified. It is never a means to becoming justified.

In verse 2 Paul stated that "the law of the Spirit of life set me free from the Law of sin and death." Paul went on to state this was possible only because of what Christ had done on his behalf. In this context the Law stands as representative of the merit system taught to a limited extent in the Old Testament. Some of the blessings of the Law were conditioned on the obedience of the individual. In Christ the Law principle is done away as having nothing to contribute to the outworking of the principle of grace (Rom. 4:4-5; 11:6; Gal. 5:4). Paul pointed out that the Law was a means by which God made sin known to His people. He prepared them to understand the grace of God which, though demanding a supernatural life (John 13:34; 2 Cor. 10:3-5; Eph. 4:30), provided such a glorious salvation through Christ entirely apart from the merit of the person receiving it. Though a believer may often fail in conflict with the world, the flesh, and the devil, this does not alter the work of God for the believer in Christ. Arminianism tends to equate the imperfect daily life of a believer as ground for being lost. The New Testament teaches that those who believe are saved from the merit system by having all its demands satisfied in Christ, and thus the believer endures forever.[373]

It may be concluded that God's salvation is never offered except as an eternal salvation, and no soul once saved can be lost. Paul stated again his conviction of the certainty of God's salvation in Philippians 1:6, "Being confident of this, that He who began a good work in you will carry it on to completion until the day of Christ Jesus." Peter introduced his epistle in a similar way. "Praise be the God and Father of our Lord Jesus Christ! In His great mercy He has given us new birth into a living hope through the resurrection of Jesus Christ from the dead, and into an inheritance that can never perish, spoil, or fade – kept in heaven for you, who through faith are shielded by God's power until the coming of salvation that is ready to be revealed in the last time" (1 Peter 1:3-5).

DELIVERANCE FROM THE REIGNING POWER OF SIN

A major aspect of God's plan of salvation is the deliverance God provides from the power of sin. Scripture clearly contemplates the fact that in saving individuals God is fully aware that they will fall short of perfection in their lives. So that believers may have victory over sin, God has provided abundantly for them by changing them into new creations each with a new nature, by indwelling them with the Holy Spirit, providing them the infinite truth of God's inspired Word, supporting them by the advocacy and intercession of Christ in heaven, and providing fellowship for them with others who have received Christ as their Savior.

As previously considered, a Christian faces three opposing forces which are sources of evil – the world, the flesh, and the devil. In his unregenerate state he was part of this and did not sense any opposing force. Once a person is saved, however, he soon discovers that he has enemies and that the world, the sin nature, and the devil are all against him.

Not only is a Christian delivered from the world, the sin nature, and the devil, but also he is delivered by the grace of God from his own human limitations. A Christian endeavoring to lead a Christian life soon discovers that just as his salvation had to be a work of God, so his deliverance from evil as a Christian has to be a work of God. The experience of Christians gaining victory over the forces of evil is stated in Titus 2:11-14. "For the grace of God that brings salvation has appeared to all men. It teaches us to say 'No' to ungodliness and worldly passions, and to live self-controlled, upright, and godly lives in this present age, while we wait for the blessed hope- the glorious appearing of our great God and Savior, Jesus Christ, who gave Himself for us to redeem us from all wickedness and to purify for Himself a people that are His very own, eager to do what is good."[374] Also, it is important to take into consideration the extensive body of truth which reveals God's ministry to a Christian who desires to be God-honoring in his life and service.

THE BELIEVER PRESENTED FAULTLESS

Believers in Christ are promised ultimate perfection at the time of their presentation in glory. Paul wrote, "To Him who is able to keep you from falling and to present you before His glorious presence without fault and with great joy" (Jude 24). God promised that believers are kept from falling or "stumbling". When presented in God's presence the church shall be a great joy to the Lord.

The same concept is declared in Ephesians 5:25-27, "Husbands, love your wives, just as Christ loved the church and gave Himself up for her to make her holy, cleansing her by the washing with water through the Word. And to present her to Himself as a radiant church, without stain or wrinkle or any other blemish, but holy and blameless."

In the present experience of the believer there is need for a constant sanctifying process to purge away imperfections. God has promised to do this. At the end of this process when a believer is presented faultless in heaven, he will have no trace of sin, age, or limitations that characterize his life on earth. From beginning to end this is the work of God for the believer rather than a work of the believer for God. The perfections that will characterize the believer in heaven which are anticipated in this life and in the prophecies of the future include the fulfillment of all that a believer yearns for in this life.

A believer's citizenship in heaven begins at the moment of his salvation. Paul stated, "Consequently, you are no longer foreigners and aliens, but fellow citizens with God's people and members of God's household" (Eph. 2:19). Though Christians have right and title to this citizenship now, the full measure of its privilege will not be realized until they get to heaven.

When a believer is resurrected or raptured, he can anticipate a renewed body as Paul expressed in Philippians 3:20-21, "But our citizenship is in heaven. And we eagerly await a Savior from there, the Lord Jesus Christ, who, by the power that enables Him to bring everything under His control, will transform our lowly bodies so that they will be like His glorious body." A similar truth is found in 1 Corinthians 15:42-57 and Ephesians 5:27.[375] Believers, in their present bodies, have the threefold problem of possessing a sin nature, of being perishable as they grow older, and of being mortal. Immediately on resurrection or translation a believer will have a new body with no trace of sin, a body that is imperishable and that will last forever, and a body with freedom from mortality. Believers in heaven will have no more tears, sorrow, or pain and will never know weariness or the limitation of this life again (Rev. 21:4-5).[376]

As stated above, part of the plan of God at the time of resurrection or translation is the eradication of the sin nature. Though believers are rescued to some extent from their estate of sin at the time of their new birth, the flesh or the old nature is still there and will not be eradicated until death or the Rapture. Believers will never experience in heaven the temptation of this life or the limitations and frailties of their present bodies.

Much is indicated in the simple phrase "like Him" (1 John 3:2). Though believers will not be omnipotent, omnipresent, or omniscient, they will have the same eternal life that is in Christ, the same sinless character, and the same quality of being everlasting. As stated in 1 Corinthians 15:49, "As we have borne the likeness of the earthly man, so shall we bear the likeness of the man from heaven." Whatever God does He does to perfection, and the Christian when fully perfected in heaven will be an everlasting token of the grace of God.

In Christ's High Priestly Prayer in John 17:24, He said, "Father, I want those You have given to Me to be with Me where I am, and to see My glory, the glory You have given Me because You loved Me before the Creation of the world." In verse 22 Christ also said, "I have given them the glory that You gave Me, that they may be one as We are One."[377] A similar truth is stated by Paul, "And we, who with unveiled faces all reflect the Lord's glory, are being transformed into His likeness with ever-increasing glory, which comes from the Lord, who is Spirit" (2 Cor. 3:18). It is also true that "our light and momentary troubles are achieving for us an eternal glory that far outweighs them all" (4:17).

The prayer of the Apostle Paul to this end, in Ephesians 1:17-21 provides a summary of this great truth, "I keep asking that the God of our Lord Jesus Christ, the glorious Father, may give you the Spirit of wisdom and revelation, so that you may know Him better. I pray also that the eyes of your heart may be enlighten in order that you may know the hope to which He has called you, the riches of His glorious inheritance in the saints, and His incomparably great power for us who believe. That power is like the working of His mighty strength, which He exerted in Christ when He raised Him from the dead and seated Him at His right hand in the heavenly realms, far above all rule and authority, power and dominion, and every title that be given, not only in the present age but also in the one to come."[378]

THE TERMS OF SALVATION

Few doctrines of the Bible are more important than the subject of the terms of salvation. As provided in Scripture, many exhortations like the one to the Philippian jailer simply, "Believe in the Lord Jesus, and you will be saved- you and your household" (Acts 16:31). Though it is common in evangelism to make appeals to "give your heart to Christ" or "invite Christ into your heart," it is questionable whether an unbeliever is able to do this until he believes.

In making faith the sole condition for receiving salvation, it should be understood that it is not simply mental assent that is called for or a superficial agreement with the facts. In view of the fact that man's personality includes intellect, sensibility, and will, when a person accepts Christ as his Savior, his acceptance is an act of the mind, the emotions, and the moral will.

Included in the concept of faith is the thought of repenting. Peter stated in his sermon at Pentecost, "Repent and be baptized, every one of you, in the name of Jesus Christ so that your sins may be forgiven. And you will receive the gift of the Holy Spirit (Acts 2:38). Because those to whom he was speaking had previously rejected Christ, he asked them to repent or to change their minds regarding Christ and place their faith in Him. This repentance is an aspect of faith. Repentance as an act of sorrow, however, is not involved nor can unbelievers be challenged effectively to change their lives before salvation.

The all-important command is to believe in Christ. Normally this includes a reversal of any previous acts of unbelief, and it includes recognizing Jesus Christ as God. Experientially many Christians do not submit to Christ as Lord of their lives until sometime after their personal salvation, though in the nature of their faith in Christ they had to accept Him as God. Accordingly all appeals to change of life and change of attitude apart from faith in Christ are not accurate Gospel presentations. In Peter's case he also asked them to be baptized, that is, to make a public confession of their faith in Christ through the ritual of water baptism. In many other passages baptism is not mentioned, but obviously baptism is public evidence of one's faith in Christ. On the Day of Pentecost the 3,000 who were saved were then baptized. Water baptism, however, was not essential to their salvation but was a confirmation of their act of faith. Obviously the thief of the cross, who accepted Christ, had no opportunity for the ritual of baptism and yet was assured that he would meet Christ in paradise.

The common use of repentance as a way of salvation following the example of Peter (Acts 2:38) needs to be studied to define its particular meaning: (1) the meaning of the word, (2) the relationship of repentance to believing, (3) the relationship of repentance to covenant people, (4) the absence of the demand for repentance from salvation Scriptures, and (5) the significance of repentance in specific passages.

"Repentance" is a translation of *metanoia* which means "a change of mind." The idea of sorrow or anguish for sin is not in the word "repentance" though sorrow and anguish may accompany faith. In 2 Corinthians 7:10 the statement is made, "Godly sorrow brings repentance that leads to salvation and leaves no regret, but worldly sorrow brings death." It is true that in some cases people who have lived wickedly will be brought to Christ partly through sorrow for these sins. However, sorrow in itself does not bring salvation as illustrated in the case of Judas Iscariot. Sorrow is a regret but not necessarily a change of mind and a decision to trust Christ. The son, mentioned by Christ in Matthew 21:28-29, first said, "I will not," but later he repented and changed his mind". This is a true example of the precise meaning of the word. The New Testament call to repentance is not an urge to self-condemnation but is a call to a change of mind, which promotes a change being pursued. This word applies especially to those who had previously rejected Christ.

Repentance is not an added feature to believing but is involved in the act of believing in Christ. If a person has previously rejected Christ, he is urged to change his mind or to believe, and therefore repentance becomes a synonym for faith. Repentance, however, should be seen not as an added requirement for salvation but rather as an aspect of true faith.

Repentance for sin focuses on sinful acts which are not the basic problem for a person who is unsaved. His sin nature is the major problem and he needs a new nature in order to be saved. This can be received only by faith.

In this discussion it has been brought out that repentance is not a good work on which to base salvation but is rather intrinsic in any act of true faith as it involves an act of the will which has not been previously exercised in regard to trusting Jesus Christ.

In Peter's sermon at Pentecost, he included baptism along with belief as a way of salvation (Acts 2:38). It should be remembered that as baptism is mentioned in Scripture, sometimes it refers to real baptism, that is, the baptism of the Holy Spirit which occurs at the moment of faith and in other cases to the ritual of water baptism. It is possible to take this verse in either sense. If it refers to real baptism, then Peter was saying that if the Jews believed and had this belief confirmed by being baptized into the body of Christ, they would be saved. Or if it refers to water baptism then Peter was saying that ritual was an outward confirmation of their faith. In any case immediately afterward, Peter baptized 3,000 (v.41), who were by this token publicly aligning themselves with Christ and indicating that they were leaving their former Jewish confidence in the Law.

In presenting the Gospel it is a subtle temptation to urge people not only to believe but also to surrender to God because of course this is the ultimate objective of their salvation. However, in explaining the terms of salvation this brings in a confusing human work as essential to salvation which the Bible does not confirm. Evidence that surrender to God is not part of the act of salvation may be approached under three aspects: (1) the incapacity of the unsaved, (2) what is involved in salvation, and (3) the preacher's responsibility.

The Arminian belief that through the reception of common grace anyone is competent to accept Christ as Savior is a rather mild assumption as compared to the idea that an unregenerate person is able to dedicate his life to God. The fact is that unbelievers are dead and unable to respond unless the Holy Spirit enables them. Accordingly the unsaved can receive the convicting work of the Spirit by which the terms of the Gospel are made known to them and may receive grace to put their trust in Christ. To add to this, however, the concept of surrendering their lives to the Lord is asking them to do something they are ill prepared to do at the time of initial salvation. Though it is clear that grace is necessary for belief (Eph. 2:8), to add the additional requirement of surrendering to God as a condition to salvation is unreasonable and contrary to Scripture.

Once a person is saved the appeal can be made to him to yield his life to Christ, but this should not be made a part of the process of the new birth.

The most subtle form of meritorious works is often found in the practice of urging unbelievers to accept the Lordship of Christ. Trusting in Christ for salvation means accepting Him as God, but the added step of yielding to Him as Lord is usually postponed until later.

An extreme case of dedication to God is involved in the death of a martyr. It is true that a Christian who has put his trust in Christ should be willing to die for Christ's sake, and in the course of human history millions have died. To make this a condition of salvation, however, is to put a stricture on the Gospel which is not natural to its offer in grace. Certainly one cannot identify Christians simply on the issue of whether they are willing to die for Christ. It is possible that those who have been born again and genuinely desire to serve the Lord have not reached that stage of spiritual maturity where they are willing to become martyrs.

Being spiritually dead an unregenerate person has no ability to desire the things of God (1 Cor. 2:14) or to anticipate what his outlook on life will be after he is saved. In presenting the Gospel the emphasis should be on appealing to the unsaved to exercise faith for salvation rather than to confuse the issue by raising problems of dedication to God.

This is where the preacher comes into play. The preacher is responsible to present the terms of salvation. Those who have this responsibility should first recognize that God uses a clear presentation which can be the basis for the convicting work of the Spirit. The Gospel must be presented as God's way of salvation and faith as the way by which this salvation can come to an individual. The issue in salvation itself is not a question of morality but a question of where the individual puts his faith. Once a Christian has accepted Christ as Savior, then he is in a position to consider the larger sphere of what he should do for God in view of what God has done for him.

In discussing the way of salvation with the unsaved people it is important that there be clarity in presenting the single issue of whether they will trust in Christ for salvation. All other issues are foreign at this point. The Holy Spirit will use a clear presentation of the grace of God that prompts salvation based on the finished work of Christ. This is the area the Holy Spirit can reveal to an unsaved person in preparation for faith.

Perhaps no verse of Scripture more accurately portrays the wonder of God's salvation than John 3:16, "For God so loved the world that He gave His one and only Son, that whoever believes in Him shall not parish but have eternal life." In this one text is marshaled the wonderful fact that "God so loved the world" even though the world was sinful and contrary to the holiness of God. This verse states that God "gave His one and only Son." In these few words the immeasurable sacrifice of the Son in dying on the cross is expressed. The third major element is stated in the words "that whoever believes in Him," which asserts that salvation is through Christ alone and is secured by faith alone uncomplicated by any work of merit. In this verse also the expression "shall not perish" contrasts the state of the saved with the state of the lost. Finally the verse promises "but have eternal life." Here the ultimate goal of salvation is to give the believer, unworthy as he is, the same kind of life that characterizes God's everlasting life.

In this incomparable text at least nine great doctrines of soteriology are included: infinite love, infinite sacrifice for the sinner, sovereign election, sovereign grace, unlimited redemption, salvation a work of God, salvation from perdition, eternal security, and salvation by grace through faith alone.

INTRODUCTION TO ECCLESIOLOGY

Ecclesiology is that branch of theology that deals with the doctrine of the church, the term coming from the Greek, *ekklesis*, meaning "assembly." In the history of Greece the assembly of citizens to consider legislation in a Greek town was called *ekklesis*, meaning an assembly of people gathered in one place. It is used in this sense of the assembly of the Jews in the desert. In the New Testament it is also used of congregations of Christians in a given locality and is used in this sense at least 100 times (Acts 9:31; m14:23; 15:41; Rom. 16:1; 1 Cor. 1:2; Gal. 1:2; 1 Thes. 1:1, etc.). In some instances, however, it is used of the church or the body of believers regardless of geographic location (Matt. 16:18; Eph. 1:22; 3:10; 5:23-25, 27; Col. 1:18).[379]

Because the Greek translation of the Old Testament uses *ekklesia* for assemblies in the Old Testament, some have argued from this that the church is also in the Old Testament. An examination of all instances of the various Hebrew words translated *ekklesia* demonstrates that the word is never used in the Old Testament in a religious sense and used only of a geographic assembly of people whether or not it has religious connotations.

A careful reading of the New Testament, however, reveals that *ekklesia*, though it refers to local assemblies which were churches, is also used in a purely religious sense of all those who were united by faith in Christ in the period beginning with the Day of Pentecost.

From Scripture, four classes of moral and rational beings are disclosed: the angels, the Gentiles, the Jews, and Christians. Each of these four classes has his own theology and program in the past, present, and future.

The angels are created beings (Ps. 148:2-5; Col. 1:1); their abode is in heaven (Matt. 24:36) their activity is both on earth and in Heaven (Ps. 103:20; Luke 15:10; Heb. 1:14); and their destiny is the celestial city (12:22; Rev:21:12).[380]   Angels do not change their essential situation though some of them fell into sin and became the demon world under Satan's direction. Each of the angels was the immediate object of God's creation, they are not increased in number, and they neither propagate not do they die. Though fallen angels are subject to eternal punishment (Matt. 25:41), they are still classed as angels.

Gentiles are a second group of rational beings. Racially the Gentiles had their origin in Adam, and they are an extensive subject of prophecy. Except for their situation in the present age, they were subordinated to Israel (Isa. 2:4; 60:3, 5. 12; 62:2; Acts 15:17).[381] From Adam to Christ, Gentiles were under a fivefold indictment, namely, they were "separate from Christ," "Excluded from citizenship in Israel," "foreigners to the covenants of the promise," "without hope," and "without God in the world".

In the present age because of the death, resurrection, and ascension of Christ and the descent of the Spirit on the Day of Pentecost, Gentiles and Jews share the same Gospel (Acts 10:45; 11:17-18; 13: 47-48), and from Jews and Gentiles alike God is calling an elect company (Acts 15:14).[382]

The Scriptures reveal that God has selected Israel as a primary race to reveal His revelation to man through prophets and writers of Scripture, through the apostles and prophets of the New Testament, and supremely through Jesus Christ. The special purposes of God for Israel are summarized in Romans 9:4-5, "Theirs is the adoption as sons; theirs the divine glory, the covenants, the receiving of the Law, the temple worship and the promises. Theirs are the patriarchs, and from them is traced the human ancestry of Christ, who is God over all, forever praised."

Though interpreters of the Old Testament were perplexed by the dual prophecies of a suffering and a glorious reigning Messiah as referred to by Peter (1 Peter 1:10-11),[383] in the New Testament it became clear that prophecies of His first coming to die have been fulfilled. The prophecies of His second coming to reign are still future. Though God's Son would die a sacrificial death (Ps. 22:1-21; 9:20-21), He would be resurrected and occupy David's throne forever (2 Sam. 7:16-29; Ps. 89:34-37). Though no one in the Old Testament understood the two comings of Christ, David apparently had some insight as he reasoned that if Christ's Son was to occupy the throne forever, He must first die and be raised from the dead and therefore freed to reign forever. This truth was featured in Peter's Pentecostal sermon (Acts 2:25-36). In His first coming Christ offered Himself to Israel as her King (Zech. 9:9; Matt. 21:50). In His second coming He will return as a conquering Ruler (Rev. 19:15-16).[384]

To avoid confusion in interpretation of Scripture, the promises given to Israel, which were repeated by Christ in His first coming, must be distinguished from the promise to the church. The church in this age is given a special place and is composed of both Jews and Gentiles. The future program for the church differs from the program for Israel as Israel's program is related primarily to the earth and to her ultimate national restoration to the Promised Land.

In His first coming Christ was rejected nationally by Israel and her leaders though many individual Israelites such as the Apostles and others put their trust in Him. Offering Himself to Israel as her Messiah, He was offering Himself in a sense as her King. Because Israel rejected this, however, the promise of the kingdom will be fulfilled at the time of His second coming. The kingdom is postponed in the same sense that the Jews, who were given the promise of the Promised Land, had their occupancy of the land postponed by their failure to trust God at Kadesh Barnea. As a result they wandered in the wilderness for 40 years until the time came for them to enter the land.

Starting with the Day of Pentecost believers are placed into the church, the body of Christ, by the baptism of the Spirit. The church continues on earth until the future Rapture. The church as a body of people distinguished from both Jews and Gentiles is given the term "Christian" (Acts 11:26).

To look at a dispensation is to look at a stage in God's progressive revelation defining a rule of life, which constitutes a distinct stewardship. Dispensations are found in different time periods (Eph. 1:7; 3:5, 9; Heb. 1:2). An age differs from a dispensation in that the age is the time period and the dispensation is the stewardship that constitutes God's rule of life in that time period. The fact that there are various ages in the history of the world is recognized in the Bible (John 1:17; 5:21-22; 2 Cor. 3:11; Heb. 7:11-12).[385]

Man's relationship to God varies in different ages. In each dispensation man is tested under different rules and invariably fails, and he is able to be rightly related to God only by grace.

In the various dispensations certain elements remain the same such as God's holy character, basic morality, and the way of salvation. Though salvation is by faith and through grace in every age, the manner in which that faith is demonstrated in life differs.

In interpreting the dispensations it is important to distinguish their primary and secondary applications. Though some instructions pertaining to a particular dispensation are superseded by later instructions, the entire Scriptures contain truths that can be applied in a secondary way as reflecting God's holy Person and what is normative in every dispensation. Accordingly there is unity as well as diversity in the dispensations.

Seven dispensations are found in Scripture: (1) innocence, (2) conscience, (3) government, (4) promise, (5) law, (6) grace, and (7) millennial kingdom. However, only three dispensations, law, grace, and kingdom, are given detailed revelation.

While not everyone recognizes seven dispensations, one must recognize the concept of dispensations in the Scriptures if a normal, literal interpretation of the Bible is employed. The attempt to erase dispensational distinctions in the Scriptures can be accomplished only by interpreting the Scriptures in a nonliteral sense.

The dispensation of the kingdom will begin with the second coming of Christ (Matt. 24; Rev. 19).[386] The time period between the Cross and the Day of Pentecost and the time period between the Rapture and the Second Coming do not form distinct dispensations but are translation periods from the Law to the kingdom with the present age of grace interposed.

Major prophecies dealing with the millennial kingdom are numerous (ps. 72; Isa. 2:1-7; 11; Jer. 33:14-17; Dan. 2:44-45; 7:9-14, 18, 27; Hosea 3:4-5; Zech. 14:9; Luke 1:31-33; Rev. 19-20).[387] Because of the special characteristics of the millennial kingdom, there will be greater manifestations of righteousness in the human race than in any other dispensation (Isa. 11:3-5). Satan will be bound and Christ will be residing supremely and visibly in the city of Jerusalem. The human responsibility in the kingdom will be to obey the King. In contrast to the age of grace the dispensation of the kingdom will be a theocratic rule. Animal sacrifices will be resumed, not to fulfill the Law of Moses but to serve as a memorial of the death of Christ (Ezek. 40-48).[388]

In spite of the unusual characteristics of the kingdom period, the millennial dispensation will end with failure (Isa. 5:20; Zech. 14:1-19), and there will be rebellion at the close of the dispensation when Satan will be loosed (Rev. 20:7-9). The dispensation of the kingdom ends with the destruction of the present earth and heavens and the creation of the new heavens and the new earth (Isa. 65:17; 66:22; 2 Peter 3:10) on which the New Jerusalem will rest (Rev. 21:1-4).[389]

In the progress of doctrine from Genesis to Revelation the Bible reveals different periods of time with different stewardship which are viewed as dispensations of God's government. As the dispensations before Moses were already history when Scripture was written, the earlier dispensations are given relatively brief revelation.

In the Mosaic Law for the first time a complete religious system was provided with at least seven distinctive features: (1) an acceptable standing of the part of man before God, (2) a manner of life consistent with that standing, (3) divinely appointed service, (4) a righteous ground whereby God may graciously forgive and cleanse the erring, (5) a clear revelation of responsibilities on the human side which lead to divine forgiveness and cleansing, (6) an effective base on which God may be worshiped and petitioned in prayer, and (7) a future hope.

In Scripture three distinct and complete divine rulings govern human action. Two are addressed to Israel. One is past and is designated the Mosaic Law, and the other is future and is Israel's required conduct in the messianic kingdom which will be set up by Christ at His second coming. A third rule of life, revealed in the New Testament, is for Christians. It directs Christians to have a standard of life in keeping with their heavenly calling. Though the saved in the present age can learn much of God's moral government by reading the Old Testament, they are given a special and more detailed revelation of their relationship to Christ for the present age in the New Testament. This rule of life for Christians differs from the rule of life for Israel.

The Mosaic system was designed to keep Israel from apostasy and to govern the nation in the land and was a temporary form of divine government administered from Moses to Christ (John 1:17; Rom. 4:9-1; Gal. 3:19-25).[390] As mentioned earlier, the Mosaic Law was divided into three divisions: (a) the commandments, which governed Israel's moral life (Ex. 20:1-17; (b) the judgments, which governed Israel's civic life (21:1-24:11); and (c) the ordinances, which governed Israel's religious life (24:12-31:18). The provisions of the Law were holy, just, and good (Rom. 7:12, 14), but they carried a penalty for disobedience (Duet. 28:58-2). Because they were not kept, Israel experienced the discipline of God in the wilderness, and in the captivities. She also is under that discipline in the present, and will be in the future.[391]

The Law did not offer a way of salvation, and heaven was not among its rewards nor was hell among its punishments. In keeping the Law a Jew could manifest his faith in God and God's provided redemption even though he only partially understood what God was providing through Christ in the future. As a specific rule of life, the Law was terminated with the death of Christ (John 1:17; Rom. 6:14; 7:2-6; 10:4; 2 Cor. 3:6-13; Gal. 3:23-25; 5:18). The Law is declared to be "done away" (kjv) and" abolished" (kjv), or "fading away" (2 Cor. 3:11-13).[392]

In the present age, Christians have the privileged position of their standing in the perfection of Christ (Rom. 3:22; 5:1; 8:1; 10:4; 2 Cor. 5:21; Gal. 3:3:22; Eph. 1:6; Heb. 10:9-14).

Both Judaism and Christianity have a future hope. Prophecy concerning Israel reaches into eternity and is based on the covenants and promises of God which are everlasting. Christians have a somewhat different eschatology in the more extensive revelation concerning their hope.

Individual Israelites were promised that they would "live long in the land the Lord your God is giving you" (Ex. 20:12) as a reward for keeping the fifth commandment by honoring their parents. In the New Testament Christians are given the hope of the imminent coming of Christ at the Rapture to take His church from earth to heaven. Christians have no prospect of possessing a land nor promise of earthly things beyond their personal needs. In the period before the second coming of Christ Israel is commanded to watch for His coming (Matt. 24:36-51; 25:13). By contrast Christians are told to "wait for His Son from heaven" (1 Thes. 1:10). Both Jews and Christians who are saved are promised that they will spend eternity in the presence of God. The eternal hope of the Old Testament saints is stated in Hebrews 11:16, "Instead, they were longing for a better country – a heavenly one. Therefore God is not ashamed to be called their God, for He has prepared a city for them." The promise of the city referring to the New Jerusalem should not be confused with the promise of their millennial kingdom on earth, Jews had hope of restoration to their earthly land as a nation, but beyond this there was the eternal hope of the heavenly city.[393]

The doctrine of resurrection is clearly taught in the Old Testament, as seen in Daniel 12:1-3. According to this Scripture Daniel's people will be resurrected following the Great Tribulation (11:36-45). Some believe the resurrection of the Old Testament saints will occur at the time of the Rapture. However, Daniel 12:1-3 and Isaiah 26:19 seem to place this after the Tribulation period. The faith of Israel in a future resurrection is illustrated by Martha (John 11:24; Heb.6:1-2).

The doctrine of resurrection for Christians includes two parts: (1) Believers have already been raised and seated with Christ (Eph. 2:6), and so are spiritually raised from the dead (Col. 3:1-3), and (2) should they die, their bodies will be raised at the Rapture when Christ comes for His own (1 Cor. 15:23; 1 Thes. 4:16-17).[394]

Prophecy concerning the future of Israel and the church should be distinguished though in some events both are involved. The Old Testament prophesies a glorious future for Israel to be fulfilled in the millennial kingdom. For the Christian the blessed hope is the Rapture of the church. Israel's particular hope is the millennial kingdom. Both Christians and Israel will inhabit the New Jerusalem and the new earth in eternity.

The doctrine of the church considered in ecclesiology is naturally subdivided into three parts: (1) the Pauline revelation of a new order or class of humanity, namely, a redeemed company of both Jews and Gentiles which together with a resurrected Christ form a new creation which is also His body and His bride; (2) the outward or visible church, the assembly of those at any place who gather in the name of Christ; and (3) the walk and service of those who are saved.

The true church has a special relation to the first Person of the Godhead who is God the Father as indicated in the New birth. Passages such as 1 John, speak of Christians as God's children. Seven figures are used in the New Testament to describe the relationship of the church to Christ as the second Person: the Shepherd and the sheep, the Vine and the branches, the Cornerstone and the stones of the building, the High Priest and the kingdom of priests, the last Adam and the new creation, the Head and the body, and the Bridegroom and the bride.

Generally speaking, Israel was appointed to live and serve under a meritorious, legal system. In contrast to the church which serves under a gracious system. The main body of prophecy relating to Israel speaks of her citizenship now and of her future millennial destiny on the earth, followed by the new earth. By contrast Christians are described as citizens and do not share the earthly promises given to Israel.

The distinction between Israel and the church is seen in the covenants God made with Israel. Those covenants pertain to (1) a national entity (Jer. 31:36), (2) a land in perpetuity (Gen. 13:15), (3) a throne (2 Sam. 7:16; Ps. 89:36), (4) a King (Jer. 33:21), and (5) a kingdom (Dan. 7:17).[395]

The church, composed of both Jews and Gentiles who put their trust in Christ, is a special body of people (Matt. 16:18) who share some things with Israel: (1) they are cosharers in the purpose of His incarnation, (2) the subjects of His ministry, (3) the objects of His death and resurrection, (4) the beneficiaries of His second advent, and (5) related to Him in His kingly reign.

Failure to understand the distinctive purpose of the church has been a serious fault of many studies in ecclesiology. As approached here, ecclesiology is considered in three divisions: (1) the church as an organism, (2) the organized church, and (3) the believers' rule of life.

THE DOCTRINE OF THE CHURCH

Though the Protestant Reformation recovered many important truths of the Bible, such as the priesthood of the believer, justification by faith, and the truth that every individual is his own interpreter of the Bible assisted by the Holy Spirit, the great truths respecting the distinctive character of the church in the present age as taught in the early church were not fully discovered. Though theology recognizes the Pauline revelation of the church, the tendency is to merge what relates to the church and what relates to Israel. However, a careful study of the New Testament reveals that they are to a large degree independent and separable.

In contemplating the church as the body of Christ in this division of ecclesiology a threefold approach should be observed: (1) general features of the doctrine concerning the church, (2) contrasts between Israel and the church, and (3) seven figures used of the church in relationship to Christ.

The word "church" is a common word in the Greek language and was used originally for a political gathering constituting the government of a particular area. In the Old Testament the same word in the sense of "an assembly" was used to characterize Israel when she was assembled in one geographic location (Acts 7:38). In the New Testament, though the word was used occasionally for a geographic assembly as in a local church, sometimes it included the entire church (9:31) whether in heaven on in earth (1 Cor. 10:32; Eph. 1:22; 5:23-25, 27, 20; Col. 1:18; Heb. 12:23). The concept of a church as a religious body without geographic location was a new use of the word in the New Testament and must be defined by the context.[396]

The fact of a new divine undertaking in which Jews and Gentiles would share alike the spiritual blessings of salvation was a thought abhorrent to Jews steeped in their theology and traditions. Paul himself was an outstanding illustration of this before his salvation, and his conversation requires a special revelation of Christ. Once Paul understood the new divine undertaking, however, he made the statement, "For there is no difference between Jew and Gentile – the same Lord is Lord of all and richly blesses all who call on Him" (Rom. 10:12).

The change from Jewish tradition to the new Christian revelation required the first church council to take up the question of whether Gentiles in the church had to follow Jewish religious laws (Acts 15:1). As recorded in verses 16-18, James affirmed that God had not forsaken His purpose to restore Israel but that in the present age Jews and Gentiles would be united in the church and this purpose would be consummated before Israel's restoration. "When they finished James spoke up: 'Brothers listen to me. Simon has described to us how God at first showed His concern by taking from the Gentiles a people for Himself. The words of the prophets are in agreement with this, as it is written: "After this I will return and rebuild David's fallen tent. Its ruins I will rebuild and I will restore it, that the remnant of men may seek the Lord, and all the Gentiles who bear My name, says the Lord, who does these things" that have been known for ages'" (Acts 15:13-18; Amos 9:1-12). It is important to observe the time sequence in Acts 15:13-18. God was "first" taking Gentiles as a people to Himself in the present age and "after this" will restore Israel. This is the order of prophetic Scripture which makes the church the present purpose of God and the restoration of Israel an event which follows this Church Age and has its primary fulfillment in the millennial kingdom.[397]

Based on this truth the decision was made that Gentiles were not required to observe the laws relating particularly to Israel in the Old Testament, but at the same time they were to avoid undue aggravation of Jews. The new divine undertaking was to include both Jews and Gentiles with their racial differences ignored (Eph. 2:14). Though it took time for some of the apostles to understand this, the council at

Jerusalem recorded Peter's statement, "Brothers, you know that some time ago God made a choice among you that the Gentiles might hear from my lips the message of the Gospel and believe. God, who knows the heart, showed that He accepted them by giving the Holy Spirit to them, for He purified their hearts by faith. Now then, why do you try to test God by putting on the necks of the disciples a yoke that neither we nor our fathers have been able to bear? No! We believe it is through the grace of our Lord Jesus that we are saved, just as they are" (Acts 15:7-11).[398]

This shows that God's purpose for the church was not His purpose for Israel and is a distinct purpose which is being fulfilled in the present age. For the present, the program of God for Israel as revealed in the Old Testament is suspended until after the Rapture of the church. Though the distinction between Israel and the church is made in the New Testament, throughout Scripture there are also some similarities, including salvation and the grace of God. The present age, however, was not foreseen by the prophets of the Old Testament (1 Peter 1:10-11).[399]

In the New Testament the first use of the word "church: as the *ekklesia* is in Matthew 16:18 where Christ said, "And I will tell you that you are Peter, and on this rock I will build My church, and the gates of Hades will not overcome it." In referring to Peter as a rock (in keeping with the name "Peter," meaning a small rock) Christ used a play on words to declare that the church would be built on a rock, referring to Himself. Though there has been some discussion as to what this means, it seems plain that in making the statement Christ pointed to Himself as the Rock on which the church would be built. This is in keeping with references to Christ as the foundation (1 Cor. 3:11) and Peter's description of the church as living stones built up on Christ (1 Peter 2:4-8).[400]

When the Old Testament closed, no fulfillment of prophecies concerning the coming Messiah and King had yet taken place. The

Incarnation had not been accomplished. Christ had not been crucified and resurrected, and the necessary preliminaries for establishing the church had not been accomplished. After Christ offered Himself as the Messiah to Israel as recorded in the early chapters of Matthew, the main body of the Jewish people rejected Christ (Matt. 12:24). Christ then stated in seven parables the characteristics of the present age (Matt. 13). This revelation was necessary because the Old Testament did not present the truth of the period between the first and the second coming of Christ.

Though many theologians do not recognize the distinctive use of *ekklesia* for the body of Christ in the present age, good reasons are advanced in Scripture to indicate that the church began at Pentecost.

1. There could be no church in the world constituted as she is and distinctive in all her features until Christ's death (Acts 20:28; Rom. 324-26; Col. 1:13-14). The death of Christ is more than a mere anticipation, but the church, the body of Christ, is based wholly on His finished work, and she must be purified by His precious blood.

2. There could be no church until Christ rose from the dead to provide her with a resurrection life (Rom. 4:24; Col. 3:1-3). This is a new feature that had not been introduced before.

3. There could be no church until Christ ascended on high to become the Head of the church (Eph. 1:19-23; Heb. 7:25; 1 John 2:1). The church is a new creation with a new Head in the resurrected Christ. As such, He is also the Head of the body of Christ, which is the church. The church in the present age could not survive if it were not for Christ's intercession and advocacy in heaven.

4. There could be no church on earth until the advent of the Holy Spirit (Acts 1:5; 1 Cor. 12:12; Eph. 4:30). The coming of the Holy Spirit on the Day of Pentecost to indwell and seal the church made the church a temple or habitation of God. Saints

had been regenerated before Pentecost but only at Pentecost was the church baptized by the Spirit into one body. Inasmuch as these important works essential to the character of the church did not occur before Pentecost, the church could not begin until that date. A church without the finished work on which to stand, a church without resurrection position or life, a church which is a new humanity but lacking a Head, a church without Pentecost or what Pentecost contributed is only a figment of theological fancy and is not the teaching of the New Testament.[401]

Though the church was not in the Old Testament as a contemporary work of God and did not have a predicted future, in the Old Testament the church was anticipated in many types. Many of the sacrifices of the old order were a foreshadowing of Christ's death. The same is true of the biblical offerings in which at least four of the seven feasts of *Yahweh* converge on the church. Some of the brides of the Old Testament are types of the church as a bride. Though the church appears in typology in the Old Testament, there were no specific prophecies concerning her until the New Testament revelation.

7 FIGURES USED IN CHURCH
RELATION TO CHRIST
(PARTS I – V)

Though almost completely neglected in most theological works, I believe the seven figures of Christ's relationship to the church are the central revelation concerning God's purpose and plan for the church. Their importance justifies a careful study of each figure.

In addition to this grouping of seven figures depicting Christ in relation to the church are two other groups of seven, namely, the seven parables in Matthew 13 and the seven letters to the seven churches in Asia (Rev. 2-3). Brief consideration of these will be undertaken before examining the seven figures.[40]

In the seven parables of Matthew 13, distinctive revelation is given of God's purpose in the present age, a subject not revealed in the Old Testament. In considering the mysteries of the kingdom of heaven it should be observed that they include the entire period from the first advent of Christ to His second advent. A major portion of this period chronologically is occupied by the church, the body of Christ. In verses 3-23 Christ characterized the present age to a harvest in which the farmer sows his seed. Four kinds of reception are given the seed, some falling on the hard, beaten path, some falling on rocky places or where there was little soil, some which fell on good soil but was chocked by thorns, and still others that fell on good soil and brought forth good fruit. This illustrates the different reception people give to the Gospel, as seen in the history of the church.[403]

In the Parable of the weeds among the Wheat (vv. 24-30, 36-43) Christ pictured the sphere of profession with the wheat and the weeds looking much alike in their early stages and inseparable until the time of judgment.

The Parable of the Yeast or Leaven (v. 33) likens the Gospel to yeast fermenting in dough. Though some Bible teachers say yeast or leaven pictures the Gospel permeating the kingdom, ordinarily the use of leaven or yeast in the Bible refers to evil. Israelites were forbidden to use leavened bread for certain sacrifices because the sacrifices were to be pure.

In the Parable of the Hidden Treasure (v. 44), some say that the treasure represents Christ and the man who found it represents individuals who put their trust in Christ. However, in salvation a person has nothing by which to purchase salvation, and in any case salvation is not secured by selling all a person has. A better interpretation is that the treasure represents Israel, which like a hidden treasure is often not acknowledged as a significant nation though it is a recognized entity in the world. Christ sold all He had in dying for Israel on the cross.

In another group of seven are the seven letters to the churches of Asia recorded in Revelation 2-3. Each of the messages is important as a message from Christ to His church. It is deplorable that so little attention has been paid to these seven letters in contrast to the much greater attention given to other letters in the New Testament. Though addressed to seven churches actually located in Asia Minor, like the Epistle of Paul addressed to churches their message goes beyond their immediate destination to the church in the present age. The messages are delivered not only to the particular churches, but to individuals who will hear, and to any church existing today that corresponds to one of the churches. Together they form a picture of the professing church in its strengths and weakness.

The term "sheep" is often applied in the Bible to people. It pictures the utter helplessness of individuals to find their own way. The term is applied to Israel as well as the Gentiles who are judged at the second coming of Christ (Matt. 25:34). In general it relates to any people who are favored of God.

In the Old Testament, Christ was truly the Shepherd of Israel (Ps. 23:1; 74:1; 79:13; 95:7; 100:3; Jer. 23:1). In the discourse of Christ in John 10 under the figure of the Shepherd and the sheep, Christ is pictured first in His relationship to Israel and then in His relationship to the church. As Israel was to find salvation in Christ, so believers in the present age who are not of the same flock as Israel will form one flock with Israel in the present age. The "Other sheep" mentioned in verse 16 are not Israel, the flock of sheep in the pen, but are present-age Gentile believers in Christ.

The doctrine of the shepherdhood of Christ introduced here is continued in His ceaseless intercession and advocacy at the right hand of the Father on behalf of His own (Heb. 7:25). Because of this, Christians can say with David, "The Lord is my Shepherd, I shall lack nothing" (Ps. 23:1).[404]

The figure of the vine and the branches in John 15 is addressed to believers in the present age. As part of the Upper Room Discourse (John 13-17), the passage looks beyond the death, resurrection, and ascension of Christ, and beyond Pentecost. It is a revelation of the relationship of Christ to His church in the present age. In the Old Testament Israel was the vineyard of God (Isa. 5:1-7; 2:21; Hosea 10:1; Luke 20:9-1). When Christ introduced Himself as the "true Vine" (John 15:1), He was presenting Himself in contrast to the vine of Israel, which was fruitless. As the true Vine, He will be fruitful through the branches that draw their life from Him. This figure illustrates the truth of communion with Christ.

The contribution which the figure of the vine and its branches makes to the doctrine of the church is to emphasize the provision of unbroken communion of the believer with the Lord, the enabling power of God resting on him both for his experience of joyous fellowship and for fruitfulness by prayer and testimony. The Vine and the branches partake of one common life—That of Christ and the church.

An obvious distinction between Israel and the church is that Israel had a temple (Ex. 25:8), and the church is a temple (Eph. 2:21). Just as God was present in the Old Testament temple, so He is present in the church indwelling those who are saved in the present age. By God's presence, the temple is purified and made holy. This fact is stated in verses 19-22, "Consequently, you are no longer foreigners and aliens, but fellow citizens with God's people and members of God's household, built on the foundation of the apostles and the prophets, with Christ Jesus Himself as the chief Cornerstone. In Him the whole building is joined together and rises to become a holy temple in the Lord. And in Him you too are being built together to become a dwelling in which God lives by His Spirit." Christ anticipated the present work of God for the church in His statement in Matthew 1:18, "On this rock I will build My church." References to the same concept are found in the New Testament (1 Cor. 3:9; Heb. 3:6; 1 Peter 2:5).[405]

The fact that the church is "a royal priesthood" (1 Peter 2:9) is one of the most significant figures related to the church. Christ is said to be typified by the Old Testament high priest, Aaron, as well as by Melchizedek to whom Abraham paid tithes. As pointed out in Hebrews 5:1-8, Christ fulfilled the typology of both Aaron and Melchizedek. In His Aaronic ministry Christ offered a sacrifice to God, the sacrifice of Himself. In this undertaking He was both Sacrificer and Sacrifice. In this He went beyond the Aaronic pattern because an Aaronic priest could not be the sacrifice himself.

Just as the Old Testament priest was sanctified and set apart by sacrifice and then having been inducted in the priest's office offered sacrifice for himself, so a believer in the present age is sanctified through the sacrifice of Christ. But as a believer he is also exhorted to sacrifice himself as stated in Romans 12:1, "Therefore, I urge you, brothers, in view of God's mercy, to offer your bodies as living sacrifices, holy and pleasing to God- which is your spiritual worship." Believers in the present age are "holy and pleasing to God" and are set apart for their priestly work just as Aaron and his sons were. When a person has been saved, he is indwelt by the Holy Spirit, is given eternal life, and is placed in the body of Christ by the baptism of the Holy Spirit. Therefore it is fitting and proper for a believer to present himself as a sacrifice to God. Apart from salvation he would not be qualified. A believer-priest may dedicate himself; but he does not consecrate himself for that is a work of God.

Just as Old Testament saints were called to worship God, so priests in the present age also should worship the Lord. As the furnishings in the tabernacle and the temple spoke of Christ, so the believers' worship in the present age is by and through Christ alone. In keeping with this a believer worships by offering himself to God (Rom. 12:1). As stated in Hebrews 13:15, a believer's service involves the worship of praise: "Through Jesus, therefore, let us continually offer to God a sacrifice of praise- the fruit of the lips that confess His name." In time as well as in eternity one of the prime functions of a believer is to offer praise to God.

As a prophet was God's representative to the people, so a priest was the people's representative to God. In the Old Testament, priest were not allowed in the most holy place of the tabernacle or temple except once a year when they were represented by the high priest who had previously offered sacrificial blood (Heb. 9:7). In the present priesthood of believers, access into God's presence is immediate through Christ their High Priest, who is now in heaven interceding for them (Rom. 8:34; Heb. 4:14-16; 7:25; 9:24; 10:19-22). Because the veil in the temple was torn at the time of Christ's death, the way into God's presence is now open to every believer-priest on the ground of the shed blood of Christ (10:19-22). The intercessory work of a priest is one of His main responsibilities (Rom. 8:26-27; Col. 4:12; 1 Tim. 2:1; Heb. 1:19-22).[406]

In contrast to Israel which was a politically organized nation (Eph. 2:12), and in contrast to the visible church or the professing church which is a human organization, the true church is an organism, a living body of believers related to Christ as the Head. The figure of the head and the body with its many members is employed in Scripture more than any other to describe the relationship between believers and Christ; (1) the church is a self-developing body, (2) the members of this body are appointed to specific service, and (3) the body is one though composed of many individuals.

The members of the body of Christ are appointed to specific service. Just as various parts of the human body are designed to function in special ways, so members of the body of Christ have differing gifts and yet function as a part of the whole. The general truth that Christians should serve the Lord effectively is brought out in many passages of Scripture. The fact that Christians are members of the body of Christ and, like members of a human body, have special functions to perform is brought out in 1 Corinthians 12, which discusses the spiritual gifts to the church. The gifts regardless of their kind should be administered in love (1 Cor. 13) and in keeping with biblical instructions (1 Cor. 14). In Romans 12:3-8 the varied contributions of members of the body of Christ are mentioned. In 1 Peter 4:7-11 various aspects of ministry are revealed which take on even more significance in view of the fact that the Lord's coming may be near. The desired end is that God will be praised through Jesus Christ in everything that Christians do.

In Ephesians 4, the fact of the unity of the body of Christ is enforced and with it is the exhortation for this unity to be observed in believers' relationship with each other. Paul stated that this unity is true because of the "one body and one spirit....one hope... one Lord, one faith, one baptism, one God and Father of all, who is over all and through all and in all" (Eph. 4:4-6). This is the spiritual unity of the church about which Christ prayed in John 17:21.[407]

7 FIGURES USED OF THE CHURCH IN HER RELATION TO CHRIST (PART VI)

An essential division of ecclesiology usually ignored in standard works is the revelation of the true church as the new creation with the resurrected Christ as its federal Head. This body of revelation is of supreme importance in understanding what God is undertaking in the present age.

At least four major themes are found in this doctrine: (1) the resurrected Christ, (2) the new creation, (3) the two creations requiring two commemorative days, and (4) the final transformation.

The new creation as a designation of the true church includes more than is comprehended in the idea that the church is Christ's body. In the new creation Christ is the all-important part whereas in the figure of the body the church is separate from and yet joined to the Head. The new creation is a unit that incorporates the resurrected Christ and that could not be what it is apart from Him.

Most theological treatments of the resurrection of Christ view the subject from the standpoint of apologetics as a proof of the deity of Christ. The relationship of Christ's resurrection to the new creation is not mentioned. The Resurrection is far more than a reversal of His death. In His resurrection Christ became the pattern of glorified saints in heaven, and Christ's relationship to His church is different from anything that existed previously. If the church were in the Old Testament and the New Testament church is merely a continuation of it, differences are ignored. The resurrection of Christ, however, made possible an entirely new creation in contrast to the old creation of Adam.

The resurrection is one of seven divine undertakings. These are: (1)

the creation of angels; (2) the creation of material things, including man; (3) the Incarnation (4) the death of Christ; (5) the resurrection of the Son of God; (6) the return of Christ to reign forever; and (7) the creation of the new heaven and the new earth. In this series of divine undertakings the resurrection of Christ is the most important. A complete treatment of the resurrection of Christ includes not only His resurrection but also the resurrection of those who are in Him. The resurrection of Christ is the center of many important doctrines.

Scripture is beyond reason inasmuch as it is a supernatural work of God who used human authors to write the Bible. If the concept of the supernatural is to be accepted there is no reasonable basis for denying the resurrection of Christ. The Resurrection is an essential part of biblical revelation viewed as prophecy in the Old Testament and presented as history in the New Testament.

In keeping with the doctrine of the Resurrection, Christ is the source of life. He had predicted, "I tell you the truth, a time is coming and has now come when the dead will hear the voice of the Son of God and those who hear will live. For as the Father has life in Himself, so He has granted the Son to have life in Himself" (John 5:25-26). He also said, "The thief comes only to steal and kill and destroy: I have come that they may have life, and have it to the full" (10:10). Christ also said of His life, "No one takes it from Me, but I lay it down of My own accord. I have authority to lay it down and the authority to take it up again. This command I received from My Father" (v. 18). So many passages refer to the resurrection of Christ that if this is removed from the Scriptures it makes impossible other doctrines revealed in connection with Christian theology. Christ was raised by the Father (Acts 2:24). In contrast to Adam who received life from God, Christ as the last Adam is the life-giving Spirit (1 Cor. 15:45). Adam brought death to the race, but the last Adam brought life (v.22). Because of the deity of Christ, it was impossible for Him to remain dead physically (Acts 2:24).[408]

In the Gospel records it is clear that the disciples could not bring themselves to believe that Christ would either die or be raised from the dead. They apparently completely forgot His predictions of resurrection once they had seen Christ die on the cross. Only overwhelming evidence would have jarred them from their unbelief to complete faith in Christ.

According to 1 Corinthians 15:45 Christ became "a life-giving Spirit," in contrast to Adam who "became a living being." In John 20:22 Christ breathed on the disciples and said, "Receive the Holy Spirit." Theologically, Christians are raised with Christ as far as their position is concerned (Vol. 2:12). Christians are exhorted to live in keeping with the fact of Christ's resurrection (3:1-4). Believers in Christ who die are promised resurrection (1 Thes. 4:13-18).[409]

In His message recorded in Matthew, Christ said "All authority in heaven and on earth has been given to Me" (Matt. 28:18). In Romans 6:3-4 the fact that the believers have been spiritually raised from the dead is presented as a demonstration of the power of Christ. In keeping with this Paul said in Philippians 4:13, "I can do everything through Him who gives me strength." Obviously the strength of a believer is derived from the power of Christ. In that power we can serve Christ acceptably (John 15:5).[410]

The resurrection of Christ introduced a new revelation of the grace of God. After the resurrection of Christ the Jews returned not to the Mosaic Law, but turned instead to the new undertaking of God beginning on the day of Pentecost which included the salvation of both Jews and Gentiles to form the body of Christ. The resurrection of Christ is a supreme illustration of the believers' own resurrection bodies. Christians have the assurance that at the Rapture of the church they will receive new bodies like the body of Christ (1 Cor. 15:51-53). This is confirmed by the revelation recorded in 1 Thessalonians 4:13-18. According to Philippians 3:20-21, believers' bodies will be transformed and made like the glorious body of Christ. To those who still may be questioning the validity of the Christian faith, the doctrine of the Resurrection is a tremendous confirmation.

The dramatic difference between a person's position in Adam and a believer's position in Christ is stated in Colossians 1:13, "For He has rescued us from the dominion of darkness and brought us into the kingdom of the Son He loves." Though formerly spiritually dead and depraved, a Christian, when he believes in Christ is born of God, becomes a member of the household and family of God, and occupies a place of an adult son. He is transferred from the fallen headship of the first Adam into the exalted and infinite headship of the last Adam. He is qualified through the imputed merit of Christ to be a partaker of the inheritance of the saints in light. Being in Christ he possesses every spiritual blessing and is made complete even to the satisfaction of God. He is justified forever. His citizenship is changed from earth to heaven. He will yet be delivered from the Adamic nature. He will receive a glorious body like Christ's resurrection body. Though personal identity continues, a Christian is totally changed when his glorification and sanctification are complete (Eph. 5:27; 1 John 3:2; Jude 24).[411] The new creation incorporates two factors, the resurrected Christ and the entire company of believers who are identified as the true church.

In the new creation the phrase "in Christ" is most important. This is a truth that is not mentioned in the Old Testament but appears in various ways in the New Testament about 130 times. The emphasis on this truth is often missing in current theological discussion. These many Scriptures combine to state the wonderful truth of a believer's present position and expectation of future glorification (Eph. 1:3-12, 15-23). In the new creation, Christians are united in the same sense that the Persons of the Trinity are united, and in a similar way all believers are united to each other as anticipated in the prayer of Christ (John 17:20-23). This truth involves the fact that the believer is in Christ and Christ is in the believer (14:20). So a believer who is in

Christ has a position, possessions, safe-keeping, and association with Christ. It is also true that Christ in the believer gives life, character, and dynamic for life. All this is anticipated in the simple phrase in verse 20, "You are in Me, and I am in you."

The New Testament clearly teaches that though the Sabbath Day was observed by Israel in keeping with the fourth commandment, Christians who accept the doctrine of the resurrection of Christ have a commemorative day on the first day of the week instead of the seventh. The deep-seated prejudices regarding the seventh-day Sabbath and the first-day celebration of the resurrection of Christ stem from a lack of comprehension of the tremendous gulf between the Mosaic Law and the present age of grace. The Mosaic Law and the Sabbath were part of the Old Testament order just as in the New Testament the observance of the first day of the week is significant of the present age as an age of grace. The failure to distinguish between God's command to the Jews and God's commands to Christians is at the root of the problem. The contrast between observing the seventh day of the week and the first day of the week is important for at least four reasons: (1) It determines an individual's conception of his blessing in grace. (2) It determines the character of the believer's conduct and the measure of comprehension of his scriptural obligation to God. (3) It is the central issue in the misleading teaching that confuses Israel and the church. (4) The enforcement of the day of rest on the first day of the week on a Christ-rejecting world has no scriptural support.

Since the Israelites failed to enter into rest under Joshua (Heb. 4:8), believers face the danger of not entering into the rest they have in Christ, which is not related to any one day of the week (vv. 9-10). Believers are urged to enter into the genuine rest they have in Christ, a rest that is not connected with the observance of a day and is related to grace rather than keeping the Law.

It is most significant that in the Epistles observance of the Sabbath is specifically prohibited. The Galatians were rebuked for turning back to the observance of laws under which the Jews lived. Paul asked, "Do you wish to be enslaved by them all over again?" (Gal. 4:9). He pointed out that they were wrongly observing "special days and months and seasons and years (v. 10). The reason for his objection was that they were departing from grace in observing the Law.[412]

The Scriptures speak of the cessation of observing the Sabbath in the age of Israel's chastisement and its reestablishment after the present Church Age is finished. According to Hosea 2:11 Israel would come to a period when all her solemn feasts and Sabbaths would cease. This is fulfilled of course by the beginning of the present age on the Day of Pentecost. As also indicated, Israel's Sabbath will be reinstated in the Great Tribulation and the millennial kingdom (Matt. 24:29; Isa 66:23). Also it is predicted that in the Millennium the Eastern Gate of Jerusalem will be shut through six working days but opened on the Sabbath and the New Moon (Ezek. 46:1).[413] The New Testament does not instruct believers in Christ to observe the Sabbath Day; instead it warns them against observing it.

In the New Testament there is no record of a Christian observing a Sabbath Day even in error. On the other hand, as has been demonstrated, the first day of the week was observed in a manner consistent with its significance.

The testimony of the early fathers is also conclusive that the first day of the week, rather than the Sabbath was observed.

Peter, Bishop of Alexandria (ca. A.D. 300), stated, "But the Lord's Day we celebrate as a day of joy, because on it He rose again, on which day we have received it for a custom not even to bow the knee: (Peter of Alexandria, Canon 15, Ante-Nicene Fathers, ed. Alexander Roberts and James Donaldson, 6:278).[414]

Justin Martyr wrote, "And on the day called Sunday, all who live in cities or in the country gather together to one place, and the memoirs of the Apostles or the writings of the prophets are read as long as time permits; then, when the reader has ceased, the president (or the official presiding) verbally instructs, and exhorts to the imitation of these good things. Then we all rise together and pray, and, as we before said when our prayers ended, bread and wine and water are brought, and the president in like manner offers prayers and thanksgivings, according to his ability, and the people assent, saying "Amen.'... but Sunday is the day on which we all hold our common assembly, because it is the first day on which God, having wrought a change in the darkness in matter, made the world; and Jesus Christ our Savior on the same day rose from the dead" (Justin Martyr, "First Apology" 67, in *Anti-Nicene Fathers*, 1:185-86).[415]

Ignatius, Bishop of Antioch (A.D. 110) wrote, "Let us therefore no longer keep the Sabbath after the Jewish manner, and rejoice in days of idleness; for 'he who does not work, let him not eat.' For say the (holy) oracles, 'From the sweat of thy face shalt thou eat thy bread.' But let everyone of you keep the Sabbath after a spiritual manner, rejoicing in meditation on the Law, not in relaxation of the body admiring the workmanship of God" (Ignatius, 'To the Magnesians" 9, *Anti-Nicene Fathers*, 1:62-3).[416]

Barnabas (A.D. 70) wrote, "Your present Sabbaths are not acceptable to me, but that is which I have made [namely this,], when, giving rest to all things, I shall make a new beginning of the eighth day, that is, a beginning of another world. Wherefore, also, we keep the eighth day with joyfulness, the day also in which Jesus rose again from the dead".[417]

In *The Teachings of the Twelve Apostles* the statement is made, "But every Lord's Day do ye gather yourselves together and break bread and give thanks having confessed your transgressions, that your sacrifice may be pure" (Didache 14; *Ante-Nicene Fathers*, 7:381.)

From these quotations it is clear that the first day of the week was observed by the early church from the first century; and the Sabbath was considered a requirement of the Jewish Law.

In observing the history of the church it is clear that devout believers, martyrs, missionaries, and countless others for 2,000 years have recognized the first day of the week as a special day. The attempts to place Christians back under Jewish Law are not supported by the New Testament nor the practice of the early church.

SEVEN FIGURES USED OF THE CHURCH IN HER RELATION TO CHRIST (PART VII)

A common source of doctrinal error is the confusion of the church with Israel. Quite common in theological interpretation is the thought that the church is the successor of Israel, a concept that is not taught in Scripture.

It is true that Israel is sometimes related to God as the wife of Yahweh who has proved to be unfaithful (Hosea 2:2). In the future millennial reign of Christ, Israel, though an unfaithful wife, will be restored as pictured in verses 13-16. By contrast, the church is described as a virgin bride already espoused to one husband who will be claimed by Christ at the time of the Rapture (2 Cor. 11:1-2). In the revelation of this truth the distinction between Israel and the church, however, is maintained. Other passages bearing on this theme are found in both the Old Testament and New Testament (Isa. 54:5; Jer. 3:1, 14, 20; Ezek. 16:1-59; Rom. 7:4; Eph. 5:25-33; Rev. 19:7-8; 21:1-22; Heb. 12:22-24.[418]

The relationship of the Bridegroom and the bride is also indicated in other Scriptures. In the Parable of the 10 Virgins (Matt. 25:1-13), Israel is related to the 10 virgins but not to the bride. While the figure of marriage is related to both Israel and the church, in general Israel is the unfaithful wife of *Yahweh* who will be restored in the Millennium while the church is pictured as the virgin bride awaiting the coming of the bridegroom.

In Ephesians 3:17-21 the Apostle Paul prayed that the Ephesian Christians may know the infinite love of God, "And I pray that you, being rooted and established in love, may have power, together with all the saints, to grasp how wide and long and high and deep is the love of Christ, and to know this love that surpasses knowledge – that you may be filled to the measure of all the fullness of God. Now to Him who is able to do immeasurably more that all we ask or imagine, according to His power that is at work within us, to Him be glory in the church and in Christ Jesus throughout all generations, forever and ever! Amen."

In connection with the love of Christ for His church in Ephesians 5:25, husbands are exhorted to love their wives as Christ loved the church. Many other contexts in Scripture reveal the love of Christ for His church (John 13:1; Romans 8:38-39; 2 Cor.5:14), a love that is true, faithful, and deep like that of a groom for his bride.[419]

The church as the bride of Christ is given an exalted position by virtue of His infinite majesty. In keeping with this, Christ announced that He was preparing a place for His bride (John 14:3). The church is also promised to be with Christ in His Glory (17:24). As the wife of Christ, the church will share in the glory of Christ which exalts Him above any creature or power (Eph. 1:20-21).

According to Romans 8:17 the church will share the glory of Christ. In keeping with this Christ referred to the glory He had with the Father in eternity past (John 17:5), the glory of His transformation (Matt. 17:1-8; Mark 9:2-13; Luke 9:28-3), and the glory He would have in His resurrection and in heaven (Rev. 1:13-18) and which would be revealed to the disciples when they too are with Christ in glory (John 17:24; Rom. 8:17; Col. 3:4). The believer in Christ is promised that his body will be made like the body of Christ in glory (1Cor. 15:43; Phil. 3:21). As the bride of Christ, the church will be glorified by Christ Himself.[420]

The meaning of the figure of the bride: In symbolism of Christ as the Bridegroom and the church as His bride, there is abundant revelation of the unsurpassing love of Christ, the unity between Christ and the church, and the authority and position to be accorded to the church in ages to come.

The figure of the bride and the Bridegroom supports the concept that there are three divisions in the human family during the present age: Gentiles, Jews, and Christians (1 Cor. 10:32). Redeemed Israelites living at the time of Christ's return to earth will share in His reign on earth. Believing Jews and Gentiles in the church will enjoy the privilege of being the heavenly bride of Christ.

THE ORGANIZED CHURCH

For the last 1,900 plus years Christians associated with other Christians in church relationships, have endured persecution and conflicts, and have received the benefits of being a redeemed people.

By the forth century of the Christian era many Christians dreamed of a conquered world by the Messiah and of a political government operating under the authority of the church. To some extent this view has been perpetuated in Romanism.

In Protestantism after the Reformation the postmillennial theory was advocated which proposes that the church will gradually extend its power until the church rules the world and Christians have triumphed over the forces of evil. When this has come about Christ will return.

Events in the twentieth century, and as we move into the twenty-first century have challenged this teaching; the concept that the church will ever rule the world seems farther from realization today than ever before. At this point, distinction should be made between the church as an organism, that is, true believers related to Christ through baptism of the Spirit, and the organized church as seen in local churches or groups of churches that are united by some organizational features. Of necessity the organized church is restricted to living persons at a given time, bound together by whatever article of agreement they accept. By contrast the universal church is an organism which includes all believers whether on earth or in heaven.

We can see that organized churches are recognized in the New Testament is seen in Acts 11:22, which refers to "the church at Jerusalem" (Acts 15:22); in Paul's epistle to individual churches (in Rome, Corinth, Galatia, Ephesus, Philippi, Colossae, and Thessalonica); and in Christ's seven messages to seven churches of Asia (Rev. 1-3). The universal church is recognized in the New

Testament by the several passages that speak of the church as the body of Christ (1 Cor. 12:12-13, 27; Eph. 1:22-23; 4:15-16; Col. 1:18; 2:19) and by Acts 9:31, which refers to "the church throughout Judea, Galilee and Samaria".[421]

The word "church" from the Greek *ekkesia* refers to a called-out assembly. In early Greek democracy citizens of a city-state were called to a central meeting place to carry on their civil business. In like manner Christians are called out from the world to form the body of Christ, and local congregations are formed from those who are called out in one locality. In local congregations, however, some who are associated outwardly with the church may not be genuine Christians. This fact, however, is never true of the church as the body of Christ.

The history of the church, the local church, or groups of churches was taken as the principal evidence of the work of Christ in the present age. Often attention is given to the organized church to the exclusion of the truth of the church as the body of Christ.

When Constantine officially recognized the church as a legal entity in the forth century, it soon expanded to a vast, super organization which later divided in the 11th century into the Roman Church and the Greek Church. With the rise of Protestant denominations thousands of individual churches have been formed with many of them being a part of a larger organization and others functioning as independent churches.

Five aspects of the local church should be considered: (1) the church and her doctrine, (2) the church and her services, (3) the church and her organization, (4) the church and her ordinances, and (5) the church and her order.

In the Protestant Reformation many churches withdrew from either the Greek Orthodox Church or the Roman Catholic Church and formed individual churches or groups of churches. Calvinists and Armenians debated the extent of the sovereignty of God. Division also occurred as to whether infant baptism and baptism by affusion were legitimate, or whether immersion of believers was indicated in Scripture. Differences of opinion in these areas often led to the execution of those who differed. Doctrinal differences led to multiple divisions in the Protestant church. The emphasis on the church as an institution often overshadowed the scriptural truth of the church as the body of Christ. Though the contentions within the organized church could not divide the church as an organism, yet divisions in the church and departure from scriptural doctrine undoubtedly hindered the progress of evangelizing the world and sanctifying the people of God with the truth of Scripture.

The command to administer baptism to Christians is clearly stated in the New Testament (Matt. 28:19). The ritual is rejected, however, by Quakers and some who hold that it is a Jewish ordinance not perpetuated after the Apostolic Age. The fact that Christ commanded baptism in connection with His command to take the message of the Gospel to the whole world has led the majority of Christians to recognize the ritual of baptism. Just as circumcision as a sign and seal of the Mosaic Covenant sets apart individuals as belonging to God in the old Testament, so baptism sets a Christian apart in the new relationship realized in salvation (Col.2:9-12).[422]

In the history of the controversy on the meaning of ritual baptism, the concept that it pictures – the baptism of the Holy Spirit – is almost totally ignored. The use of the word "baptism" for both the baptism of the Spirit and baptism by water signifies that water baptism refers to baptism by the Spirit or the joining of the Christian to Christ. Included in the concept of baptism is the fact that the rite is a symbol of purification, an outward sign that the individual is the object of divine grace, by which he has received regeneration and forgiveness of sin and has been set apart to a new life in Christ.

A major problem in discussions on baptism is the question of its mode. About one third of all Protestant churches hold that baptism is by immersion only and usually of adult believers only. A small number of churches practice "tri-baptism," in which the individual is immersed three times, in the name of each Person of the Trinity. About two thirds of the churches hold that the rite of baptism includes the application of water by other means such as sprinkling or pouring. Most who hold this view also recognize immersion as valid baptism. For many centuries the controversy has continued.

The controversy over the mode of baptism depends largely on the definition of the word *biptizo*, which means "to dip," that is, to place into and remove, is never used of the ritual of baptism. So they hold that the rite of baptism indicates the placing in or initiation of a Christian in his new relationship to God and to his fellow believers. He is placed in this new relationship and not taken out of it again. Others who argue for immersion point out that when Jesus was baptized, He "went up out of the water" (Matt. 3:1) and that when the Ethiopian eunuch was baptized he "came up out of the water" (Acts 8:39).[423]

Because of the numerous arguments used by both affusionists and immersionists, it is difficult for anyone to attempt to solve this problem, and ultimately the choice has to be made as to which evidence is received and which is rejected. Controversy in the Christian church over the mode of baptism has been largely fruitless. It is more important to recognize the significance of the rite of baptism as related to the baptism of the Spirit and believers' initiation into their new life in Christ.

The early church was a fellowship rather than an organization, and converts were numbered in the thousands before any clear church organization took place. The suggestion that the local church was organized after the model of the synagogue is not supported in Scripture. The inference that the church today must follow rigidly the customs of the early church is also subject to question. In reading the Acts and the Epistles, however, certain major factors emerge.

Undoubtedly the apostles provided leadership for the large church at Jerusalem, but as churches were established through the missionary work and evangelization of Paul and others, control was often in the hands of those who evangelized the church in the early stage. Only as the church matured were structures established. In Acts seven men were set aside to assist the apostles in caring for the widows and similar needs in the early church (vv. 1-5). These men were set aside with prayer and laying on of hands by the apostles) v. 6). It is probable that these servants were later called deacons.

In Scripture there are frequent references to the apostles and elders as the church leaders responsible for maintaining order and discipline. Basic requirements for an elder or bishop are stated in 1 Timothy 3:1-8, and qualifications for deacons are given in verses 8:13. Elders had to be above reproach morally and models of godly leadership in their own homes. Their Christian experience had to be mature, and they had to have a good reputation in the community. Deacons were to have similar requirements of maturity, morality, and ability.[424]

The New Testament makes no distinctions between clergy and laity though it does recognize that individual believers differ in their spiritual gifts and that some persons were set apart for leadership over others.

In contrast to the church, the body of Christ is universal and is addressed as a single unit. Local churches consisted of professing believers in locality who met for worship and service. Local churches are frequently mentioned in the New Testament (Acts 9:31; 15:41; 16:5; Rom. 16:4; 1 Cor. 11:1; 14:34, 19; 2 Cor. 8:1, 18-19, 23-24; 12:13; Gal. 1:2, 22; 1 Thes. 2:14; Rev. 1:4, 11, 20; 2:7, 11, 17, 23; 3:, 13, 22; 22:1). Though these churches recognized the leadership of apostles, there is no indication that the churches were organized into denomination or some form of regional government. On the other hand the Scriptures do not forbid churches relating to each other in their common task.

In contrast to the church in the sense of the body of Christ which is universal whether in earth or heaven, the visible church which consists of professed believers in the world is often recognized without reference to locality (Acts 12:1; Rom. 1:16; 1 Cor. 4:17; 7:17; 11:16; 14:33-34; 15:9; 2 Cor. 11:28; 12:13; Gal. 1:13; Phil. 3:6; 2 Thes. 1:4). The visible church is also a subject of prophecy (2 Thes. 2:3; 1 Tim. 4:1-3; 2 Tim. 3:1-8; 4:3-4; 2 Peter 2:1-3:18; Rev. 2:1-3:22).

THE FUTURE KINGDOM ECONOMY

According to premillennial interpreters, the second coming of Christ will be followed by a reign of Christ on earth for 1,000 years. The Second Advent will introduce an economy of dispensation distinct from the Mosaic economy and from the economy of grace in the present age. The premillennial view is based on the Davidic Covenant in which God promised David's descendants that his kingdom would endure forever. "When your days are over and you rest with your fathers, I will raise up your offspring to succeed you, who will come from your own body, and I will establish his kingdom. He is the one who will build a house for My Name, and I will establish the throne of his kingdom forever. I will be his Father, and he will be My son. When he does wrong, I will punish him with the rod of men, with floggings inflicted by men. But My love will never be taken from him, as I took it away from Saul, whom I removed from before you. Your house and your kingdom will endure forever before Me; your throne will be established forever" (2 Sam. 7:12-16).[425]

This covenant with David is interpreted by premillenarians, as a literal promise of a political government over which one of David's descendants would reign forever, that is, as long as the earth is in existence. Though a descendant of David has not sat on a throne in Israel continuously without interruption, the Davidic Covenant does affirm that a descendant would reign from time to time until the end of the earth, that is, till the end of the Millennium. Twenty descendants of David beginning with Solomon (1 Kings 1:28-30, 43) and continuing through Zedekiah (2 Chron. 36:11-14) ruled in Jerusalem until the Babylonian Exile (vv. 15-21). The next Descendant will be the Messiah, Jesus Christ, who will reign from Jerusalem for 1,000 years in the millennial kingdom. Jesus Christ is qualified to sit on the throne of David forever (Luke 1:32; Rev. 1:5-

7), and this is what repeated promises in the Old Testament affirm.[426]

The Old Testament anticipated a New Covenant that would replace the Mosaic Covenant (Jer. 31:31-34). The gracious promises of God which stem from the fact that Christ died on the cross for the sins of the whole world are applied to the church in the present age, but the same gracious principles will be applied to Israel in the Millennium. At that time according to verses 31-32 it will replace the Mosaic Covenat, and the Law of God will be written on their hearts instead of tables of stone. The proclamation of the truth about the Lord will no longer be necessary because "they will know Me, from the least of them to the greatest' declares the LORD"(v. 34). This promise is said to be as certain as the decree of the moon and the stars, and as long as they remain, Israel will continue as a nation (vv. 35-36).

As presented particularly in the Synoptics, Christ is introduced as the King who will sit on David's throne. The concept is introduced early in Matthew where the lineage of Christ through Joseph is traced back to David because David was the legal progenitor of Christ. And in Luke 3:23-38 the genealogy of Mary is traced back to David to show that Christ had a physical link with David and the tribe of Judah. In connection with the birth of Christ, Mary was informed by the angel that her Son was to be named Jesus and that "He will be great and will be called the Son of the Most High. The Lord God will give Him the throne of His father David, and He will reign over the house of Jacob forever; His kingdom will never end"(1:32-33). It should be obvious that Mary understood this as a literal fulfillment of the promise given to David that she would have a Son who would reign over the house of Jacob forever.

In both the Old and New Testaments the concepts of the kingdom rule of God is presented in various ways. As it relates to the eschatological program of God, it is primarily a concept in which Christ would reign politically with Jerusalem as His capital in the period after His second coming.

In referring to the doctrine of the kingdom, Matthew often used the term "kingdom of heaven" in contrast to the term "kingdom of God, " as used in the rest of the New Testament and a few times by Matthew himself. Most scholars hold that these two concepts are one and the same as a rule of God over human beings on earth. However in Matthew the "kingdom of heaven" refers to the kingdom as a sphere of profession in which there are both wheat and weeds that look like wheat (Matt. 13:4-30, 36-43). The kingdom of heaven is also compared to a net full of good and bad fish which will be separated at the end of the age (vv.47-50). By contrast the kingdom of God is always represented as including only those who have been redeemed by salvation and holy angels. This contrasts with the kingdom of heaven which never includes angels but does include those who are professing Christians but are not saved. Though most scholars ignore this distinction, it does give added light on the character of the kingdom on earth as including not only the saved but also some who outwardly appear to be saved but are not.

If the premillennial view is correct, the future kingdom will have a different rule of life than the present age, and the present age is distinct from either the Mosaic era or the future kingdom. If the amillennial and postmillennial views are correct, this distinction will be blurred, and a legalistic quality to the present age will be introduced, an emphasis that contradicts the gracious rule of life presented in the New Testament.

THE PRESENT GRACE ECONOMY

In the present age salvation of those who believe in Christ places the saved one in the position of a Son of God, a citizen of heaven, and a member of the family and household of God. Such a position demands a corresponding manner of life. Grace in the present age not only provides a perfect salvation and eternal keeping for one who believes in Christ, but grace provides more divine enablement than in previous economies for the daily life of the one who is saved. This is accomplished through the indwelling Holy Spirit, the completed Word of God, and Christ's intercession in heaven.

Though there is a measure of grace in every dispensation, as salvation is always by grace, the rule of life under the present Church Age or age of grace contrasts sharply with that required in the Old Testament or with what will be required in the future kingdom. The Bible as a Book from God for all people of all ages reveals the will of God concerning the manner of life in various dispensations in keeping with their particular covenants with God. The daily life of those who are saved by grace in this dispensation is in effect from the time of the death of Christ to the second coming of Christ. The gracious rule of life in the teachings of grace is more complete than other dispensations.

In contrast to the requirement of the Mosaic Law to love one's neighbor as himself, Christ stated in John 13:34-35, "A new command I give you: Love one another. As I have loved you, so you must love one another. All men will know that you are My disciples if you love one another." In Matthew 5:43-46 the requirements that were greater than the Law of Moses are stated, "You have heard that it was said, 'Love your neighbor and hate your enemy.' But I tell you, Love your enemies and pray for those who persecute you, that you may be sons of your Father in heaven. He causes His sun to rise on the evil and the good, and sends rain on the righteous and the unrighteous. If you love those who love you, what reward will you get? Are not even the tax collectors doing that?"

Love under grace is a "fruit of the Spirit" (Gal. 5:22), a work of the Spirit which enables Christians to love others as God loves them. Scripture declares, "God has poured out His love into our hearts by the Holy Spirit, whom He has given us" (Rom. 5:5). Love under grace is especially revealed as the dynamic for willing souls. Paul's statements in 9:1-3 are typical of this point. "I speak the truth in Christ- I am not lying, my conscience confirms it in the Holy Spirit -I have great sorrow and unceasing anguish in my heart. For I could wish that I myself were cursed and cut off from Christ for the sake of my brothers, those of my own race." Though in the Mosaic Law as well as in the future kingdom, evangelicalism is not required, Israel was to be the Light to Gentiles (Isa. 42:6).[427]

The new enabling power of the Spirit characterizes this age in contrast to "the old way of the written code" (Rom. 7:6). Under the Law circumcision was of the flesh. Under grace circumcision is of the heart (2:29). The challenge in the age of grace is for believers to adjust their lives to the holy presence of the Spirit and to live in an unbroken attitude of dependence on Him. In a believer's struggle between the sin nature and the new nature he can be victorious only as the Spirit of God gives grace. Many Scripture passages speak of the special character of the present grace economy (John 7:37-39; Acts 1:8; Romans 6:14; 8:4; 1 Cor. 12:4-7; 2 Cor. 10:3-5; Gal. 5:16; Eph. 6:10-11; Phil. 2:13; Col. 2:6).[428]

Divine grace imparted by the indwelling Holy Spirit issues in a manifestation of the graciousness of God in the heart of the believer. It is not an imitation of God's graciousness but is produced by the extensive doctrine in the New Testament (Rom. 12:3-6; 15:15; 1 Cor. 1:4; 3:10; 15:10; 2 Cor. 1:12;4:15; :1-3; 8:1, 6-7, 9; 9:8, 14; 12:9; Gal. 2:9; Eph. 3:2-8; 4:7; Col. 3:16; 4:6; 2 Thes. 1:12; 2 Tim. 2:1; Heb. 4:1;

12:15; James 4:6; 2 Peter 3:18).

The Christian's daily life is one of adjusting to certain important relationships. The distinctive features of the grace order are based on the threefold truth that the believer is appointed to uphold (1) relationships to the Person of the Godhead; (2) a relationship to the world system; and (3) relationship to other Christians who are fellow members in the body of Christ. These major relationships are supported by many exhortations in the New Testament.

If a Christian brother should err, fellow Christians have an obligation from God to minister to that erring brother or sister. A number of passages indicate that Christians have a special responsibility to treat an erring brother or sister properly. They should approach him with a spirit of meekness (Gal. 6:1), with appropriate warning for the unruly, and special support of those who are weak (1 Thes. 5:14). Christians should not participate with unruly brethren who create dissension (2 Thes. 3:, 11-15), with disorderly believers who are careless in their Christian conduct. A sincere believer, however, may disagree with another in matters of biblical interpretation without necessarily causing a problem. Believers should not be separated over minor questions of doctrine in major areas (2 John 9-11).

The goal in dealing with an erring brother or sister is restoration. However, those who are needlessly contentious should be avoided (Rom. 16:17-18). Fellow Christians should consider not only their own consciences but also the consciences of others. In relation to a weak brother they should not put a stumbling block in his way by their own exercise of freedom. Exhortations to Christians in this situation are found in Romans 14:1-4, 15-23.[429]

INTRODUCTION TO ESCHATOLOGY

The last major division of systematic theology is called eschatology from the Greek *eschoto* meaning "last" or "farthest." Eschatology is the science of last things.

Of all the fields of theology eschatology has been the most neglected. Even capable theologians such as Charles Hodge confess that prophecy is not within their area of study and that prophetic interpretation involves scholarship that specializes in the doctrine. In discussing the Second Advent Hodge stated:

"This is a very comprehensive and very difficult subject. It is intimately allied with all the other great doctrines which fall under the head of eschatology. It has excited so much interest in all ages of the church, that books written upon it would of themselves make a library. The subject cannot be adequately discussed without taking a survey of all the prophetic teachings of the Scriptures both of the Old Testament and of the New. This task cannot be satisfactorily challenged by any one who has not made the study of prophecies a specialty. The author knowing that he has no such qualifications for the work, proposes to confine himself in great measures to a historical survey of the different schemes of interpreting scriptural prophecies relating to this subject (systematic Theology. New York: Charles Scribner's Sons, 1892, III, p. 790).[430]

Not only do theologians tend to avoid eschatology, but also courses of instruction in theological seminaries often include little instruction on eschatology. This is in spite of the fact that Christianity does not make logical sense if it does not have a future for all eternity.

Among conservative theologians a literal second coming of Christ is usually affirmed, followed by the judgment of all men and heaven and hell. Disagreements arise principally from the doctrine of the Millennium in the Old and the New Testaments.

The neglect of prophecy has no reasonable basis. Approximately one forth of the Bible was prophetic when it was written and about one half of these prophecies have already been literally fulfilled. A fair introduction would be that unfulfilled prophecies will be fulfilled in the same literal way as prophecy was fulfilled in the past.

The premillennial interpretation considers prophecy as revealing a literal 1,000- year reign of Christ on earth following His second coming. Accordingly it is properly labeled premillennial. In the early history of the church it was called chiliasm from the Greek word *chilias* meaning "one thousand."

One of the two other major views of the Millennium is amillennialism, which denies a literal political kingdom of Christ on earth. Amillenarians interpret Scriptures relating to the future kingdom as (1) applying to the present age, (2) applying to the believer's intermediate state in heaven, (3) as finding fulfillment in present earth or heaven, or (4) as finding fulfillment in the new heaven and new earth in eternity. Each of the various approaches to amillennialism are negative or contradictory to premillennialism. Even though each view differs greatly from the others, they unite in denying a literal millennial reign of Christ on earth after His second coming.

The postmillennial view is similar to some forms of amillennialism in that it holds that the millennial kingdom will occur before the Second Coming, and the Second Coming therefore will be after the Millennium. Postmillennialism becomes a leading interpretation in the 18th and 19th centuries and embraces the idea that the Gospel would be so effective that the entire world would be Christianized, resulting in a thousand years of a golden age in which Christ would be honored and Christianity would be the dominant theory of society. Because no such age has actually begun, postmillenarians usually hold that the Millennium is still future but about to begin at any time. In the 19th century postmillennial views were combined with organic evolution as a major means of bringing about the golden age. All conservative theologians oppose evolution. Great prophecy conferences were held in the last quarter of the 19th century and the opening of the 20th century as a means of combating postmillennial evolution. These conferences which earlier included all three conservative millennial views gradually became limited to those who upheld the premillennial interpretation.

The Bible college movement was largely premillennial because this offered a sensible and consistent interpretation of the entire Bible. Premillennialism was not adopted by theological seminaries or denominations until the 20th century. Neglect of prophecy has led to neglect of the Bible as a whole and has often opened the way for liberal theological concepts which are destructive of historic Christian theology.

The importance of the study of prophecy is stated by George N.H. Peters:

"The history of the human race is, as able theologians have remarked, the history of God's dealings with man. It is a fulfilling of revelation; yea, more: it is an unfolding of the ways of God, a comprehensive confirmation of, and an appointed aid in interpreting the plan of redemption. Hence, God Himself appeals to it, not merely as the evidence of the truth declared, but as the mode by which we alone can obtain a full and complete view of the divine purpose relating to salvation. To do this we must, however, regard past, present, and future history. The latter must be received as predicted, for we may rest assured, from the past and present fulfillment of the Word of God, thus changed into historical reality, that the predictions and promises relating to the future will also in their turn become veritable history. It is this faith, which grasps the future as already present, that can form a decided and unmistakable unity." (The Theocratic Kingdom. Grand Rapids: Kregal Publications, 1952, I, p. 13).[431]

Knowledge of biblical prophecy qualifies all Christian life and service. In prophecy one comes to know the faithfulness of God by His Word. When men of faith like Daniel believe implicitly in the accuracy and literalness of the Word of God (Dan. 9), it should lead to the same conclusion on the part of those who study the Bible today. Prophecy is intended to be illumination, comforting (1 The. 4:18, and sanctifying (John 17:17) in presenting the wonderful expectation of Christ's promised return.[432]

Eschatology is studied in the following divisions: (1) general features. (2) the seven major highways of prophecy, (3) major themes of Old Testament prophecy, (4) major themes of New Testament prophecy, (5) predicted events in their order, (6) the judgments, and (7) the eternal state.

A BRIEF HISTORY OF CHILIASM

Chiliasm is the historical word referring to the concept of a Kingdom Age of 1,000 years which will follow the second coming of Christ. Compared with other views, the distinctive feature of this doctrine is that Christ will return before the 1,000 years. During this 1,000 year period He will be personally present on the earth, exercising His rightful authority as King and securing and sustaining all the blessings on earth ascribed to that period.

The history of the premillennialism as a doctrine may be approached under seven time periods.

The future millennial kingdom is important for it is the fulfillment of many promises given to Israel – a glorious period of righteousness and peace when her Messiah will come. During the kingdom Christ will sit on David's throne in Jerusalem and rule over Israel as well as over the entire world (PS. 89:19-37; Jer. 23:5-6). In the discussion to follow, additional revelation will be considered on the important doctrine of the future kingdom.

When Christ began His public ministry, it was commonly believed by the people of Israel that the Messiah would deliver them from their enemies and bring in the literal kingdom on earth in which they would be honored. No one seems to have understood the difference between the first and second coming of Christ until after His ascension into heaven.

In presenting Himself to the people of Israel Jesus clearly claimed to be the Christ and to be the One who fulfilled Old Testament prophecies. In offering Himself He presented to them the kingdom as being at hand.

The Gospel records clearly testify that Christ was rejected by the religious leaders of His day as well as by many of the common people, though some were His loyal followers. Some contentions has arisen over the idea that if Christ offered to bring in the future kingdom this would make unnecessary His death and resurrection. Such criticism fails to distinguish that what is offered in a genuine way was also rejected. This was part of God's plan from eternity past.

The Children of Israel went through a similar experience at Kadesh Barnea when on their journey from Egypt to the Promised Land they failed to trust God and rejected the leadership of Moses. The result was that they spent 40 years wandering in the wilderness before the promise was realistically fulfilled. Yet the offer of God to bring them into the land flowing with milk and honey was genuine even though in the sovereign plan of God the offer would be rejected.

In like manner Christ made a genuine offer of Himself as the King of Israel and stated the moral principles of His Kingdom in the Sermon on the Mount (Matt. 5-7). The argument that by this act He was making His death unnecessary does not take into proper consideration the difference between the divine and the human viewpoints. God can make a genuine offer of salvation to an unsaved person even though God knows that he is not elect to salvation.

Premillenarians believe that their interpretation of the Scriptures is a self-consistent, justifiable conclusion from interpreting prophecies of the future in a literal way. As the early church tended to do this, the evidence supports the fact that the early church was premillennial. Some internal evidences from the Scriptures confirm that the early church followed the premillennial interpretation of prophecy.

In the church council held in Jerusalem (Acts 15) the problem raised was whether Gentile believers had to be circumcised. The record of the meeting not only presents the problem but also the solution as recorded in verses 5-11, "Then some of the believers who belonged to the party of the Pharisees stood up and said, 'The gentiles must be circumcised and required to obey the Law of Moses.' The apostles and elders met to consider this question. After much discussion, Peter got up and addressed them: 'Brothers, you know that some time ago God made a choice among you that the Gentiles might hear from my lips the message of the Gospel and believe. God, who knows the heart, showed that He accepted them by giving the Holy Spirit to them, just as He did to us. He made no distinction between us and them, for He purified their hearts by faith. Now then, why do you try to test God by putting on the necks of the disciples a yoke that neither we nor our fathers have been able to bear? No! We believe it is through the grace of our Lord Jesus that we are saved, just as they are.'"

The solution to the problem was to recognize that Gentiles in the present age are being blessed of God. They came to the conclusion that the ultimate time for Israel's blessing would be in the future kingdom period. In the present time God does not make a distinction between saved Jews and Gentiles in the church but gives them the same spiritual blessings and the same salvation.

In the years that followed the apostolic period there were many centuries in which spiritual darkness characterized the world. The Middle Ages are often called the "Dark Ages." In the period immediately following the Apostolic Age, however, there is clear evidence of premillennial faith as the normal orthodox position of the church.

It was Justin Martyr who testified, there have always been those who rejected the second coming of Christ and the millennial kingdom to follow, but they were not considered orthodox. In the modern world these denials have appeared in three areas. (1) Liberalism tends to belittle the Scriptures bearing on the theme, considering the subject of the Millennium itself as unworthy of scholarly investigation. (2) The scholarship of those who defend the premillennial interpretation is attacked. (3) Even in relatively conservative scholarship there seems to be a tendency today to belittle the evidence for premillennialism in the early centuries.

The School of Theology at Alexandria attempted to combine Christian theology with the philosophy of Plato, a pure idealist. The viewpoint of Plato was so contrary to Scripture that the only way any resemblance could be noted would be by taking the Scripture in a nonliteral sense. The result was that most of the important doctrines of the faith were subverted and with it the premillennial teaching. Scholars of every viewpoint of eschatology agree that leaders of the School of Alexandria were Gaius (or Caius), a third-century theologian; Clement, who taught in Alexandria from 193 to 220; his pupil Origin (185-254), who was an outstanding advocate of amillennialism; and Dioysius (190-265). The teachings of Clement and Origen are well established as in opposition to premillennialism.

The establishing of a different hermeneutic for eschatology from the method used in interpreting other Scriptures is questionable especially when the nonliteral interpretation arbitrarily selects the millennial kingdom as the doctrine to be spiritualized while holding that other prophecies are literal. It is obvious that rejection of the Millennium was based not so much on lack of evidence in the Bible as resistance to the doctrine itself.

The period between Augustine and the Protestant Reformation was largely a time of spiritual darkness. Though a few bright lights appeared as devoted souls who believed the Scriptures, for the most part the rank and file of those in the church as well as out of the church had limited comprehension of scripture doctrine. Opponents of premillennialism often revealed ignorance of the doctrine itself even though there were competent scholars in other areas. It was not until the Protestant Reformation when the principle of every man being his own interpreter of the Bible as led by the Holy Spirit was established that the groundwork was laid for individual study of the Scriptures leading to the premillennial view.

The main leaders of the Protestant Reformation such as Martin Luther and John Calvin were amillennial and interpreted prophecy concerning endtime events as being fulfilled. They viewed the Roman Catholic Church as the best of Revelation 13 and the apostasy of the

Roman Church as fulfilling the prophecy of apostasy in the endtime. Even though not premillennial, Luther and Calvin anticipated the possibility that Christ might return in their lifetime.

THE BIBLICAL CONCEPT OF PROPHECY

Only God knows the future; therefore human writers of Scripture were enabled to write prophecy through God's supernatural guidance and revelation. Though the Bible does not give the details of endtime events, what is revealed helps make life meaningful.

Under these circumstances it is amazing how many neglect prophetic Scriptures almost entirely. Though requiring careful study to decide what the Scriptures teach on the subject of prophecy, even a simplistic approach to Christianity provides a basis for faith in important future major events.

In studying the biblical concept of prophecy, six general subjects are examined: (1) the prophet, (2) the prophet's message, (3) the prophet's power, (4) the selection of prophets, (5) the fulfillment of prophecy, and (6) the history of prophecy.

The Prophet: In general, prophets in Scripture were those who spoke for God. A prophet was God's voice to the people in contrast to the priest who represented the people in approaching God. In Christ both activities unite for He is both the Prophet and the Priest.

Prophecy does not necessarily always concern the future, for prophets often delivered a message for a contemporary situation. Prophecy is both forthtelling and foretelling.

In the New Testament, prophets had a different role. They had less of the role of patriot, reformer, and revivalist and more the role of communicating truth from God. In 1 Corinthians 14:3 it is stated, "Everyone who prophesies speaks to men for their strengthening, encouragement, and comfort." The gift of prophecy is included as a ministry gift (Eph. 4:11). Some who had the gift of prophecy, that is, having the gift of foretelling events or bringing a communication from God, were not always fully recognized as prophets who executed this office regularly, such as Paul, Peter, and others.

The Prophet's message: In Scripture all truth is prophecy in the sense that it came from God, but many prophecies were predictive in their character. This is true of the great biblical covenants such as the Abrahamic, Palestinian, Davidic, and New Covenants. Prophecies related to various peoples including Israel. Prophecies about Gentiles were presented by Nahum, Obadiah, and Jonah though that was not their main burden of revelation. The greatest treatment of prophecy pertaining to the Gentiles is seen in Daniel chapters 2,7, and 8, which spoke of the great empires of the future from Daniel's perspective.[433]

Great chapters on prophecy include the predictions of Moses concerning the future of Israel (Deut. 28-30). In Psalm 2, the second coming of Christ is predicted, and Daniel 2 and 7 mention the four great world empires. It is obvious that prophecy of future events as well as proclamation of present truth characterize Scripture.[434]

The Prophets Power: In the Old Testament, prophets were often seen as equal to, or, greater than kings, though humanly speaking, kings had the power to kill prophets. On the other hand prophets would often dictate to kings, and divine protection would be given them. A number of Scriptures support this concept.[435]

The Selection of Prophets: The prophets who were chosen by God carried the authority of being His choice. The prophets were not always in sympathy with their message as illustrated by Saul (1 Sam. 10:11; 19:24), Balaam (Num. 23:5-10), and Caiaphas (John 11:52). The prophetic office in the Old Testament seems to have existed for a lifetime.

The Fulfillment of Prophecy: As a divine test of a prophet's authenticity as appointed by God, prophecies had to be fulfilled (Deut. 18:21-22). In the New Testament frequent reference is made to fulfilled events as spoken by the Lord through a prophet, which emphasizes the character of true prophecy in all Scriptures.[436]

Prophecies in the Bible are so specific and numerous that skeptics can hardly account for prophecies as mere conjecture by man. It would be impossible, apart from divine revelation, for a prophet to be right consistently in his predictions. An outstanding illustration is Dan 11:1-35 in which there are approximately 135 prophecies, all of which have been literally fulfilled.

The History of Prophecy: The prophetic story of prophecy especially as it relates to the Old Testament largely revolves around the Abrahamic, Palestinian, and Davidic Covenants. These prophecies center on Israel and are in contrast to the church, which has a heavenly purpose and will be consummated in heaven according to Hebrews 2:10.

In the fulfillment of Old and New Testament prophecies the principle is illustrated again and again that the natural, literal, and grammatical meaning is what is intended. Little support is given for the notion that prophecy should not be interpreted in a literal way. It is unreasonable to suppose that predictions yet unfulfilled will be realized in some spiritualized manner when prophetic events now already fulfilled have been completed literally.

.

MAJOR THEMES OF
OLD TESTAMENT PROPHESY

From Adam to Abraham mankind is presented as Gentile. After Abraham mankind is divided into two major divisions consisting of (a) Jacob, his 12 sons, and their descendants, and (b) the rest of mankind. This division of Jew and Gentile was continued until the New Testament when a third element was introduced – those who are included in the church. As least seven major aspects of Gentile prophecy are revealed in the Old Testament.

Though there were general predictions concerning the coming of the Messiah as early as Genesis 3:15 when it was predicted that an offspring of Eve would crush Satan, there were also predictions that the ground would be cursed and man would labor to produce his food. In Genesis 9:25-27 God predicted that the three sons of Noah would be the progenitors of the entire human race. Details which itemize the descendants of the three sons are given in Genesis 10.

The term, found in the New Testament in Luke 21:24, is a period of extensive predictions in the Old Testament especially in relationship to Israel. The times of the Gentiles is defined as the period in which Jerusalem will be under the general rulership of Gentiles. This began with the fall of Jerusalem to Nebuchadnezzar and his armies in 605 B.C. and will continue until the second coming of Christ. This period, which is not defined as to the extent of years, includes the period in the Old Testament from 605 B.C. and continues through the present age to the end of the Great Tribulation and up to the second coming of Christ. This period is interrupted by a parenthetical time period devoted to the calling out of the church from the Day of Pentecost to the Rapture. During this period Israel temporarily had possession of Jerusalem for brief periods of time as is true today, but even in these circumstances her possession was not secure, and as is true at the present time it was only possible by the help of Gentile nations such as the United States. Prophecy indicates Israel will lose control of Jerusalem especially in the period of the Great Tribulation preceding the Second Coming.

The succession of monarchies in the times of the Gentiles was a major prediction in the Old Testament. According to Daniel 2, 7-8, four world empires would be prominent in the times of the Gentiles beginning with the empire of Babylon, followed by the empire of the Medes and the Persians beginning in 539 B.C., to be followed in the fourth century B.C. by the conquest of Alexander the Great and the empire of Greece. The empire of Rome gradually developed in the second and first centuries B.C. Daniel mentioned by name the empires of Babylon, Medo-Persia, and Greece, but the great empire which followed Greece, though un-named, was obviously that of Rome, the greatest of all world empires in its geographic extent as well as in duration.

The times of the Gentiles are being interrupted by the present Church Age from Pentecost to the Rapture, and the times of the Gentiles will be resumed with the seven years mentioned in Daniel 9:27 climaxing in the second coming of Christ when Gentile rule will be destroyed (Rev. 19). If the earlier empires of Egypt, and Assyria are added to the four that Daniel predicted there will be six major world empires. The sixth empire of Rome in such a series will have a final consummation in the world empire preceding the second coming of Christ. The seventh great empire would then be the millennial kingdom which will occupy the entire world. Though these empires are called world empires, it is obvious that the first five empires did not cover the entire globe. The last three and one half years of the Roman Empire which is yet future will be worldwide and will be brought to its close by the second coming of Christ.

The early history of Israel beginning with the call of Abraham and the subsequent birth of Isaac and Jacob and his 12 sons is presented in Genesis as the beginning of the nation Israel. Many of these prophecies have already been fulfilled, but others, such as Israel's ultimate possession of the land (Gen. 12:7), await the second coming of Christ for their complete fulfillment. In addition to the role of Abraham, Isaac, and Jacob, the Scriptures speak of Israel's Egyptian bondage, and release (15:13-14), the character and destiny of Jacob's sons (49:1-28), Israel's conquest of Palestine following the Egyptian bondage (Deut. 28:1-67; Lev. 2:3-46; Deut. 30:1-3; Ps. 106:1-48; Jer. 9:16; 18:15-17; Ezek. 12:14-15; 20:23; 22:15; Neh. 1:8; James 1:1). It is evident in tracing the history of Israel that they are a chosen people selected sovereignly by God to be a channel of blessing to the world.[437]

Beginning with the Abrahamic Covenant (Gen.12:1-3; 13:14-17; 15:1-7, 18-21; 17:1-8) and continuing throughout the Old Testament many predictions were made concerning Israel. These promises include a national entity (Jer. 31:3), a land (Gen. 12:7; 13:15), a throne (2 Sam. 7:16; Ps. 89:36), a king (Jer. 33:21), and a kingdom (Dan. 7:14). Though other dispensations followed the dispensation of Abraham, the divine blessings promised in the Abrahamic Covenant continue throughout human history. The Scriptures predicted, however, that the blessings of the covenant may be suspended from time to time if the people do not respond and walk with God. But such interruptions are only temporary and constitute a chastisement of the nation Israel. Their sins, however, do not abrogate the eternal promise of the Abrahamic Covenant. The many references to her possession of the land that characterizes the Old Testament revelation concerning the future of Israel whether in times of revival or apostasy make clear that the ultimate fulfillment of the promise of the land is yet to take place at the second coming of Christ.

Three dispersions of Israel and three returns to the land were predicted in the Old Testament. The first of these was fulfilled when

Israel went down to Egypt at the time of Jacob to escape the famine in Palestine. Their return from Egypt constituted the first return to the land. Their second dispersion occurred in the eighth, seventh, and sixth centuries B.C. during the Assyrian captivity of the 10 tribes and the later Captivity of the two remaining tribes in Babylon. Extensive prophecies are given in Scripture for these events.[438]

In the first advent of Christ Israel as a nation rejected her Messiah (Matt. 23:37-39). As a result, the national chastisement will continue until Christ comes again. In a similar way Israel at Kadesh Barnea rejected God's promise of the land, and the wilderness experience was extended 38 years. Though the deliverance of Israel in both cases was delayed, ultimate fulfillment of the promise was assured. When Christ comes again He will complete the regathering of the godly remnant of His people into their own land and cause them to enter into the glory and blessedness of every covenant promise God made concerning them.[439]

From 1 Peter 1:10-11 it is clear that the prophets of the Old Testament were unable to distinguish the two advents of their Messiah. There does not seem to be anyone who distinguishes the first and second comings of Christ with an age between until after His ascension into heaven following His first advent. Even the disciples, who were closely associated with Him for more than three years, could not understand the death and resurrection of Christ and His ascension into heaven for they were expecting that somehow He would bring in the glorious Kingdom Age predicted in the Old Testament.

Throughout the Old Testament there is anticipation that there would be unprecedented Tribulation before the second coming of Christ (Deut. 4:29-30; 12:1; Ps. 2:5; Isa. 26:16-20; Jer. 30: 4-7). The New Testament adds many additional prophecies about that awesome time period. Because the Rapture will occur before the endtime events, after the Rapture and before the Second Coming mankind will include only Jews and Gentiles and not the church, the body of

Christ. The endtime prophecies that will be fulfilled after the church is raptured will complete the time of the Gentiles as well as the last seven years of Daniel 9:24-27. When Christ returns there will be complete destruction of Gentile power and institutions (Rev. 17-18; 19:17-21). In the Great Tribulation the Gentiles will be judged, and Israel will experience her final hour of affliction (Ezek. 2:33-44; Matt. 24:37-25:30).

The extended period of the Day of *Yahweh* beginning with the Rapture includes the endtime events preceding the Second Coming as well as the 1,000-year kingdom which will follow the Second Advent. In keeping with the use of this term throughout the Old and New Testaments the Day of *Yahweh* is a period that deals with direct judgment on human sin. Various periods of judgment in the Old Testament were called the Day of *Yahweh*, but prophecies spoke specifically of that which will precede the second coming of Christ.

MAJOR THEMES OF
NEW TESTAMENT PROPHECY

The Gospel of Matthew opens by introducing the genealogy of Christ (Matt. 1:1). The record of His birth in 2:1-2 as well as Luke's description of the background of His birth and His birth itself, sets the stage for the dramatic events to follow (Luke 1:1-2:20). In New Testament revelation additional information is given including a number of New Testament themes: (1) the new age, (2) the new divine purpose, (3) the nation Israel, (4) the Gentiles, (5) the Great Tribulation, (6) Satan and the forces of evil, (7) the second coming of Christ, (8) the messianic kingdom, and (9) the eternal state.

The New Testament introduced a new dispensation not anticipated in Old Testament prophecy. Its major features described as mysteries in Matthew 13, introduced the revelation of the many new features that characterize the age between the first and second coming of Christ. In the Bible a mystery is a truth hidden in the Old Testament but revealed in the New (Rom. 11:25; 1 Cor. 15:51; Eph. 3:1-6; 5:25-32; Col. 1:27; 2 Thes. 2:7).

In describing the present age Matthew used the expression "the kingdom of heaven" which described a rule of God on earth including both those who are genuinely saved and those who profess salvation. The rule continues through the present age and also in the Millennium.

Though many scholars make the kingdom of heaven equivalent to the kingdom of God, in its usage in the New Testament the kingdom of God includes only those who are saved and also includes the holy angels. The kingdom of God does not have any weeds (Matt. 13:25) nor bad fish (v. 48). The kingdom of heaven includes both the saved and professing Christians, but not angels. The aspect of the kingdom of heaven and the kingdom of god fulfilled in the present age are called mysteries because they were not formerly revealed. Matthew 13 states in seven parables the features of the new age relating to the church, Israel is seen as a "treasure" hidden in the field (v. 44). The church is indicated by the pearl which the merchant, referring to Christ, purchased with "everything he had" (vv. 45-46).

The present age is characterized by the dual development of both good and evil (vv. 24-30, 3-43). As the age progresses, evil also matures, as mentioned frequently in the New Testament (2 Thes. 2:1-12; 1 Tim. 4:1-3; 2 Tim. 3:1-5; James 5:1-10; 2 Peter 2:1-3:8; Jude 1-23; Rev. 3:14-22; 4-18). In contrast to the postmillennial anticipation of a gradually improving world the Scriptures instead predict that things will get worse and worse as the age progresses, and in no sense will a converted world await Christ on His return (Matt. 13:1-50; 24:38-39; 2 Tim. 3:13).[440]

The New Testament introduces the church as a new classification of humanity in addition to the Jews and the Gentiles (1 Cor. 10:32). The word "church", first used in Matthew 16:18, refers to all who are born again in this age. By being baptized by the Holy Spirit they are in Christ, and form with Christ the new creation including both Jews and Gentiles (Eph. 3:1-6).

The New Testament resumes the history of Israel where the Old Testament left them, a disorganized and scattered people, some of whom were dwelling in the land but not possessing it. In the present dispensation Israel nationally is set aside and there is no progress politically. But as individuals they are on the same plane before God as Gentiles (Rom. 3:9; 10:12). During the present age Jews have the same offer of salvation by grace alone. Their former exalted position above Gentiles in the Old Testament is mentioned by Paul in Romans 9:4-5.[441]

During the present age Israel as a nation is hidden (Matt. 13:44); hardened or spiritually blinded (Rom. 11:25); broken off (v.17);

without her national center Jerusalem (Luke 21:24); and scattered (James 1:1). In the coming Great Tribulation the Jews will be hated and persecuted (Matt. 24:9), and in the kingdom they will be regathered (v. 31; Ezek. 39:25-28) and delivered from her enemies (Rom. 11:26).

At His second coming Christ will occupy the throne of David (Matt. 25:31; 2 Sam. 7:16; 1 Chron. 17:12; Luke 1:31-33; Acts 15:16-17). The Apostle Paul prophesied Israel's spiritual and national restoration (Rom. 11:22:31). In the coming time of Tribulation preceding the Second Coming 144,000 Israelites will be kept alive through the period (Rev. 7:3-8; 14:1-5), but many others will be martyred (7:9-17; Zach. 13:8-9). The godly remnant of Israel will enter the millennial kingdom including those who survived the Tribulation as well as those Old Testament saints and Tribulation saints who will be resurrected from the dead (Rev. 12:13-171 20:4-; Dan. 12:2).

The Old Testament contains many references to the future of the Gentiles. From the standpoint of the New Testament the times of the Gentiles (Luke 21:24) which began with the Babylonian Captivity in 605 B.C., will continue until the second coming of Christ (Dan. 2:44-45).

The progress of the times of the Gentiles is interrupted by the Church Age during which the Roman Empire gradually faded from history. When the Church Age is ended, the Gentiles history is resumed with the revived Roman Empire in the form of 10 nations banded together as a political unit (Rev. 13:1; 17:16; Dan. 7:7, 20, 24). The Gentiles will be judged at the second coming of Christ (Matt. 25:31-46; Rev. 19:15-21).

The future period of the Great Tribulation prophesied by Christ (Matt. 24:9-28) is described by the Apostle Paul (1 Thes. 5:1-9; 2 Thes. 2:1-12); and John recorded at length the details of the tremendous divine program leading up to the second coming of Christ (rev. 3:10; 6:1-19:6). The entire period between the Rapture and the

Second Coming is a time of Tribulation, but the last three and one half years are called "the Great Tribulation" (Matt. 24:21-27; Dan. 12:1). When Christ returns, the times of the Gentiles will cease with God's judgments on the Gentile political power. Steps will be taken to assure the absolute reign of Christ on earth for 1,000 years.

Prophecy concerning Satan began in the Old Testament (Isa. 14:12-17; Ezek. 28: 11-19). Satan will be expelled from heaven and will be restricted to earth (Rev. 12:7-12) three and one half years before the Second Coming. At Christ's second coming Satan will be bound and confined to the Abyss (20:1-3). At the end of the Millennium Satan will be allowed to lead a final revolt against God (vv. 7-9) and then will begin his eternal doom in the lake of fire (v. 10). Along with the revelation of the power of Satan is the fact that his power is communicated to the future world ruler (13:2-4) and will empower the world ruler as "the man of lawlessness" (2 Thes. 2:3; Dan. 7:8' 9: 24-27; 11:36-45). The final world ruler is described by Paul as desecrating the restored temple, declaring himself to be God, and then being destroyed at the glorious appearing of Christ (2 Thes. 2:1-12). The Apostle John predicted the world ruler's governmental power and final doom (Rev. 13:1-10; 19:20; 20:10).[442]

The major themes of both the Old and New Testament prophecy should be approached from the standpoint of the major highways of prophecy running from Genesis to Revelation, disclosing God's plan for salvation, for the great nations of the world, for Israel, for the church, and the climax of human history in eternity to come.

PROPHECY CONCERNING
THE LORD JESUS CHRIST

In the major works of Christ, the Father and the Holy Spirit participate, but early in Scripture the focus of divine revelation is on Jesus Christ. In the fall of Adam and Eve from their pristine purity in their partaking disobediently of the tree of the knowledge of good and evil, Jesus Christ is introduced as the Offspring of the woman who would crush the head of the serpent (Gen, 3:15). This is the first intimation of God's plan for a redeemed people who would share the blessings of eternity with the Triune God. Early in the history of the race Abel's offering of the firstborn of the flock introduced the theme of blood redemption which runs as a scarlet thread from Genesis to Revelation. The depravity of the race was revealed in Cain's human race except for Noah and his family.

The human race continued its downward course leading to the Tower of Babel. It was then that God turned to His special purpose for Abraham, Isaac, Jacob, and the 12 sons of Jacob. Through their line would come the promised Savior and the people of Israel through whom God would speak by means of their prophets, the writers of Scripture, the 12 Apostles, and preeminently, Jesus Christ, thus fulfilling the promise to Abraham that his descendants would bring blessing on all peoples of the earth (Gen. 12:1-3).[443]

Moses predicted that the coming Messiah would be the greatest of the prophets, "The Lord your God will raise up for you a Prophet like me from among your own brothers. You must listen to Him. 'I will put My words in His mouth, and He will tell them everything I command Him. If anyone does not listen to My words that the Prophet speaks in My name, I Myself will call him to account'" (Deut. 18:15, 19-19). Knowledge of this prophecy was widespread in Israel at the time of Christ. Because they revered Moses as their great prophet, his prediction of another prophet was easily linked to their expectation of the Messiah. To this expectation Philip referred as recorded in John 1:45, "Philip found Nathaniel and told him, 'We have found the One Moses wrote about in the Law, and about whom the prophets also wrote- Jesus of Nazareth, the son of Joseph.'" Peter quoted the same prophecy in his sermon (Acts 3:22-23). In Stephen's address before his martyrdom he also quoted this prophecy. "This is He that Moses who told the Israelites about, 'God will send you a Prophet like me from your own people'" (7:37).[444]

Jesus Christ in His public ministry assumed the role of a prophet. He said He was delivering a message from God (John 7:1) and that what He said was given to Him by God the Father. "When he looks at Me, he sees the One who sent me. I have come into the world as a light, so that no one who believes in Me should stay in darkness. As for the person who hears My words but does not keep them, I do not judge him. For I did not come to judge the world, but to save it. There is a judge for the one who rejects Me and does not accept My words; that very word which I spoke will condemn him at the last day. For I did not speak of My own accord, but the Father who sent Me commanded Me what to say and how to say it. I know that His command leads to eternal life. So whatever I say is just what the Father has told Me to say" (12:45-50). Christ again and again referred to His message as a message from God the Father (14:24; 17:8).[445]

Though the Old Testament predicted the coming of Christ as a Priest (Ps. 110:1-4), most of the references to Christ in His future priestly work are seen in the types of the priesthoods in the Old Testament. Generally speaking, before the Mosaic Law was given, the head of the family was the priest for that family. With the coming of the Mosaic Law Aaron and his descendants were made into a special priesthood. Unique among the Old Testament references to priesthood was Melchizedek to whom Abraham brought tithes. "Then

Melchizedek king of Salem brought out bread and wine. He was priest of God Most High, and he blessed Abram, saying, 'Blessed be Abram by God Most High, Creator of heaven and earth. And blessed be God Most High, who delivered your enemies into your hands.' Then Abram gave him a tenth of everything" Gen. 14:18-20). In Psalm 110:4 the psalmist wrote of Christ, "You are a Priest forever, in the order of Melchizedek." From the Old Testament itself it is obvious that Christ fulfilled the qualifications both of Melchizedek and his priesthood and the Aaronic priesthood which was an integral part of the Mosaic Covenant.

The Aaronic priesthood does illustrate some of the works of Christ as Priest (Heb. 8:1-5). Not only in His office was Christ perpetually a Priest, but also His one offering was sufficient for all time in contrast to the Aaronic offerings which were constantly repeated (9:23-28). The intercession of Christ as our High Priest continues forever (John 17:1-2; Rom. 8:34; Heb. 7:25). Because as God all of Christ's attributes are infinite, as the believer's High Priest He can give His full attention to the needs of one believer while at the same time giving His full attention to the needs of all other believers. His intercession is such that when a Christian prays he in effect joins a prayer meeting already in session in heaven. Believers in Christ, who also constitute a priesthood (1 Peter 2:9) serve as priests under Jesus Christ as their High Priest.[446]

As early as Genesis 17:1, God predicted concerning Sarah, "I will bless her and will surely give you a son by her. I will bless her so that she will be the mother of nations; kings of people will come from her." It was not until the final years of Samuel as judge that the elders of Israel came to Samuel and said, "You are old, and your sons do not walk in your ways; now appoint a king to lead us, such as all the other nations have" (1 Sam. 8:4). Though warned that a king would not meet their needs, God appointed Saul as recorded in 9:17, "When Samuel caught sight of Saul, the Lord said to him, 'This is the man I spoke to you about; He will govern My people.'"

Saul, though he had a good beginning as king, soon proved to be disobedient to the Lord, and Samuel was informed that Saul would be replaced as king (16:1-13). After David killed Goliath and became the hero in Israel, Saul attempted to kill him suspecting that David might be his successor.

God made a Covenant with David, and let him know that his kingdom would never end. Before Jesus was born, Mary was informed, "You will be with child and give birth to a Son, and you are to give Him the name Jesus. He will be great and will be called the Son of the Most High. The Lord God will give Him the throne of His father David, and He will reign over the house of Jacob forever; his kingdom will never end" (Luke 1:31-33). Mary understood this as referring to an earthly rule of the son of David, and this was the common belief of the nation of Israel. If a literal interpretation of the Davidic Covenant were in error, it is unexplainable why the angel would have given this prediction to Mary, thus perpetuating what the amillenarians considered to be an erroneous interpretation.

In His earthly ministry Christ repeatedly affirmed that He is the King of Israel, and only after His rejection did He reveal the character of the present age (Matt. 13) and announced the fact that He was to be crucified. The disciples who followed Christ for more than three years did so with the anticipation that He was the King who would sit on the throne of David and redeem Israel. They did not understand until after His ascension into heaven that there would be a time period between the first and second comings of Christ and that the promise of the earthly reign would not be fulfilled until Christ returned the second time .

Christ, however, assured the disciples of the certainly of the future kingdom. He said to them, "I tell you the truth, at the renewal of all things, when the Son of man sits on His glorious throne, you who have followed Me will also sit on 12 thrones, judging the 12 tribes of Israel"

(19:28). When the mother of Zebedee's sons came to Jesus requesting that her sons sit on His right and left in His kingdom (20:20-21), Christ did not tell her she was mistaken about an expectation of an earthly political kingdom. Instead He said, "These places belong to those for whom they have been prepared by My Father" (v. 23).

When Christ returns to earth, "He will sit on His throne in heavenly glory" (25:21). It would reflect unduly on the integrity of Christ if these prophecies were not taken in their literal sense. According to 1 Corinthians 15:24-28, Christ will first destroy all dominion, authority, and power and put all enemies under His feet. When this is accomplished He will hand over the kingdom to God the Father. This final victory can only come after He has reigned for 1,000 years and vanquished Satan and those who follow him in the rebellion in Rev. 20, after He has judged all the wicked in the judgment of the Great White Throne, and then has established the new heavens, the new earth, and the New Jerusalem. In this sense Christ will continue to rule even as God the Father does, but its mediatorial government will have been brought to its conclusion with literal fulfillment of all the promises.

The second coming of Christ has the distinction of being the first prophecy recorded as uttered by man (Jude 14-15). It was also the last message from the ascended Christ as well as the last word of the Bible (Rev. 22:20-21). The second coming of Christ is unique because it occupies more Scripture than almost any doctrine and is an outstanding theme of both the Old and New Testaments. All other prophecies of Scripture to some extent cluster around either the first advent or the second advent of Christ.

In the highway of prophecy concerning the Second Advent there are at least 44 major predictions, beginning with the first direct mention of it in Deuteronomy 30:3 and continuing to the last promise of the Bible. In addition to this large volume of Scripture are also many other passages that refer to the Rapture of the church which is distinguished in the New Testament from the formal second coming of Christ.

At least seven distinct achievements are consummated in the Second Advent: (1) Christ Himself will return as He went, in the clouds of heaven and with power and great glory. (2) Christ will sit on the throne of His father David, which is the throne of His glory, and reign forever. (3) Christ will come, not to a converted world, but to the earth in rebellion against God and His Messiah, and will conquer it by His own infinite power. (4) At Christ's coming, judgment will fall on Israel, the nations, Satan, and the lawless one. (5) Christ's coming will be accompanied with the convulsion of nature which will be released from the curse. (6) Christ's coming will provoke Israel's long-predicted repentance and bring her to salvation. (7) At His coming Christ will establish His kingdom of righteousness and peace, with converted Israel regathered to her land, united and blessed under her King, and with Gentiles, as a subordinate people, sharing in that kingdom.

The coming of Christ for His church, an important prophecy concerning Him, will be treated in connection with prophecy concerning the church.

PROPHECY CONCERNING ISRAEL'S COVENANTS

The Mosaic Law was given to Israel by Moses (Ex. 20:1-31:18; John 1:17) and governed three major areas of her life: (1) the commandments dealing with God's moral law (ex. 20:1-26); (2) the judgments, which covered the social life of Israel (21:1-24:11); and (3) the ordinances, which instructed them concerning their religious life (24:12-31:18).[447]

The promises of the Mosaic Law were conditional, depending on Israel's obedience. Moses told the children of Israel that if they obeyed the Law they would be blessed of God and if they did not they would be cursed and disciplined (Deut. 28:1-68).

The Law was not a way of salvation but was a rule of life. Its application was limited to Israel. The Mosaic Law terminated at the time of the death of Christ.

By indicating conduct that was sinful in God's sight the Mosaic Law was preparatory provision for Israel which would lead them to Christ.

In Galatians 3:19 Paul raised a question about the purpose of the Law. He stated, "What, then, was the purpose of the Law? It was added because of transgressions until the Seed to whom the promise referred had come. The Law was put into effect through angels by a mediator." The Law characterized sin as transgression, but before the Law came the sin was not attributed to them (Rom. 5:13). The purpose of the Law was not only to prove that sins were forbidden but also to prove the sinfulness of man (7:11-13). From Galatians 3:19 it is clear that the Law was an interim provision. Because the Law could only condemn and not save, it was a means to bring people to recognize the necessity of Christ as their Sin Bearer. The Law was intended to be a discipline leading people to holy lives. This goal could only be fulfilled by becoming a disciple of Christ (Matt. 11:29; John 17:6-8; Titus 2:11-13). In Galatians, Paul pointed out that the Law was not a means to salvation and that it was not a means to sanctification. Both salvation and sanctification are to be found only in Jesus Christ and are obtained through grace, not the Law.

The Mosaic Law was limited to those who were in covenant relationship to God by physical birth as descendants of Jacob. With the coming of Christ, grace as a rule of life superseded Law as a rule of life (John 1:17).[448]

The covenant God made with David (2 Sam. 7:11-16) is like the gracious covenant He made with Abraham; both are unconditional and everlasting in their duration. The Davidic Covenant guaranteed that a descendant of David would sit on his throne forever. The details of the covenant in 2 Samuel 7 include the fact that David was to have a child not yet born who would succeed him on the throne. This son who was Solomon would build the temple that David desired to build. The throne of Solomon's kingdom would continue forever, and it would not be taken away from him even if he sinned. The covenant included the fact that through David's posterity, his throne, and his kingdom would be established forever.

Because the Mosaic Covenant was intended to be a temporary covenant the Old Testament promised that it would be superseded by a new covenant, "The time is coming,' declares the LORD, 'when I will make a new covenant with the house of Israel and with the house of Judah. It will not be like the covenant I made with their forefathers when I took them by the hand to lead them out of Egypt, because they broke My covenant, though I was a husband to them,' declares the LORD. 'This is the covenant I will make with the house of Israel after that time,' declares the LORD. 'I will put My law in their minds and write it on their hearts. I will be their God, and they will be My people. No longer will a man teach his neighbor, or a man his brother, saying, "Know the LORD," because they will all know Me, from the least of them to the greatest,' declares the LORD. 'For I will forgive their wickedness and will remember their sins no more'" (Jer. 31:31-34).

The fact of a New Covenant is recognized by all conservative scholars. The coming of Christ brought in a new order (John 1:17) which is supported by the designation Old and New Testaments in which the Scriptures are divided. Interpretation of the New Covenant has varied according to whether the millennial view of the interpreter is postmillennial, amillennial, or premillennial.

Conservative postmillnarians regard the promise of the New Covenant as fulfilled in the glory of the last 1,000 years of the present age in which the Gospel will be triumphant and the world will become Christianized.

The New Covenant is confirmed in two other Old Testament passages, Isaiah 61:8-9 and Ezekiel 37:21-28. In these passages the New Covenant in relation to Israel's includes promises of the everlasting character of the covenant, Israel's regathering, the rejoining of the 10 tribes of the kingdom of Israel and the 2 tribes of the kingdom of Judah who will be ruled by one King, their spiritual revival, their living in the land forever, God's presence with them, and their having a testimony that they are a nation blessed by God. If the promise and provisions of the covenant are taken in the normal, literal sense, they require a millennial kingdom (in addition to the present age) to allow for a literal fulfillment.

It is important to observe that the great covenants of God, which continue forever and which provide blessing in the millennial kingdom as well as in the eternal state, are all based on His gracious provision through Jesus Christ by His sacrifice on the cross. He is able to end the Mosaic Law and introduce the New Covenant of grace in which God gives those who trust Him blessings they do not deserve in time and in eternity.

ISRAEL'S 490 PROPHETIC YEARS

The opening verses of Daniel 9 recording the first year of the Medo-Persian rule of Babylon (539 B.C.) describes Daniel's excitement at finding in the writings of Jeremiah 29:10 the prophecy that the desolations of Jerusalem would continue for only 70 years. As approximately 7 years had already elapsed since Jerusalem fell to Nebuchadnezzar (605 B.C.), he pleaded with God to restore His people, the city of Jerusalem, and the sanctuary in keeping with the prophecy (Dan 9:4-19). The answer to Daniel's prayer is found in the Book of Ezra when 50,000 returned to the land of Israel.

This introduction to this important prophecy of Daniel 9:24-27 is most significant for it reveals that Daniel was on good grounds in praying that God would fulfill His promise. As Daniel continued his petition to the Lord, the Angel Gabriel came to him with a special message from God.[449]

Most Christological interpreters agree that the prophecy of Daniel relates to Jesus Christ though a variety of explanations are given regarding the combination of the nine sevens at the time of Christ's public ministry and death. The problem is complicated by the fact that there is no general agreement as to the beginning of the 490 years. Four decrees were given relative to the rebuilding of Jerusalem: (1) the decree of Cyrus to rebuild the temple (2 Chron. 36:22-23; Ezra 1:1-4; 6:1-5); (2) the decree of Darius, which confirmed the decree of Cyrus (vv. 6-12); (3) the decree of Artaxerxes (7:11-2); and (4) the decree of Artaxerxes given to Nehemiah relating to the rebuilding of the city (Neh. 2:1-8).[450] Though various facts can be presented in support of each of these interpretations, the fact is that the wall of Jerusalem was not built until approximately 444 B.C. when Nehemiah returned to Jerusalem. The beginning of the 70 sevens is most easily understood as the year 444 B.C.

Using the 444 B.C. as the starting point of the 70 sevens, and computing the first 9 sevens or 483 years as composed of 12 months or 360 days (as is normal in the Old Testament), this prophecy allows for the time of Christ's birth and life on earth, and the 483 years can be seen as terminating before the death of Christ. The current trend of scholarship to date the death in A.D. 28-29 allows ample time for the prophecies to be fulfilled literally.

The main problem in the interpretation of Daniel 9:24-27 is how the last seven years should be interpreted. At lest five theories may be considered.

Three Christological views have been advanced by conservative scholars. One view is that the last seven years of Daniel's prophecy is an indefinite period which does not have its fulfillment until the consummation of human history. However, if the first 483 years are interpreted literally there is no justification for turning to a completely nonliteral interpretation of the last seven years. As a matter of fact, nothing has happened in history to correspond to what was predicted in Daniel 9:27.

A second Christological view, however, which attempts literal fulfillment of the seven years, computes the 483 years as being completed at the time of the baptism of Christ. From this interpretation the first half of the seven years is fulfilled in Christ's ministry before the cross. Those holding this view say that the prediction that sacrifice and offering will cease at the middle of the seven-year period was fulfilled in Christ's crucifixion. Having come to this point in literal fulfillment, however, they are at a loss to explain literally the final three and one half years.

Daniel wrote that two events will occur after the 483 years but they are not said to be part of the 7 years. This is strong support for the next view, the view that there is a period of time between the end of year 483 and the beginning of the last 7 years. In addition to the prediction that the Messiah will be cut off, the prophecy is made, "The people of the ruler who will come will destroy the city and the sanctuary" (Daniel 9:26). The most plausible explanation of this destruction is that it refers to the destruction of Jerusalem which occurred at least 35 years after the death of Christ in 70 A.D. Both of these events are described as being after the 69th week but are not included in the 70th week.

"The ruler who will come" is related to "the people" who destroyed Jerusalem in 70 A.D., but the ruler himself is yet future and probably refers to the final world ruler. He will make a seven-year covenant with Israel. Though amillenerians resist the concept of the interval between the 9 sevens and the 70th seven, the premillennial interpretation provides for the most literal interpretation and is superior in explaining all the prophecies relative to this important period in Israel's history, the last seven years before the Second Advent.

In view of the prophecy of Daniel 9:24-27 it is evident that Daniel was given the remarkable assignment of not only defining the period of Israel's history including her last seven years before the second coming of Christ but also the massive revelation of the four major empires beginning with Babylon which would culminate at the second coming of Christ and be followed by the kingdom from heaven. Daniel's prophecies continue to be the important key to understanding the prophetic future as well as the fulfillment of prophecy in the past.

PROPHECY CONCERNING
THE GENTILES

After Cain's murder of his brother Abel, judgment on Cain and his descendants was prophesied (Gen. 4:10-12). In Genesis God declared His purpose to wipe out the human race except for Noah and his family by a great Flood. These predictions about the Flood have been completely fulfilled (7:1-8:18). After the Flood God declared, "Never again will I curse the ground because of man, even though every inclination of his heart is evil from childhood. And never again will I destroy all living creatures, as I have done. As long as the earth endures, seedtime and harvest, cold and heat, summer and winter, day and night will never cease (8:21-22).[451]

In Genesis 9 God blessed Noah and made a covenant with him in which He promised that animals, birds, and fish were given into Noah's hands (v. 2). Also He gave Noah green plants for food and for the first time authorized the eating of meat (vv. 3-5). For the first time He gave the law that if man sheds the blood of another person, his own blood should be shed (v. 6). God also promised that never again would life on earth be destroyed by a flood (vv. 11-17).[452]

Following Noah's drunkenness, predictions were given about his three sons and their descendants. Noah pronounced a curse on Canaan the sons of Ham and Canaan's descendants because of Ham's disrespect for his father (vv. 24-25). Noah declared that Canaan would be Shem's slave (v.26) and that Japheth would have extended territory on earth and that Canaan would also be Japheth's slave (v.27). These prophecies are being fulfilled throughout the period of human race on earth.[453]

Before the later empires of Assyria and Babylon were formed Egypt was already an advanced nation nourished by the rich Nile Valley.

Egypt already had an advanced culture, its own literature, and a history that extended over hundreds of years. It was to Egypt that Jacob and his sons went for relief from famine in Canaan when Joseph was a major administrator of the Egyptian nation.

Egypt already was a nation of the past when Moses wrote the Pentateuch. The first mention of Egypt in Scripture is in Genesis 10:6 where Mizraim is mentioned; Mizraim is another name for Egypt (v. 13). Some believe that the modern title of Egypt came from a king by the name of Egyptus who lived about 1485 B.C. The Egyptians called their own land Kemmet, meaning "The Black Land," and Egypt was also mentioned as "the land of Ham" referring to the fact that Egyptians were descendants of Ham the son of Noah.

Abraham went to Egypt because of famine in Canaan (12:10); He was clearly out of the will of God in going to Egypt. But God delivered him from his deception that Sarah was his sister. This was a half truth (which is a lie), as she was his half-sister as well as his wife. From this trip to Egypt, Hagar the handmaid was taken back to the Promised Land where she ultimately became the mother of Ishmael (16:1-). In 26:2 Isaac was told not to go to the land of Egypt as Abraham had done. But Hagar took a wife for Ishmael from Egypt (21:21).

In Scripture, Egypt has a prominent place among the nations of the world. She was the first great empire of history and a land that nurtured the children of Israel during a period of their growth from a family of 70 to a nation of probably three million or more people. Later Egypt provided a place of safety for Jesus when Joseph and Mary fled from the wrath of Herod (Matt. 2:13-15).[454]

Assyria is another nation that is important in biblical prophecy primarily as the nation that carried out God's judgment on the 10 tribes of Israel. Assyria first exacted tribute from Israel (2 Kings 15:19-20). When the Assyrians carried off the 10 northern tribes of Israel into captivity (vv. 29-30), this fulfilled Moses' prediction of one of God's judgments on Israel for her sin (Deut. 28:15-8). The account of Assyria's dealings with Israel is detailed in 2 Kings 15:19-36 and 2 Chronicles 28:1-33:11. Isaiah recorded the attempt of Assyria to conquer the two remaining tribes of Judah and Benjamin and God's deliverance of them (Isa. 3:1-37:37; 38:6). Though Judah successfully avoided surrender to Assyria, more than a century later Nebuchadnezzar attacked Jerusalem in 605, 597, and 586 B.C. and took Judah into the Babylonian Captivity.

Another important factor is the prophecy given through Daniel concerning Israel's history, beginning with her return to their land after Babylon was conquered by the Medes and Persians in 539 B.C. Later the reconstruction of Jerusalem was begun in 444 B.C. as described in the Book of Nehemiah. Daniel prophesied the background of Israel's history beginning with the fall of Jerusalem to Babylon in 605 B.C. and climaxing with the end of the times of the Gentiles at the second coming of Christ (Dan. 7:11-13, 26-27: Rev. 19:11-21).[455]

In all three major visions (Dan. 2; 7-8) Daniel saw Gentile times running from the time of Babylon to the consummation of the second coming of Christ. He also prophesied the death of Christ (9:2). Daniel did not predict the period between the first and second coming of Christ though such a period is partially intimated in verse 2, which depicts the two events of the death of Christ and the destruction of Jerusalem. Daniel had no information about the formation of the church as the body of Christ in the important period from Pentecost to the Rapture.

The New Testament references to Babylon present three major facts about the nation: (1) Babylon will be a city, (2) Babylon will be a political power, and (3) Babylon will be a false religion.

Some believe that the city of Babylon will be the capital of the world government during the three and one half years of the Great Tribulation preceding the second coming of Christ. This would require that Babylon be rebuilt on its ancient site. Others believe Babylon as the city refers to Rome as a possible center of political and religious power in the endtime,

Religiously Babylon represents many of the pagan doctrines and customs that were incorporated in the Roman Catholic Church. These will be supremely manifested in the false religions of the endtime and the future world church. The religious aspect of Babylon and the destruction are described in Revelation 17-18.[456]

Though scholars have various opinions on Revelations 18, the destruction of the great city may be one of the results of the earthquake described in 16:19-21, a passage which mentions Babylon. Taken as a whole, Babylon is the political and religious power of the ancient world and in the final endtime form of world religion.

Daniel 11:3-35 gives a detailed prophetic revelation of the various political movements of the kingdom of Greece after Alexander's death. In this amazing section more than 100 prophecies are made, all of which have been literally fulfilled, including those that refer to Antiochus Epiphanes. These prophesies are so detailed that many scholars who deny the possibility of accurate prophetic revelation advance the theory that the Book of Daniel was a forgery written after the events had happened. Many conservative scholars have supported the authenticity of Daniel's prophecies as written by Daniel in the sixth century B.C. and regard them as authentic prophecies of future events.

While the prophecies relating to the empire of Greece were being fulfilled, including the prophecies of Antiochus Epiphanies, the forth empire revealed to Daniel was gaining power. After conquering all of Italy, Rome then defeated Sicily in 242 B.C., thus demonstrating her rising power. Roman conquests were then directed at Spain and Cartage, which came under complete Roman control and eventually were destroyed in 146 B.C. The Mediterranean Sea was already being surrounded by countries conquered by Rome as early as the beginning of the second century B.C.

In Daniel's first revelation of the forth world empire (2:40-43) he referred to Rome by saying "As iron breaks things to pieces, so it will crush and break all the others" (v. 40). Though Daniel did not identify Rome by name, history makes it plain that the great empire of Rome which followed that of Greece was anticipated in these prophecies. In 7:7 Rome as the forth beast was described as "terrifying and frightening and very powerful. It had large iron teeth; it crushed and devoured its victims and trampled underfoot whatever was left."

Though some have attempted to deny that the forth empire is Rome, there is no plausible explanation of the forth empire other than to identify it as Rome. Since the empire of Greece, Rome was the only world empire that emerged and it continued for almost 1,000 years, leaving and influence on culture, government, architecture, and literature that was unprecedented by any previous empire. Only those who refuse to acknowledge the accuracy of literal prophecy can avoid the conclusion that the forth empire was Rome.

A problem that remains is to identify the fulfillment of the last stage of the Roman Empire defined in Daniel 2 as having "feet partly of iron and partly of baked clay" (v.33) and the beast with 10 horns (7:7).[457]

The revival of the Roman Empire will be in three stages. The first stage will be the emergence of the 10 kingdoms once controlled by the ancient Roman Empire. The 10 horns of Daniel 7:7 and Revelation 13:1 are said to be simultaneous kingdom banded together in a political union (Dan. 7:24). Their names are not given in Scripture, but presumably they were once controlled by the ancient Roman Empire. They may refer to the major countries surrounding the Mediterranean Sea including Spain, France, Italy, Greece, possibly Syria in western Asia, and Egypt and Libya in northern Africa and others.

The second stage of the revival of the Roman Empire will be the emergence of a man revealed in verse 8 as "another horn, a little one, which came up among them," with the result that "three of the first horns were uprooted before it." This little horn will be a king, as described in verse 24. "Another king will arise, different from the earlier ones; he will subdue three kings." He apparently will soon conquer the seven remaining kingdoms for they are regarded as part of his political power from then on (Rev. 17:16). The second stage then will be a consolidation of 10 countries into one political unit dominated by a dictator.

The third stage of the revival of the Roman Empire will be an expansion of its power to the entire world, beginning in the middle of the last seven years of Daniel's prophecy for Israel (Dan 9:27) and continuing for three and one half years or 42 months (Rev. 13:5; Dan. 7:23; Rev. 13:7).[458]

As a world empire, who will be Satan's masterpiece of substitution for Jesus Christ as God and King of kings, the final world ruler will be the little horn of Daniel 7:8, the king who "will exalt and magnify himself above every god" (11:3), the one who will be the "man of lawlessness" (2 Thes. 2:3), a head of the beast coming out of the sea (Rev. 13:2-3), and the beast who will be destroyed by Christ and cast into the lake of fire at His second coming (19:20). According to Daniel 9:26 the "people of the ruler… will come and will destroy the city and the sanctuary" and "will confirm a covenant with many of the one 'seven'" (v. 27). His world empire will begin at the middle of the last seven years leading up to the second coming of Christ. This will be the beginning of 42 months or three and one half years of world domination (Rev. 13:5).

The first half of the final seven years will feature a world church, symbolized by the "great prostitute" of Revelation 17. It will be seceded by a world religion consisting of the worship of the world dictator and of Satan (13:4), which will continue for the last 42 months preceding the second coming of Christ. The power of this world dictator will extend to the control of the total economy of the world so that no one can buy or sell except by his authority (v.17).

The final form of world religion will actually be Satan's masterpiece of substitution for the worship of Jesus Christ. The future world ruler will claim to be God and will abolish all religions including the worship of Christ (Dan 11:3-37). The only power he will recognize will be the power of Satan and military power (vv. 38-39).

Though Satan knows he cannot win, he will be driven nevertheless by his own evil nature to oppose God in every possible way. The result will be that he will be cast into the Abyss and rendered inactive during the millennial kingdom (20:1-3).

At the end of the 1,000 years Satan will be released and he will incite a rebellion against God (vv. 7-9). But God will destroy those who surround Satan and support his cause. Satan will then be cast into the lake of fire, where the world ruler and false prophet were cast, 1,000 years before. All three "will be tormented day and night forever and ever" (v. 10), a dramatic proof of eternal punishment. The fact that the beast and false prophet will still be in the lake of fire refutes the idea of annihilation. As Gentile power will come to its end at the time of the Second Coming, so all satanic power will come to its end with Satan and the demon world judged at the beginning of the eternal state (Rev. 21-22).

SATAN, EVIL, AND
THE MAN OF LAWLESSNESS

Scripture describes not only the origin of evil but also its final disposition by a righteous God. The Scriptures make clear that evil did not begin with man and will not be solved by man. History and prophecy testify to the all-sufficiency of God in power and wisdom to permit evil to the extent that it is good and wise in God's judgment and to bring it to final judgment and disposition in His time. The answer of biblical theologians to the great problem of evil is that God has permitted it as a means to display His own infinite perfections and glory. God did not create evil; He is permitting it for a time.

In judgment on sin God demonstrates His righteousness and power. By His introduction of grace into the human situation (where men can be saved by grace through faith in Christ in keeping with His righteousness), God demonstrates as well His wisdom, love, and goodness. Though it is beyond man's understanding how God could tolerate evil in the world – evil that resulted in the death of His own Son on the cross- the only plausible answer is that this ultimately will display God's infinite perfections.

As we bring Satan into the picture, we find that Satan was originally created as a holy angel and given a high place of authority over the angelic world. Sometime before man was created, Satan's desire to be like God resulted in his being judged. The angels who supported and sinned with him were also judged, and they became the demon world. Some were bound and are awaiting judgment (Jude 6). Others like Satan were allowed some freedom in keeping with God's providential purpose (1 Peter 5:8).[459]

The order of God's execution of judgment on Satan is as follows: (1) Satan was judged at the Cross. (2) He will be cast out of heaven when defeated in the angelic war which is yet to come (Rev. 12: 7-12). (3) He will be cast into the Abyss, which will be sealed for 1,000 years (20:1-3). (4) He will be loosed for a short time for his wickedness to reach its consummation (vv. 3, 7-9). (5) He will be cast into the lake of burning sulfur (v. 10). The first of these events as sovereignly decreed by God has been fulfilled. The others are yet to be fulfilled.

Evil is revealed in Scripture as predetermined to follow in this program. But, rather than evil being gradually overcome by human effort, it can be conquered only by God Himself. The essential features of God's dealing with evil are these: (1) Israel's transgression will be finished when her Messiah returns and she enters into the kingdom (Dan. 9:24; Rom. 11:26-29). (2) Whatever evil will exist in the Millennium will be judged instantly by the King (Isa. 11:3-4). Though mere profession of faith that does not openly challenge Christ as King of kings will be permitted, unbelievers will be judged at the end of the Millennium. (3) Evil will be banished forever from the new heaven and the new earth and righteousness will dwell in eternity (2 Peter 3:13; Rev. 21:27).[460]

In Daniel's vision of the four great empires, the forth empire identified as Rome was described as having 10 horns in its later stage (Dan. 7:7). An eleventh little horn is spoken of in verse 8. He will gain control of all 10 kingdoms which the horns represent (vv. 8, 11, 20-21, 23-24). This ruler will receive his power from Satan (Rev. 13:2; Luke 4:5-7).[461]

When this ruler gains power over the 10 kingdoms, he will impose a peace treaty on Israel (Daniel 9:27) for seven years which will enable people to identify him. In the middle of the seven years he will become a world ruler (7:23, Rev. 13:7). Christ referred to him as "standing in the holy place" and desecrating the temple by "the abomination that cause desolation, spoken of through the Prophet Daniel" (Matt. 24: 15).

The man of lawlessness is the ultimate substitute for Jesus Christ as

King of kings and Lord of lords. The ruler will be empowered by Satan to dominate the whole world in the 42 months preceding the second coming of Christ (Rev. 13:5).

A most significant reference to this lawless leader is found in Daniel 9:24-27, where he is referred to as the "the ruler" (v. 26). He will make a covenant with Israel for the last seven years leading up to the second coming of Christ. According to verse 27, "He will confirm a covenant with many for one 'seven,'" but "in the middle of that 'seven' he will put an end to sacrifice and offering. And one who causes desolation will place abominations on a wing of the temple until the end that is decreed is poured out on him." Opinions differ on the identification of this person who will make the covenant.

A literal interpretation of prophecy strongly suggests that a future seven-year period prior to the second coming of Christ is by far the best way to explain these prophecies.

Other substantial prophecies support the concept of a future fulfillment of Daniel's last seven years before the second coming of Christ. In 2 Thessalonians 2:1-10, an extended revelation is given concerning the activities of the lawless one:

2 Thes. 2:1-10, " Concerning the coming of our Lord Jesus Christ and our being gathered to Him, we ask you, brothers, not to become easily unsettled or alarmed by some prophecy, report, or letter supposed to have come from us, saying that the Day of the Lord has already come. Don't let anyone deceive you in any way, for that day will not come until the rebellion occurs and the man of lawlessness is revealed, the man doomed to destruction. He opposes and exalts himself over everything that is called God or is worshiped, and even sets himself up in God's temple, proclaiming himself to be God. Don't you remember that when I was with you I used to tell you these things? And now you know what is holding you back, so that he may be revealed at the proper time. For the secret power of lawlessness is already at work; but the One who now holds it back will continue to

do so till He is taken out of the way. And then the lawless one will be revealed whom the Lord Jesus will overthrow with the breath of His mouth and destroy by the splendor of His coming. The coming of the lawless one will be in accordance with the work of Satan displayed in all kinds of counterfeit miracles, signs, and wonders, and in every sort of evil that deceives those who are perishing. They perish because they refuse to love the truth and so be saved".

Here Paul was correcting the false teachings the Thessalonians had received from certain Bible teachers that they were already in the Day of the Lord, the time of trouble. Paul points out that the Day of the Lord had not begun because the major events of the day had not been fulfilled.

The lawless one will be revealed after the Rapture of the church and will increase in power until he is finally a world ruler for the last 42 months preceding the second coming of Christ. He will be part of Satan's imitation of the Trinity in which Satan takes the place of God the Father, the lawless one takes the place of Christ, and the false prophet takes the place of the Holy Spirit.

PROPHECY CONCERNING
THE GREAT TRIBULATION

In the period between the Rapture and the second coming of Christ three specific time periods can be observed: (1) a time of preparation between the Rapture and the emergences of the ruler of the 10 kingdoms; (2) 42 months of peace for Israel, the first half of the last seven years (Dan. 9:27; (3) the Great Tribulation, the time of unprecedented trouble which will be fulfilled in the 42 months leading up to the second coming of Christ, the last half of the seven year period offered by the treaty with Israel. Only the last 42 months of the trouble before the Second Coming are called "the Great Tribulation (Rev. 7:14). Christ referred to this period as the major sign of the second coming of Christ when He predicted, "For then there will be great distress, unequaled from the beginning of world until now – and never to be equaled again. If those days had not been cut short, no one would survive, but for the sake of the elect those days will be shortened" (Matt. 24:21-22).[462]

After gaining control of the 10 kingdoms, composed of 10 countries forming a revival of the ancient Roman Empire, the king will attempt to solve the problem of Israel in relation to the other countries of the Middle East. He will impose a peace treaty on Israel (Dan. 9:27), which will be hailed as a great step forward toward peace (1 Thes. 5:3). Though Scripture does not describe the details of the peace treaty, it obviously is an imposed peace, not a negotiated one; undoubtedly it will fix the boundaries of Israel; it will provide them protection from attack; and it will restore normal trading relations with Israel's neighbors. The period of peace will continue for 42 months.

Scholars differ as to what will cause the abrupt change from the time of peace to the period that follows, but a plausible explanation is that the prophecies of Ezekiel 38:29 will be fulfilled at that time.[463] This unusual prophecy predicts an invasion of Israel from the north by a small group of nations joining with a great army from the "far north" of the Holy Land (28:6). This reference could be to no country other than Russia because this is the only nation that is to the "far north" of Israel.

The prophecy describes a strange war in which there will be no opposing army, but God Himself will interpose with a series of catastrophes including a great earthquake, a plague, a torrent of rain including hailstones, and the showering of the invaders with burning sulfur (vv. 19-22). The result will be that the entire invading force will be wiped out (39:1-4). After the battle it will take Israel seven months just to bury the dead (v. 12).

As the dictator of the entire world, the ruler of the 10 kingdoms will assume all the power of his position, ruling over every group of people (v. 7) and demanding that all worship him as god or be killed (vv. 8, 15). He will be supported by another person referred to as "another beast, coming out of the earth" (v. 11). In order to buy or sell everyone will be forced to receive a mark on their right hand or forehead indicating they are worshipers of the beast (vv. 16-17). Because the ruler will persecute anyone who will not worship him, the great catastrophes pictured in Revelation 6-18 will follow.[464]

In addition to the great catastrophes inflicted as judgments of God will be the massacre of those who will not worship the world ruler as god. Only the limitation of the period to 42 months will make impossible for him to carry out his program completely. Gentile and Jewish survivors will be on earth when Christ returns.

In addition to the detailed prophecies of Revelation the final time of Tribulation is described in many passages of Scripture.[465]

Other features of the Great Tribulation are also discussed in Scripture. The role of Israel in the Great Tribulation is described in Rev. 12:1-6 as a time of trouble from which she should flee. In answering the questions of the disciples about the end of the age, Christ exhorted the Children of Israel to flee to the mountains (Matt. 24:16) when their temple will be desecrated at the beginning of the Great Tribulation. Christ described the Great Tribulation as a time of such distress that if He did not come back in the Second Coming the entire human race would be wiped out (v. 22).[466]

The possibility of going through the Great Tribulation and being raptured at the end hardly fulfills the description given in Titus 2:13 of "the blessed hope."

PROPHECY CONCERNING THE CHURCH

The course of the true church on earth is traced through the Acts and the Epistles and the climax is found in Revelation 2-3 where messages to seven churches in Asia Minor are recorded. The church is not seen in Revelation 4-18 because the church is in heaven during that period. At the second coming of Christ the church will return with Christ to share in the millennial kingdom.

At least seven major features form the theme of prophecy concerning the future experiences of the church. These seven events include (1) the last days of the church in the world, (2) the Rapture of the church including the resurrection of the dead in Christ and the translation of the living saints, (3) the Judgment Seat of Christ, (4) the marriage of the Lamb, (5) the return of the church with Christ at His second coming, (6) the reign of the church with Christ at the Millennium, and (7) the church in the New Jerusalem in the eternal state.

The Bible includes references to seven people who were restored to life such as the son of the widow (1 Kings 17:22), the son of the Shunammite (2 Kings 4:35), the dead man restored by Elisha (13:21), the resurrection of Jairus' daughter (Matt. 9:25; Mark 5:42), the son of the widow of Nain (Luke 7:15), Lazarus of Bethany (John 11:44), and Dorcas (Acts 9:40). It may be presumed that all these, when raised from the dead, were restored to their former lives and eventually died the second time. An exception to this rule of death and resurrection are Enoch and Elijah (Gen. 5:24; 2 Kings 2:11; Heb. 11:5), who were caught up to heaven without dying.

The Scriptures are clear that all men continue to exist forever whether removed from this life by death or the Rapture (Dan. 12:2; John 5:28-29; Acts 24:15).[467]

One of the erroneous concepts is the teaching that all people will be raised at the same time and then will be judged. The Scriptures are clear that while all will be raised, each will be raised in his own order with the various resurrections differing in time and circumstances as well as results. At least seven resurrections to an immortal body are recorded in Scripture.

The first Person to receive a resurrection body that will never die is Jesus Christ. This is referred to frequently in Scripture. The resurrection of Christ is a subject of prophecy (Ps. 16:10; Matt. 16:21; 26:32; Mark 9:9; John 2:19; Acts 2:22-23). His resurrection was announced by angels (Matt. 28:6; Mark 16:6; Luke 24:6), and was accompanied by evidence of its reality (Matt. 27:66; Luke 24:39; John 20:20; Acts 1:30).

Christ was resurrected with a new body that would be immortal, that is, that would never die (Mark 16:14; Luke 24:33-49; John 20:19-23). As such the body of Christ at His resurrection is the pattern that will be followed by all the saved. This is the pattern that will be followed by all the saved at the time of their resurrection (1 John 3:2).

The third resurrection will occur at the Rapture of the church (1 Cor. 15:52; 1 Thes. 4:16). The resurrection of the "dead in Christ" (v. 16) seems to limit this resurrection to those who have been baptized into the body of Christ by the Holy Spirit at the time they became a part of the church (1 Cor. 12:13). Though Old Testament saints were in Christ representatively, they were not a part of His body, the church, and apparently their resurrection will occur later.

In Revelation 11, prior to the seventh trumpet, two witnesses will have three and one half years of prophetic ministry (vv. 3-13). They will be kept alive supernaturally and will prophecy for 1,200 days. At the end of this period God will permit their enemies to kill them, and their bodies will lie in the streets of Jerusalem for three and one half days. They will then be raised from the dead and ascend to heaven (vv. 7-12). It may be debated whether their three and one half year period of prophecy is the first half or the second half of the last seven years leading up to the second coming of Christ, but the context seems to point to the Great Tribulation before the seven bowls of wrath of God (Rev. 16) will be poured out in rapid succession immediately before the second coming of Christ.

A very important item in the prophetic future is the question of when the Rapture of the church will take place. Liberal theologians have omitted this doctrine almost entirely by their rejection of some of the literal aspects of resurrection and judgment. Among premillemarians, however, at least four views have been advanced: (1) the preteibulation Rapture, (2) the midtribulation Rapture, (3) the partial Rapture, and (4) the postribulation Rapture. The problem of determining which is the correct interpretation of Scripture involves a comprehensive review of the doctrine of the church as a distinct body of saints and the consideration of various New Testament Scriptures. In the 20th century a number of comprehensive treatments of the pretribulational Rapture and of the posttribulational Rapture have been written.

Until A.D. 190 the early church fathers were almost unanimous in holding to the premillennial interpretation of Scripture. They were confused by the fact that the Bible affirms that major events will take place before the Second Coming such as the appearance of the Antichrist and a single worldwide government. On the other hand they recognized the teaching of the Scriptures that the coming of Christ for the church is imminent. The early church fathers accordingly were confused and often they spoke of the Rapture as imminent and then later affirmed that some event must take place first which would deny its imminency. The doctrine of the Rapture as a separate teaching was not clarified in the early centuries of the church and was obscured completely as the amillennial view became dominant in the second, third, and fourth centuries and became the majority view of the church. In a climate where premillennialism itself was being attacked and discredited there was no proper basis for considering such a doctrine as the pretribulation Rapture.

With the Protestant Reformation building is eschatology largely on Augustine, who embraced a nonliteral interpretation of prophecy; little attention was paid then to the doctrine of the Rapture. However, one of the central doctrines of the Reformation that every believer may be his own interpreter of Scripture provided a basis for future Bible study which eventually reconsidered the whole question of the Millennium, the Rapture, and the second coming of Christ.

The major arguments of the controversy between pretribulationalism and postribulationalism involves a number of important issues. Prominent in the discussions by postribulationists is the argument that posttribulationism is an old doctrine extending from the first century until now. However, Paul labeled postribulationism a false doctrine in 2 Thessalonians 2. The Thessalonians had been informed by false teachers that they were already in the Day of the Lord or in the Tribulation. But Paul stated that they were not in the time of Tribulation and that in fact they would not enter this period.

In 1 Thessalonians 5:9 Paul had written, "For God did not appoint us to suffer wrath but to receive salvation through our Lord Jesus Christ." In 2 Thessalonians 2:7 he wrote that the coming of the man of lawlessness will not occur until after what is holding back or restraining sin "is taken out of the way." Though scholars differ on the identity of the restrainer force in the world today, it is the church indwelt by the Holy Spirit. The removal of what is restraining could only be the Holy Spirit. The removal of what is restraining could only be accomplished by the Rapture.

The principles of interpretation or hermeneutics play an important part in the doctrine of the pretribulational Rapture. Those who spiritualize prophecy including the time of Tribulation have assumed a point of view that makes impossible a pretribulation Rapture. Only those who are willing to accept prophesy as literal and who distinguish God's program for Israel from His program for the church are in a position to consider a pretribulational Rapture.

The nature of the Tribulation period is an important facet in pretribulationalism. In the last 35 years or so, there has been a remarkable turn to a more literal view of the Tribulation period which is the entire period of more than seven years between the Rapture and Christ's Second Coming.

If the church has to go through the Great Tribulation and be decimated by the catastrophes and judgments that will occur, with only a fraction of the world's population surviving, it is difficult to support the concept that the believer's hope of the Rapture at the end of the Tribulation is a "blessed hope" (Titus 2:13). The hope of survival through the Great Tribulation is hardly a comforting message or one that is imminent. Such a view makes Paul's comforting message to the Thessalonians (1 Thes. 4:13-18) incredible because they would not see their loved ones until after the Tribulation. If the Tribulation is literal the pretribulationalists have by far the better explanation of the blessed hope extended to the church.

The doctrine of imminency is another area of the discussion related to the Rapture question. Every passage referring to the Rapture speaks of it as an imminent event, an event that could occur at any moment, in contrast to the passages referring to the Second Coming which speak of numerous events that will precede it (Matt. 24:15-30; Rev. –18). Exhortations relating to the Rapture lose most of their significance if the Rapture is not imminent.[468]

Survivors of the Tribulation will be in their natural bodies and in the Millennium will carry on normal activities (Isa. 65:20-25). If all the Tribulation saints were raptured at the time of the Second Coming, there would be no one to occupy the earth and fulfill these prophecies in the Millennium.

Another significant passage is Matthew 25:31-46, which describes a judgment following Christ's second coming and the establishing of His throne on earth. At that time the sheep, representing the saved, will be separated from the goats, representing the unsaved. If a Rapture had taken place in connection with Christ's coming from heaven to earth, this separation of believers from non believers would have already taken place before Christ arrived on earth and this judgment of the Gentiles would be unnecessary. Also the judgment of Israel (Ezek. 20:34-38), to occur soon after the Second Coming, will be unnecessary if the saved in Israel were already separated from the unsaved by the Rapture of the church.[469]

In keeping with the fact that judgment follows resurrection, the Scriptures indicate that the church will experience a special judgment in heaven following the Rapture. The central passage on this doctrine is 2 Corinthians 5:10, "For we must all appear before the Judgment Seat of Christ, that each one may receive what is due him for the things done while in the body, whether good or bad."

Is this judgment on sin? The Roman catholic church teaches the doctrine of purgatory, the necessity of further cleansing from sin after death before one can enter heaven. Protestants have generally held to the doctrine of justification by faith, the teaching that all who are saved are completely justified and declared righteous by God. The present position of the church before God is seen as being positionally in contrast to their spiritual state in which they still experience sin and temptation.

At the Judgment Seat of Christ sin will not be the subject of consideration. At that time believers will be perfect, with no sin nature, and will never sin again in thought, word or deed. Therefore any concept of discipline because of previous sins is unnecessary and would be unfruitful. The question of their righteousness before God was settled when they were justified by faith. The Judgment Seat of Christ deals with works, not with sin. Believers will be judged on whether their works were good (worth something) or whether they were bad (worthless).

Paul used several illustrations in speaking of the believers' judgment at the Judgment Seat of Christ. In 1 Corinthians 3:11-16 he wrote about constructing a building with Christ as the foundation and believers using either gold, silver, and costly stones, or wood, hay, and straw—worthless works – will be reduced to ashes whereas the gold, silver, and costly stones – worthy works – will remain. Gold may be typical of anything that glorifies God. Silver seems to represent redemption and may speak of soul-winning. Costly stones represent all other things that believers can do, even simple and humble tasks that may reflect the glory of God. According to 4:4 every Christian will apparently receive some reward, "Therefore judge nothing before the appointed time; wait till the Lord comes. He will bring to light what is hidden in darkness and will expose the motives of men's hearts. At that time each will receive his praise from God."

A second illustration is found in 9:24-27. Here Paul used the figure of a race. Believers are urged to run the race of life and lay aside anything that would hinder their receiving "a crown that will last forever" (v. 25).

A third illustration, found in Romans 1:10-12, pertains to a trusteeship or stewardship. Christians are exhorted not to belittle or judge their fellow Christians because the matter of evaluation of their lives is God's doing. The fact is each Christian will give an account of himself to God as stated in verse 12, "So then, each of us will give an account of himself to God." This judgment is not a comparative one in which one Christian will be compared to another. It relates to the gifts and opportunities God has given each Christian. Every Christian has equal opportunity for reward for the judgment will be based not on what others have done but on what he himself has done as God's steward. It is most encouraging for those who labor obscurely and in minor roles in the church to know that their opportunity for service and reward is the same as those who are prominent and successful. Every Christian at the Judgment Seat of Christ will be saved (1 Cor. 3:15), but his reward will be determined on the quality of his life.[470]

The church is the bride waiting for the coming of Christ, her

Bridegroom. In Bible times a wedding had three steps. The first stage was reached when the parents of the bridegroom gave a dowry to the bride's parents. The second stage would usually follow a year later, when the groom and his male friends went in procession at midnight from his home to the bride's home. The bride would be waiting there with her friends and then they would join the procession, returning to the home of the groom. The third stage was the wedding feast illustrated at the wedding of Cana in John 2:1-11. The feast might extend for days, depending on the wealth of the people involved.

The church is already married to Christ. From the time when a person is saved, Christ Himself paid the "dowry" in His sacrifice on the cross. The coming of the Bridegroom for His bride will occur at the Rapture of the church, and the wedding feast will follow. When used as an illustration in Scripture weddings normally are seen as occurring on earth as in Matthew 22:1-14. In Revelation 19:9 the wedding feast is announced in connection with the second coming of Christ. This may suggest that the feast had not occurred yet. Though not stated explicitly in Scripture, the wedding feast may be fulfilled in the early years of the millennial reign of Christ in which millions of saints will attend Christ and the Church, His bride. Though the first two stages of the marriage are relatively literal, the distinction between the church and angels and saints of other ages is preserved in this illustration.

The Church which will be caught up in the Rapture to Heaven will return with Christ in His second coming to the earth when He will establish His millennial kingdom. Paul wrote of the Church in Colossians 3:4, "When Christ, who is your life, appears, then you also will appear with Him in glory." The Church, having been glorified at the Rapture, will appear at the Second Coming as the glorified Savior. Reference to this event is found in other passages also (1 Thes. 3: 13; Jude 14; Rev. 19:9, 14). The Church will be a part of that grand procession which may require many hours for all church believers to come from Heaven to the earth (vv. 11-21) with the destination being the Mount of Olives for all the church believers (Zech. 14:4). Following this return stupendous events of judgment and reward will occur. Members of the Church will experience the promises given in 2 Timothy 2:12 that they will be fittingly honored in the millennial kingdom and throughout eternity.

Just as the Church will be with Christ throughout His millennial reign, so the Church will also have her place in the New Jerusalem in the eternal state. The saints of all ages will be there along with the holy angels and the glorious presence of God Himself. In the New Jerusalem, however, the individuality of individuals and groups will again be observed with Israel treated as Israel, the Church as the church, and others as "the spirits of righteous men made perfect" (Heb. 12:23). The presence of Israel in the New Jerusalem is seen in the fact that the names of the 12 tribes are inscribed on the 12 gates (Rev. 21:12). The fact that the Church is in the New Jerusalem is indicated in Hebrew 12:23 where "the church of the firstborn" is said to be in the heavenly city. When prophecy is taken as a whole, it presents a marvelous picture of God's plan for the future in which every child of God will participate. This great sequence of events will begin for the Church when in the Rapture Christ comes for His own.[471]

THE JUDGMENTS

Of the eight judgments pronounced in the Bible one is past, two relate to the present, and five are future. As indicated in the study of soteriology, three fractures of divine judgment are related to Christ's death on the cross: (1) the judgment of the sin of the world, (2) the judgment of the believer's sin nature, and (3) the judgment of Satan.

The divine judgment on the sin of the world in the cross of Christ reveals on the one hand the infinite extent of the problem of sin and on the other hand the complete answer that God provides in the cross of Christ. Though it is true that Christ died with a view to saving the elect, the purpose of His death related to the whole world in that the infinite value of His death was sufficient for all and made the entire world savable even though it is applied only to those who believe (John 10:11; Eph. 5:25-27; 1 John 2:2). No human being goes to eternal punishment because Christ has not died for him but rather because he as an unbeliever has not availed himself of what Christ has done for him in dying on the cross.[472] The judgment of the believer's sin nature was also accomplished by Christ on the cross. This judgment is related only to those who are saved but is far reaching in its significance (Rom. 6:1-10).[473] In dying on the cross Christ provided a divine remedy for the believer's sin nature in the form of divine judgment on Christ (Rom. 6:1-10; Gal. 5:24; Eph. 4:22-24; Col. 3:9-10).[474]

Though Scripture does not reveal all the details about the relationship of angels to God, various instances of conflict with Satan and the fallen angels reveal God's superior power. In the protevangelium of Genesis 3:15 the superior of God is indicated. Again in Christ's temptation in the wilderness (Luke 4:1-14) the superior power of Christ the Son of God over Satan is revealed. In the war in Heaven Satan will be cast out in the middle of the last seven years leading up to the second coming of Christ (Rev. 12:7-12), and at Christ's second coming Satan and the demon world will be rendered powerless (1 Cor. 15:25-26; Rev. 20:1-3). The judgment of Satan by Christ as He died on the cross is also mentioned frequently in Scripture (John 12:31; 14:30; 16:11; Col. 2:14-15).[475]

It is necessary for believers to judge their own sins in the light of Scripture. Extended revelation of this truth is given in Hebrews 12:3-15. In this passage it is revealed that every son in the Father's household is subject to chastisement when sin intrudes on his Christian life. In verse 6 believers are said to be both chastised and scourged. Scourged seem to reflect a once-for-all conquering of human will. Chastisement on the other hand may be repeated many times in dealing with lesser problems of the believer in his spiritual life. In John 15:2 Christ said that the branches of the vine had to be pruned in order to bring forth more fruit. This pruning refers to discipline. Those who do not judge their own sins partake of the Lord's Supper unworthily (1 Cor. 11:30). Also revealed is the truth that "if we judged ourselves, we would not come under judgment." When we are judged by the Lord, we are disciplined so that we will not be condemned with the world (1 Cor. 11:31-32).[476]

A Christian who does not judge his own sin requires God's chastening to bring him back in fellowship with God and to identify him as a child of God in contrast to the unsaved in the world. If a believer judges himself, he will not need this chastening judgment. And if he does not judge himself he will experience God's discipline (1 John 1:9).

Though believers are under no condemnation in respect to their sins, having been justified by faith (John 3:18; 5:24; Rom. 8:1, 13-17), they are subject to judgment at the Judgment Seat of Christ in relation to their works. At the Judgment Seat of Christ believers' works will be evaluated to demonstrate whether they were good or bad, and rewards will be conferred (2 Cor. 5L10; Rom. 14:10-12; 1

Cor. 3:9-15; 9:24-27). The goal of the Christian in his life is to be pleasing to God whether in time or eternity. The Judgment Seat of Christ is not related to salvation but to the bestowal of rewards, and every Christian is assured that he will receive some rewards (1 Cor. 4:5; Eph. 6:8; 2 Tim. 4:8; Rev. 22:12).[477]

The saved who have died will be resurrected, and those who are living will be judged relative to their salvation and their works. The practical application of the second coming of Christ to Israel is seen in Matthew 24:32-25:30. The unsaved in Israel who will be living on earth at the time of the Second Coming will be purged out, according to Ezekiel 20:33-44. The righteous will be resurrected and rewarded (Dan. 12:2-3). This is in keeping with the fact that all the righteous, regardless of the dispensation in which they lived and whether resurrected or living in mortal bodies, will participate in the millennial kingdom and will be rewarded in a similar way as the church will be rewarded at the Judgment Seat of Christ (Mal. 3:1-18). On the one hand the fact that all are saved by grace in every dispensatation is upheld; on the other hand the importance of works on the part of those who are saved is specifically taught and relates to Israel and the saved Gentiles of the Old Testament as well as to the church.[478]

Scripture reveals that God will judge the Gentiles for their sins and in particular will judge Gentiles living at the time of the second coming of Christ. At the judgment of the Gentiles Christ will separate the sheep, representing the saved, from the goats, representing the lost (Matt. 25:21-46). Though salvation is by grace and through faith, the saved who come out of the Great Tribulation will be identified by their works in befriending their Jewish brothers. In the universal anti-Semitism of the Great Tribulation one who befriends Jews will by this evidence manifest his salvation.

In the millennial kingdom Satan and the demon world will be rendered inactive. At the end of the Millennium Satan and the demonic world will once again be released (Rev. 20:7-10). When Satan and the fallen angels are cast into the lake of fire (v. 10), the final judgment on sin in the angelic world takes place (2 Peter 2:4; Jude). Then all opposing forces of God will be dealt with in judgment as indicated in 1 Corinthians 15:24-2, "Then the end will come, when He hands over the kingdom to God the Father after He has destroyed all dominion, authority, and power. For He must reign until He has put all his enemies under His feet."

The judgment of the Great White Throne which will occur before the eternal state begins is the final judgment on the wicked. All whose names are not written in the Book of Life will be cast into the lake of fire. The tragedy of this judgment is that Christ died even for the unsaved people, but they did not avail themselves of God's gift of grace and therefore will eternally experience God's righteous judgment on them (Rev. 20:11 -15).[479]

The itemization of the judgments of God, some of which are past, some present, and some future, make clear that the concept that there is only one general final judgment is not supported in Scripture. Though it is true that everyone will be judged, angels and men will not be judged at the same time, at the same place, or on the same basis.

THE ETERNAL STATE

As used in theology, the term "intermediate state" refers to the state of human souls in the interval between their death and resurrection. Those who will be translated at the Rapture of the Church will not enter the intermediate state, but apart from them the order of death, and intermediate state, and resurrection are universal. The Scriptures are clear that death is not an unconscious condition for either the saved or the unsaved. Several aspects of this important teaching are revealed in Scripture.

The Old Testament word *sheol* and the New Testament word *hades* are identical in meaning, referring to the place where those who die go. In some passages they refer to the grave in which the body is placed and in others to the place where the souls are waiting for the resurrection of the body as indicated in the intermediate state. Neither of these terms is ever used for the eternal destiny of men. Both the saved and the unsaved at death have bodies that are subject to burial. The intermediate state of the unsaved is one of the torment and suffering (Isa. 14:9-11; Ezek. 32:21; Jonah 2:2). In contrast, the intermediate state of the righteous is one of bliss and peace (2 Sam. 22:; Ps. 18:5; 116:3). The rich man in hades was fully possessed of all his faculties and was in a suffering state, in contrast to Lazarus who was in a state of bliss (Luke 1:19-31).

The separation of the unsaved who have died from the saved is eternal, and no change of their situation is indicated until the Judgment of the Great White Throne. The state of the saved is represented as being in paradise (13:43) or being with Abraham (16:22).

Some believe that paradise before the resurrection of Christ was a place distinct from heaven though it was a place of joy and peace. Beginning with the resurrection of Christ the Scriptures are clear that the saved are in heaven itself in the presence of God. The change in situations for the saved is believed to be revealed in Ephesians 4:7-10, "But to each one of us grace has been given as Christ apportioned it. This is why it says: 'When He ascended on high, He led captives in His train and gave gifts to men.' (What does 'He ascended' mean except that He also descended to the lower, earthly regions? He who descended is the very One who ascended higher than all the heavens, in order to fill the whole universe.)"

Others on the basis of Daniel 7:9-10 believe that paradise is identical to heaven even in the Old Testament. The New Testament is clear that at least since the ascension of Christ those who are saved go immediately to heaven at death, and when the resurrection of the dead in Christ and the Rapture of the living church is consummated, they will go immediately into the presence of Christ (1 Thes. 4:17) in bodies suited for eternity.[480]

Created beings are subject to a fourfold classification – angels, Gentiles, Jews, and Christians. These can be further divided into 12 subdivisions or classes: (1) unfallen angels, (2) fallen angels, (3) saved Gentiles, (4) unsaved Gentiles, (5) Gentiles of the kingdom, (6) Gentiles barred from the kingdom, (7) Jews saved by entry into the church, (10) Jews condemned for rejecting the Gospel, (11) the unsaved as a whole, and (12) Christians.

The unfallen angels are those who have maintained their holy estate. Though tempted at the same time as Satan and the fallen angels, when they resisted this temptation they apparently were rendered secure for all eternity and no further departure from God has occurred among the angels.

Fallen angels, these angels are those who were created holy but when Satan sinned they fell with him (Rev. 12:9). As fallen angels they are identified with Satan in his work opposing God. Their destiny is sealed, and with Satan they will be forever in the lake of burning sulfur (Matt. 24:41; Rev. 20:10).

In the Old Testament saved Gentiles include believers who were not Jews, such as Adam, Enoch, Noah, Job, and Melchizedek. They will share eternity with others who are saved in later dispensations.

Most of the Gentiles in the Old Testament were unsaved. They will be resurrected at the Great White Throne Judgment and cast into the lake of fire (Rev. 20:14-15).

Gentiles in the kingdom refer to those who will live during the time of the millennial kingdom and will be saved by faith in Christ. After the Millennium those Gentiles will walk by the light of the eternal city and will have part in the New Jerusalem with the saints of all ages in the eternal state.

Gentiles who will be barred from entering the millennial kingdom are those who are lost and who will ultimately be subject to eternal punishment (Matt. 25:41-46).

Jews in the millennial kingdom are those who in Israel will put their trust in Christ and be saved. Some of these will have come out of the Tribulation time, and others will be born in the kingdom. They will share the New Jerusalem with others who are saved. They are distinguished from those in Israel who do not put their trust in Christ and will be subject to eternal judgment (Dan. 12:2-3; Ezek. 20:33-44; Matt. 24:37-25:30).[481]

Jews excluded from the kingdom will include those who are not saved at the time of the second coming of Christ and so will not be allowed to participate in the kingdom period. Other references to unsaved Jews are found in Matthew 24:50-52; 25:10-12.[482]

Jews saved in the church between the time of Pentecost and the Rapture are baptized into the body of Christ and have equal place with Gentiles who are saved. Though the church was largely Jewish in its early years, in the centuries since then Gentiles have become dominant in number. But Jews and Gentiles alike share the blessed promises in grace for those who are saved in the present Church Age.

The condemned Jews are the ones condemned for rejecting the Gospel and are unsaved just as the unsaved Gentiles are (John 3:18;

8:24). The unsaved as a whole are also treated in Scriptures as one category and without recognition of the various classes otherwise indicated. Even though Christ died for them they are lost and excluded from the glory of the redeemed. "Christians" refers to both Jews and Gentiles who are saved in Christ in the present dispensation. They form the one body of Christ, are branches of the vine, and share the eternal blessings of God as pronounced on the church. In the church, Jews and Gentiles have equality and are exhorted to maintain in their experience the same unity that is true of their position in Christ (John 17:21-23; Eph. 4:1-4).[483]

In general Scripture recognizes two classes of humanity, those who are saved and those who are unsaved. For them there are two spheres of existence in eternity, heaven and the lake of fire.

In many Bible passages, there is distinction between the millennial kingdom and the new earth and the new heavens. Though in one sense Christ will deliver the kingdom up to God at the end of the Millennium (1 Cor. 15:24-28), there is also a sense in which His rule as the Son of David will continue forever (Isa. 9:6-7; Dan. 7:14; Luke 1:31-33; Rev. 11:15). In the eternal state these who dwell in the heavenly city, the New Jerusalem, will include all the saved of every dispensation (Heb. 12:22-24). In the New Jerusalem, however, they will retain their individual as well as their corporate identities in accord with the dispensation in which they lived and in keeping with the promises God has given them.[484]

Human speculation on life after death is almost as old as the human race. Many ignore divine revelation and engage in speculation which is without supporting facts. As many as seven theories have been advanced. (1) Some believe in death as the cessation of existence, a view known as mortalism. (2) Another view is the transmigration of the soul. This view has been advanced by a number of religions, including Hinduism, Buddhism, and Jainism. The idea is that the soul passes from one incarnation to another. There is no ground for this belief and it arises from pure speculation. (3) Conditional immortality has come about because of the natural aversion in human thought to the concept of eternal punishment. Conditional immortality is widely held by liberals who do not accept the truth of the Bible about life after death. The thought is that those who die will never be resurrected. A variation of this view is the concept that the unsaved will be resurrected, judged, and then annihilated, and that this is the meaning assigned to the second death (Rev. 20:14-15; 21:18). (4) The concept that all men will be resurrected is called universalism. (5) Another variation of universalism is restitutionalism. This concept is that all created beings will be reconciled to God including the fallen angels and Satan. (6) The concept of purgatory is held by the Roman Catholic Church. This advances the idea that Christ's death was a satisfaction for sins committed before baptism, but those who sin after baptism must atone for those sins in purgatory unless they are cared for in life. Because no one can confess all his sins, everyone must pass through this experience of purgation. On this theory prayers for the dead and contributions to the church for offering up prayers are offered as a remedy. In effect this view denies the fact that Christ is the propitiation for the believer's sin (1 John 2:2) and it denies the truth of justification by faith (Rom. 5:1). (7) Nirvana refers to the condition in which a human life is extinguished like a lamp being blown out and is the belief of Buddhists. This belief is built on the concept that the immaterial part of man is absorbed into the divine and that this may begin even in this life by the renunciation of all personal desires. In contrast the Bible teaches eternal punishment, as is considered in the doctrine of hell.

Though the doctrine of eternal punishment is a teaching that many question or deny, the doctrine does not originate in human reason nor is it a product of human sympathy. It is taught in the Bible and therefore is to be accepted as part of God's revelation to man. It is difficult for man to realize the awfulness of sin and the infinite holiness of God and to face objectively the fact that an infinitely holy God must require infinite punishment for sin. In this doctrine as in many others God has not revealed everything (Deut. 29:29).

God's permission of sin in the universe, in which He is sovereign and in which He as the holy God hates sin, is difficult for one to understand. The Scriptures state that sin has done much damage to multitudes of beings, including, both angels and men. The Scriptures also affirm that human sin demanded of God the greatest sacrifice He could make in giving His Son to be crucified for the sins of the whole world. It was necessary for Christ as a man to enter into the awful experience on the cross as He quoted Psalm 22:1, "My God, My God. Why have You forsaken Me?"

To understand the doctrine of evil in the universe one must understand three facts: (1) Evil caused God to will the doom of multitudes of men and angels, which is an essential feature in the final solution of the problem. (2) By faith man must accept the revelation of Scripture that God's answer to the problem of sin is the best that the infinite God devised and that God was wholly free from any wrong motive in the condemnation of the wicked. (3) In keeping with scriptural revelation man must believe that God has done everything in perfect righteousness and that His punishment of sin is justified and in fact demonstrates His holiness and infinite glory. In the end those who believe the Bible must accept the doctrine of eternal punishment with the same finality as they accept the doctrine of eternal heaven as being in keeping with God who is at the same time a God of infinite love and righteousness.

Just as heaven is viewed as both a place and a relationship to Christ so the eternal state of the lost is referred to as a place and separation from God. In Scripture a distinction must be observed between the temporary place of the lost before the Judgment of the Great White Throne and the eternal place of their condemnation. In the New Testament the common word used for eternal punishment is "gehenna". In Hebrew, gehenna means the Valley of Hinnom and refers to the valley south of Jerusalem, where human sacrifices were sometimes made (2 Chrom. 33:6; Jer. 7:31). At the time of Christ it was a place where rubbish was burned continuously and accordingly became a synonym for judgment (Matt. 5:22; 29-30; 10:28; 18:9; 23:15, 33; Mark 9:43, 45, 47; Luke 12:5). This same word is used in James in reference to constant fire.[485]

As these references indicate, "gehenna" is equivalent to the "lake of fire" and in Mark 9:48 it is described as a place where "their worm does not die, and the fire is not quenched." The lake of fire or the lake burning sulfur is equivalent to "gehenna" (Rev. 14:10-11; 19:20; 20:10, 14-15; 21:8). Revelation 14:11 states that "the smoke of their torment rises forever and ever." In 19:20 the beast and the false prophet, who will be thrown into the lake of burning sulfur before the Millennium, will still be there in conscious torment at the end of the Millennium. "And the devil, who deceived them, was thrown into the lake of burning sulfur, where the beast and the false prophet had been thrown. They will be tormented day and night forever and ever." (20:10) The pronoun "they" refers to the beast and the false prophet who were cast into the lake of burning sulfur at the beginning of the Millennium as well as the devil who is cast into the lake of fire at the end of the Millennium. In verse 14 the lake of fire is made equivalent to "the second death." In Matthew 25:46 the goats representing the unsaved who will be living at the second coming of Christ will be cast into "eternal punishment," or "eternal fire".

Attempts to avoid the doctrine of eternal punishment have caused untold problems and misunderstandings regarding this doctrine. I believe that Greg Gilbert, senior pastor of Third Avenue Baptist Church in Louisville, KY got it right when he wrote: "I won't belabor this point. Others have made this case with crystal clarity. Suffice it to say that medieval bishops didn't invent the doctrine of hell as a way to scare the serfs; they got it from the apostles. And the apostle didn't invent it to scare the pagans; they got it from Jesus. And Jesus didn't borrow in from the Zoroastrians to scare the Pharisees; he was God, so He *knew* it to be real, and said so. And besides, hell's reality had already been revealed in the Old Testament.

At the most basic level, therefore, if we claim to be Christians and believe that the Bible is the Word of God, we have to recognize that the Bible teaches the reality of hell. But there's more.

There is no doubt that the doctrine of hell is horrible. The doctrine is horrible because the reality is horrible. But that's not a reason to avert our eyes and ignore it, much less to reject it.

There are those who think that, by rejecting or at least ignoring the doctrine in their preaching, they are making God more glorious and more loving. Far from it! What they are really doing is unwittingly stealing glory from the Savior Jesus Christ, as if what He saved us from was…well, is not so bad after all.

In fact, the horrific nature of what we have been saved from only intensifies the glory of what we have been saved to. Not only so, but as we see ever more greater worship to the One who endured that hell for us and saved us". By: Greg Gilbert-senior pastor-Third Baptist Church-Louisville, Kentucky. Crossway, 2010.[486]

Attempts to avoid the doctrine of eternal punishment often emphasize God's attribute of love while ignoring His attributes of Holiness, righteousness, and justice. Though in the wisdom of natural man this would be a desirable conclusion, the Scriptures are clear on the subject of eternal punishment. This doctrine remains a motivation for evangelism ("Knowing therefore the terror of the Lord, we persuade men," 2 Cor. 5:11, KJV) and for responding to the Gospel in faith.

The creation of the new heavens and new earth will follow the destruction of the present heavens and earth. "Then I saw a new heaven and a new earth, for the first heaven and the first earth had passed away, and there was no longer any sea" (Rev. 21:1).

The few references to the new earth do not give much information except that it will not have any oceans. Because directions on the new earth are said to be north, south, east, and west in reference to the gates of the city of Jerusalem, it may be inferred that the new earth will be round as the only other alternative would be a flat earth which is out of keeping with anything known in the physical world today. Life on the new earth, however, was described in detail in verses 3-4, "And I heard a loud voice from the throne saying, 'Now the dwelling of God is with men, and He will live with them. They will be His people, and God Himself will be with them and be their God. He will wipe every tear from their eyes. There will be no more death or mourning or crying or pain, for the old order of things has passed away.'" The new earth will be the dwelling place of the saints of all ages who will have their home in the New Jerusalem.

Three distinct heavens are identified in Scripture. The first is that of the atmosphere about the earth in which are the birds and the clouds of heaven. The second is the world of planets and stars which is the abode of the angels. The third is the celestial realm where God abides in supreme glory. In the eternal state nothing is revealed about the new heavens except that no sun or moon will be there (Rev. 21:23). As the earth will be bathed in the glory of God and there will be no night, it would be useless to place stars in the heavens which could not be seen. As far as scriptural revelation is concerned, the glory of God will be seen supremely in the New Jerusalem.

Paul also confirmed the fact of heaven in 2 Corinthians 12:1-9 where he recorded his experience of being caught up into heaven which he equated with paradise (v.4). Some believe this experience occurred when Paul was stoned at Lystra and was left for dead (Acts 14:19). Paul referred to being in heaven as being away from the body and being with the Lord (2 Cor. 5:8). Paul stated again that being in heaven is far better than being on earth (Phil. 1:23). Though he was not permitted to state what he saw in heaven (2 Cor. 12:4), he was nevertheless an experienced witness who could testify to the reality of heaven.[487]

The Scriptures clearly reveal that heaven is far better than earth (2 Cor. 5:8; Phil. 1:23). In heaven the child of God will be made sinless and will be given a body similar to that of Christ's body (Rom. 8:29; Phil. 3:20-21; 1 John 3:1-3).

The location of the third heaven, the home of the Triune God, is not specified in Scripture, but in eternity it will be the same as the New Jerusalem on the earth. When believers die they go at once to be with Christ (2 Cor. 5:8: Phil. 1:23). At the end of the Millennium they will be with Him in the New Jerusalem.

A believer in Scripture can only exclaim in keeping with the words of Paul the greatness of the revelation that God has given, "Oh, the depth of the riches of the wisdom and knowledge of God! How unreachable His judgments, and His paths beyond tracing out! 'who has known the mind of the Lord? Or who has been His counselor? Who has ever given to God, that God should repay him? For from Him and through Him are all things. To Him be the glory forever! Amen" (Romans 11:33-36).

END NOTES

1. . 1 Cor. 2:13
2. . 2 Tim 3: 16-17
3. . PS. 148:2-5; Col. 1:16
4. . Matt. 24:3
5. . Ps. 103:29; Luke 15:10; Heb. 1:14
6. . Heb. 12:22; Rev. 21:12
7. . Matt. 25:41
8. . Acts 10:48; 11:17-18; 13:47-48
9. . Acts 15:14
10. Isa. 0:3, 5, 12; 2:2; Acts 15:17
11. Rev. 21:24, 26
12. 1 Cor. 15:20-57; 1 Thes. 4:13-18
13. 1 Cor. 3:9-15; 9:18-27; 2 Cor. 5:10-11
14. Rev. 19:7-9
15. Luke 12:35-36; Jude 15:15; Rev. 19:11-16
16. Heb. 12:22-24; Rev. 21:1-22:5
17. Ex. 2012; Matt. 23:38; Acts 15:16; Isa. 2:1-4; Ps. 137:5-6; Luke 1:31-33; Acts 1:6-7; Matt. 2:2; 1 Tim. 1:17; 6:15; Heb.13:10-14
18. Gen. 9:24-27; Deut. 28:1-33
19. Ezek. 39:25-29; Amos 9:11-15
20. Eph. 2:12; Dan. 2:36-44; Acts 10:45; 11:17-18; Matt. 25:31-46; Isa 2:4; 60:2; Acts 15:17; Matt.25:34; Rev. 21:24-26
21. Matt. 1:18; Acts 15:14; Rom. 11:25; 2 Cor. 5:10; 1 Thes. 4:13-18; Rev. 19:7-9; Jude 14-15; Rev. 19:11-16; 20:6
22. Matt. 2:13
23. Acts 17:26-27
24. Phil. 3:7-11
25. B.B. Warfield; Bibliotheca Sacra 51 (1894) pp. 615-16
26. Duet. 28
27. Duet. 11: 24-25
28. Matt. 22:29

29. Matt. 22:44
30. Matt. 5:18
31. Acts 1:16
32. Acts 4:25
33. Acts 28:27
34. Rom. 9:2-4
35. Dan. 12:8-9
36. Phil. 2:13
37. E.D. Schleiermacher (1768-1834
38. Dr. Benjamin Warfield; Bibliotheca Sacra 51 (1894) pp. 23-24
39. Jn. 1:1; 14; 1Jn. 1:1; 5:7; Rev. 19:13
40. Jn. 14:6; 17:17; Ps. 119:19; Matt.24:34-35; 1 Peter 1:25; Jn. 11:25; Acts 16:31
41. 2 Tim. 3:16-17
42. 2 Tim. 3:15
43. 2 Peter 3:16
44. Duet. 25:4; 1 Tim. 5:18; Luke 10:7
45. Mark 1:9-29; Jn. 7:53-8:11
46. B.F. Westcott and F.J.A. Hort; The New Testament in the Original Greek- Cambridge: Macmillan and Co., 1881 !:2 Conservative
47. A Companion to the Greek Testament and the English Version. Harper and Brothers, 1883, p. 177
48. Holy Bible; Matthew, Mark. Luke. John
49. Jn. 14:
50. Rev. 1:5
51. Rev. 3:14;
52. Jn. 18:37
53. Rev. 22:18-20
54. Eph. 4:11; 2:20; 1 Cor. 14:3
55. Eph. 6:17; 1 Tom. 4:1
56. 1 Cor. 2:14
57. 1 Cor. 2:10
58. Luke 24:13-35
59. The Holy Bible; Matthew, Mark, Luke, John

60. 2 Tim. 3:16
61. Nim. 15:32-36
62. Matt, 5:29-30
63. Jn. 5:24; 2 Cor. 5:10-11
64. Matt. 16:28-17:13
65. 1 Cor. 2:9-10; 9:27
66. 2 Cor. 4:2
67. Psalm 19:7-9
68. Psalm 119:86- 172
69. Jn. 17:17; 2 Tim.3:16; Heb. 4:12
70. 1 Pet. 1:23
71. 2 Tim. 4:2
72. Rom. 10:17
73. 2 Tim. 3:15
74. 2 Pet. 1:4
75. Jn. 3:5; Titus 3:5; 1 Pet. 1:23
76. Jn. 17:17
77. I Pet. 2:2
78. 1 Thes. 2:13
79. Acts 20:32
80. Eph. 5:26; Ps 37:31; 119:11
81. Isaiah 55:10-11
82. Jer. 23:29
83. 2 Tim. 4:2
84. Jn. 4:24
85. Duet. 33:27
86. Jn. 10:29; Isaiah: 1; 2 Chronicles 1:9; Isaiah 59:1; 58:14; Ex. 33:11, 29; 2 Sam. 22:9, 1
87. John Miley; Systematic Theology. Hunt and Eaton, 1892, 1:173
88. Gen. 1:1; Job 11:7-9; 36:26; 37:5, 23; Ps. 77:19; 92:5; 97:2 ; 145:5; Prov. 25:2; Isa. 40:28; Jer. 10:10-1; Matt. 11:27; Rom. 11:33-34
89. Ps. 139:6
90. 1 Tim. 6:15-16; Col. 1:15; 1 Tim. 1:17; Jn. 1:14, 18; Matt. 5:48; 1 Pet. 1:16

91. Westminster Confession of Faith; Chapter 2, The Constitution of the Presbyterian Church of the United States of America. Philadelphia: Presbyterian Board of Publications and Sabbath-School Work, 1907, pp. 16-20

92. The American College Dictionary

93. Jer. 31:3

94. Ex. 3:5; Lev. 19:2; 1 Sam. 2:2; Job 15:15; Pss. 22:3; 47:8; 111:9; Isa. 6:3; 57:15; 1 Jn. 1:5; Rev. 4:8; 6:10; 15:4

95. Jn. 4:24; 1 Jn. 1:5; 4:8

96. Becoming Friends with God; Leith Anderson. Bethany House 2001 pp.27 ,Matt. 11:27

97. Rom. 3:4

98. Ps. 12:6; Num. 23:19; Heb. 10:23

99. The American College Dictionary

100.   Psalm 102:24-27; Isaiah 46:9-10; James 1:17

101.   Westminster Shorter Catechism- Question 7, Westminster Confession of Faith, Inverness, Scotland: Free Presbyterian Publications, 1981, p. 288

102.   Acts 15:17-18

103.   Ps. 76:10

104.   Rom. 11:33

105.   Isa. 40:13-14

106.   Derek W.H. Thomas, How the Gospel Brings Us All the Way Home; published be; Reformation Trust, 2011.

107.   Dr. Greg Gilbert Senior Pastor of the Third Avenue Baptist Church in Louisville, KY What is the Gospel September/ October 2010

108.   Strong's Exhaustive Concordance of the Bible

109.   Israel My Glory; David Levy – The Uniqueness of God's Word. 2011

110.   Ex. 3:14-15

111.   Col. 1:3; 2 Cor. 1:3; Rom. 8:15; Matt. 6:26; Heb. 12:9; John 17:11, 25; James 1:17; Eph. 1:17

112.   Philip Schaff, the Creed of Christendom. Grand Rapids: Baker Book House, 1983, II, pp. 58-59

113.   W.L. Alexander, System of Biblical Theology. Edinburgh: T. & T. Clark, 1888, 1:104

114.   JN. 8:29

115.   JN. 17:24

116.   JN. 17:5

117.   Rev. 21:23

118.   JN. 10:15; Matt. 11:27; Rom. 8:27; 1 Cor. 2:10

119.   JN. 14:11

120.   Eph. 3:14-15

121.   Malachi 2:10

122.   Acts 17:29

123.   1 Cor. 8:6

124.   Ex. 4:22-23

125.   2 Sam. 7:14

126.   Ps. 103:13

127.   2 Cor. 11:31

128.   Matt. 27:4

129.   JN. 20:17

130.   JN. 3:16; 20:17; 1 Peter 1:23

131.   Eph. 2:8-9

132. Arian heresy: Tricia Ellis-Christensen: May 20, 2011-Conjecture Corp.

133. JN. 1:14-15, 18,30; 3:13, 16-17, 31; 6:33, 42, 50-51, 57-58; 7:29; 8:23, 42; 9:39; Phil. 2:8; Heb. 2:14

134. JN 1:1-4, 14

135. JN. 6:33, 38, 41, 50-51, 58, 62

136. JN. 3:13, 31

137. JN 6:62

138. JN. 8:56;58

139. JN. 17:5

140. Phil. 2:6-7

141. Gen. 18:1-33; 32:24-32; Ex. 24:9-11

142. Ex. 33:9-23

143. Josh. 5:13-15; Ezek. 1:1-28; Dan. 10:1-21

144. Ps. 83:18; Isa. 42.8; Zech. 12:10

145. Isa 40:3

146.Matt. 3:1-5

147.The New Strong's Exhaustive Concordance of the Bible; James Strong LLD., S.T.D. Thomas Nelson Pub. 1984

148.Matt, 11:19; 12:40; 20:18; 24:37-44; 26:2; Luke 12:40; 19:10

149.JN. 1:51

150.Matt. 10:6; 23; John 5:22-27

151.Strong's Exhaustive Concordance of the Bible- James Strong. LL.D., S.T.D.- Thomas Nelson Pub. 1984

152.Rom. 1:7; 1 Cor. 1:3; 2 Cor. 1:2; Gal 1:1; Eph. 1:2; :23; Phil. 1:2; Col. 1:2; 1 Thes. 1:1; 2 Thes. 1:1; 1 Tim. 1:2; 2 Tim. 1:2; Titus 1:4; Phile. 3

153.The Constitution of the Presbyterian Church in the United States of America, The Confession of Faith, Philadelphia: Presbyterian Board of Publication and Sabbath-School Work, 1907, pp. 1-19

154.JN. 1:3; 10; Col. 1:16-17; Heb. 1:10-11; Ps. 102:25

155.Matt. 12:31; 27:46; Mark 10:17; 12:31; 13:32; 15:34

156.B.B. Warfield- Christology and Criticism. New York: Oxford University Press, 1929, pp. 189-90

157.Col. 1:1; Gen. 1:1-31; JN. 1:14; 19:30; Matt. 28:5-6; Rev:11-16; 21:1; Isa. 65:17

158.Eph. 1:20-21; Phil. 2:9-11; Heb. 1:3

159.JN

160.. 1:1-2;14

161.Phil. 2:-6-8

162.Col. 1:13-17; 1 Tim. 3:16

163.Heb. Chapters 1 thru chapter 10

164.Lk. 1:35

165.JN. 8:29

166.Heb. 10:5; Matt. 2:38; Mark 2:8

167.Isa. 9:6-7

168.1 Sam. 2:35

169.Acts 20:28; Heb. 10:4-10; JN. 2:9

170.Psalm 22 and Isaiah 53

171.Acts 2:33; 5:31; 7:55-56; Rom. 8:34; Heb. 7:25

172.Phil. 2:5-11

173.Strong's Exhaustive Concordance of the Bible- James Strong, LL.D.,

S.T.D.

174. John 13, 19:30; Rev. 19:11

175. 2 Cor 5:19

176. Charles L. Feinberg, Bibliotheca Sacra 92 (October – December 1935): 415-18; and John F. Walvoord, Jesus Christ our Lord (Chicago: Moody Press, 1969), pp.138-45

177. Strong's Exhaustive Concordance of the Bible- James Strong, LL.D., S.T.D.

178. The New UNGER's Bible Dictionary- Merrill F. Unger-1984 –Moody Press

179. Philip Schaff= Creeds of Christendom. New York: Harper Brothers, 1983. II, pp. 62-63

180. John Miley, Systematic Theology (New York: Hunt and Eton, 1894, II, pp. 5-7

181. 1 Tim. 3:16

182. Matt. 28:19

183. Luke 4:18; 1 Cor. 6:11; Num. 11:29; Jud. 3:10 Ps. 139:7; Isa. 1:1; Matt. 10:20; 2 Cor. 3:33; Gen. 6:3; Rom. 8:9,11; Phil. 1:19; 1 Peter 1:11; Acts 5:9; 8:39

184. Eph. 4:4; Rev. 1:4; 3:1; 2 Cor. 3:18; Heb. 9:14; 1 Peter 4:14; Rom. 8:2; Ps. 51:11; Matt 1:20; Luke 11:13; 1 John 2:20; Eph. 1:17; Isa. 11:2; John 14:17; Heb. 10:29; Rom 8:15; John 14:16, 26; 15:26; 16:7

185. Ezek. 36:25-27

186. Isa. 32:15; 44:3; Ezek. 39:29; Joel 28:29

187. Isa. 11:2

188. 1 Cor. 12:13

189. 2 Cor. 5:18-19

190. 2 Cor. 4:3-4

191. JN. 1:7-11

192. JN. 3:5

193. JN. 7:38-39

194. 1 Cor. 12:13

195. Matt. 3:11; Mark 1:8; Luke 3:1; JN. 1:33; Acts 1:5; 11:16; Rom. :1-4; 1 Cor. 12:12-13; Gal. 3:27; Eph. 4:4-6; Col. 2:9-13; 1 Peter 3:21; Mark 16:16

196.Rom. 7:15-25

197.Rom. 8:2

198.Gal. 5:22-23

199.Balancing the Christian Life- by; Dr. Charles Ryrie- 1969- Moody Press

200.Eph. 4:30

201.Ps. 119:11

202.The Tozer Pulpit- Dr. A.W. Tozer-Christian Publications, Inc.
    Harrisburg, PA 1968- pp.107

203.Heb. 7:26

204.JN. 13:3-11; 15:3

205.Luke 15:11-32

206.Col. 1:16; 1 Peter 3:22

207.Jude 6; 2 Peter 2:4

208.Eph. 6:12; 2 Kings 6:17; Col. 2:18; Rev. 22:8-9

209.Psalm 8:4-5; Heb. 2:6-7

210.Gen. 1:27

211.Cor. 6:3

212.Matt. 18:10; 24:36

213.Matt. 22:28-30

214.Matt. 13:41-42

215.Matt. 28:2-4

216.Dan. 9:21; Isa. 6:1-6

217.Dan. 9:21; Gal. 1:8; Rev. 20:3; 9:1-3,11; 21:-22; Matt. 25:41

218.Dan. 7:10; Luke 2:13-14; Heb. 12:22

219.Jude 9

220.2 Sam. 24:15-16

221.Col. 1:16; Luke 21:26; 2 Thes. 2:9; 1 Peter 3:22

222.1 Tim. 5:21

223.Heb. 1:14

224.Gen. 18:1-2; Ps. 91:11-12; Dan. 3:25; 6:22; Acts 7:53; Gal. 3:19; Job
    38:7

225.1 Tim. 3:16

226.Luke 15:10; Rev. 14:10-11

227.1 Cor. 6 :3

228.Job 38:7; Gal. 3:19; Acts 1:10; 7:53; Heb. 2:2; Luke 2:13; Matt.

4:11;28:2; 13:37-39; 24:31; 25:31; 2 Thes. 1:7

229.Gen. 15:16; Matt. 13:30; 2 Thes. 2:6-8

230.Rev. 9:20; 12:7; 20:19; 1 Tim. 4:1; James 2:19;

231.Leith Anderson- Becoming Friends with God Bethany House-
Minneapolis, MN-2001- pp192

232.Ezek. 28:1-19

233.Isaiah 14:12-17

234.Balancing the Christian Life- Dr. Charles Ryrie-pp.124- Moody Press-
1969

235.Job 1-2; Rev. 12:7-9

236.1 Tim. 3:6; Gen. 14:19

237.Matt. 4:1; 13:39; JN. 6:70-71; 8:44; 13:2,27; Mark 4:15; Luke 22:3

238.Halley's Bible Handbook (New Revised Edition) Dr. Henry H. Halley;
Zondervan Pub. 1965 pp. 723

239.Col. 1:15-22' 2:14-15

240.JN. 12:31; 16:11

241.Rev. 20.10

242.Rev. 12:7-20:10

243.1 Tim. 3:6-7

244.2 Peter 2:11; Jude 9; 2 Tim. 2:26

245.JN. 8:44; 1 JN. 3:8

246.Gen. :3; 2 Thes. 2:7; Dan. 7:8, 20, 24-25

247.Rev. 19:11-21; 20: 7-9

248.Luke 22:31-31; 1 Cor. 5:5; 1 Tim. 1:20

249.John 12:46; cf. 1:6-11; 16:8-11; 17:14; 18:36; 1 Cor. 1:21; James 1:27; 2
Peter 1:4; 2:20

250.Strong's Exhaustive Concordance

251.1 JN. 4:9; JN. 3:16; James 4:4; John 13-17

252.JN 12:31; 14:30; 16:11; Eph. 2:2; 2 Cor. 4:4; Eph. 6:12, 16; 1 JN. 5:19

253.1 JN. 2:2; 2 Cor. 5:19

254.Isaiah 14:12, 1-17; Job 1:13-19; 2:7; 2 Thes. 2:9-10; Rev. 13:1-17

255.1 Cor. 2:8; Rom. 3:10-12; Jn. 14:30; Rom. 12:2; Gal. 1:4; Col. 1:13;
James 1:27; 4:4; 2 Peter 1:4; 2:20; 1 JN. 4:3; 5:4

256.1 JN. 3:17; Mark 4:19; 1 Cor. 7:29-31; James 2:5

257.Psalm 2; Dan 2:35; Matt. 25:31-4; 2 Thes. 2:8; Rev. 6-18; 1 Cor. 7:31;

2 Peter 3:10; 1 JN. 2:17

258. Ezekiel 28:2-9

259. Isa. 14:14; Rev. 12:9; 13:14; Rev. 20:3,8,10

260. JN. 16:33; 2 Tim 3:12; 1 JN. 3:13

261. Eph. 6:11-12; JN. 17:15

262. Rev. 13:13-15

263. Rom. 5:10; JN. 3:16

264. Matt. 12:22-29; 25:41; Rev. 12:9

265. 2 Cor. 4:4; Matt. 9:34; 12:24; Mark 3:22; JN. 12:31; 14:30;16:11; Eph. 2:2

266. 2 Peter 2:4; Jude 6

267. 1 Cor. 10:21-21

268. Matthew, Mark, Luke, and John

269. Matt. 9:32=33; 12:22; Luke 8:26-35; Matt. 17:15; Luke 8:29; 13:11-17

270. Gen. 1:27; 2:20-23

271. James Ussher , 1581-1656- James Ussher Annales Veters Testament; John Lightfoot Chronology 1642-1644

272. Merrill F. Unger, Unger's Bible Dictionary, Chicago: Moody Press, 1957, p. 373

273. Ed Uthman, MD- Diplomat, American Board of Pathology- The Elemental Composition of the Human Body- Feb. 14, 2,000

274. 1 Cor 15:47-49; Gen 2:7; 3:19

275. James 2:26; 2 Cor. 4:16; 5:6-8; 2 Peter 1:13-15; Matt. 10:28; Hebrews 9:27

276. 1 Cor. 15:51-52; Acts 24:15

277. Phil. 3:20-21; Rev. 20:12

278. Gen 22:5; Job 19:25-27; Isa. 26:19; Dan. 12:2, 13; Hosea 13:14; Luke 24:1-8; JN. 10:18; Matt. 27:52-53; Lev. 23:15; JN. 5:28; 1 Cor. 15:22-23; 1 Thes. 4:14-17; Rev. 20:4; JN. 5:25-29; Rev. 20:11-13; Rev.20:5; I Cor. 15:50-53; Phil. 3:20-21; Rev. 20:7-17

279. Heb. 10:5; Rev. 1:13-18; 5:6; 19:12

280. Gen. 2:7; Ezek. 28:15

281. Eph. 2:4-7

282. Phil. 3:21; 1 JN. 3:21

283. 1 Cor. 15:44; 1 Thes. 5:23; Heb. 4:12

284.Gal. 5:19-21

285.Rom. 8:13; Gal. 5:24-25; 6:8; Col. 2:11; Jude 20-23

286.Rom. 7:25; 8:6-7; Titus 1:15

287.Gen. 2: 9; 16-17; 3:3; 6; 4:5; 6;

288.1 JN. 2:16; 1 Tim. 2:14

289.Genesis Chapter two and three

290.Gen. 2:17; Matt. 25:41

291.Mark 7:20-23

292.Hab. 1:13; 1 JN. 1:5; James 1:13

293.Julius Muller and Augustus Strong- Theology Today, July 1987

294.Matt. 22:37-40

295.Gal 5:16-21; Ps. 51:5

296.Rom 8:31-35; 9:22; Eph. 2:7

297.1 Tim. 1:13; Matt. 5:27-28

298.2 Cor 5:19; Rom. 3:23; Gal 3:22; 1 JN. 1:10

299.Gen. 1:25

300.Gen. 2:17; Rev. 20:14

301.W.G.T. Shedd- Comprehensive discussion of the sin nature 2:198-200

302.Gen. 8:21; Ps. 14:2:3; 51:5; Jer. 17:5,9; JN. 3:6; Rom. 1:18-8:13; 1 Cor.
7:14; Gal. 5:17-21; Eph. 2:3

303.Gen. 6:5; Job 11:12; 15:14-16; Ps. 58:2-5' 94:11; 130:3; 143:2; Prov.
21:8; Ecc. 7:20; 9:3; Isa. 64:6; Jer. 13:23; 16:12; Hosea 6:7; Matt. 7:11;
12:34; 15:19; 16:23; Luke 1:79; John 3:18-19; 8:23; 14:17; Rom. 3:9;
6:20; 1 Cor. 2:14; 3:3; Gal. 3:22; Vol. 1:13, 21; 2:13; 3:5-7; 2 Tom. 3:2;
1 Peter 1:18; 4:2; 2 Peter 1:4; 1 John 1:8; 2:16; 5:19

304.Rom. 8:1

305.The American College Dictionary

306.Strongs Exhaustive Concordance of the Bible- James Strong, LL.D.,
S.T.D. 1984

307.Commentary on the Epistle of the Romans. Charles Hodge New York:
A.C. Armstrong and Son, 1909, pp. 279-80

308.Heb. 7:9-10; 1 Cor. 15:22; Rom. 5:13-14; 20-21

309.Rom. 3:9; 3:22; 7:14; 9:3-5; 10: 11-13; Gal. 3:22; Acts 15:9

310.Rom. 3:24; 8:29; Eph. 1:6; 2:7; Col. 2:10; JN. 3:16; Isa. 53:11; Heb.
2:10; 1 JN. 3:2

311.2: Cor. 5:17; Eph. 2:10; Rom. 4:4-5; 11:16

312.1 JN. 1:7-9

313.Strongs Exhaustive Concordance of the Bible- James Strong, LL.D., S.T.D. 1 JN. 5:4; Rom. 7:18-20

314.Eph. 2:2; Rom. 7:7-25; James 4:7; John 15:5; 2 Cor. 10:3-5; Phil. 2:13; 4:13; 1 Peter 5:9

315.Ps. 119:11; JN. 15:7; 2 Tim. 3:16-17; JN. 17:17

316.Eph. 4:32; Col. 3:13; Matt. 6:14-15

317.1 Cor. 11:31-32

318.Romans 7:7-25

319.Romans 8:2, 4

320.Romans 8:12-14

321.Romans 6:13; 23; 8:1; 38-39; JN. 3:18; 1 Cor. 11:32; 15:55-57

322.Ps. 32: 3-6; 8-10

323.Heb. 12:6

324.1 Cor 15:24-28; 54; Rev. 20:11-15

325.JN. 14:2; Rev. 21:2, 10; Heb. 12:22-24

326.2 Peter 3:7-13; Heb. 1:10-12; Rev. 21:3-4; Rom. 11:33-36

327.Strong's Exhaustive Concordance of the Bible

328.Gal. 3:13; JN. 3:36; 1 Thes. 5:9; 2 Cor. 7:10; 2 Thes. 1:9

329.2 Peter 3:18; JN. 16:14

330.Isa. 7:14; 9:6-7; Micah 5:2; Luke 1:30-35; JN. 1:1-2, 14; Phil. 2:6-8; Col. 1:13-17; 1 Tim. 3:16

331.1 Tim 6:15-16; Heb. 7:25; Rev. 1:13-18

332.JN. 2:13; 1 JN. 3:2; Isa. 63:1-6; Dan. 7:13-14; Matt. 34:27-31; Acts 15:1-18; 2 Thes. 1:7-10; Rev. 19:11-16

333.1 Cor. 15:24-28; Isa. 9:6-7; Ezek. 37:21-25; Dan. 7:13-14; Luke 1:31-33; Rev. 11:15

334.Rom. 8:29; Col. 1:15, 18; Heb. 1:6; Rev. 1:5

335.Matt. 8:29; 9:6;11:19; 12: 23; 13:55; 15:22

336.Matt. 1:1; Luke 3:23-34; 19:9; 28:18-20; Gen. 12:3;

337.Acts 20:28

338.Rom. 3:26; 4:5; 1 Cor. 1:18-19; 23-24; Gal. 6:14

339.John 12:31; 14:30; 16:11; Col. 2:14-15

340.Gen. 22:8; Ps. 22:1; 69:20; Matt. 27:46; Mark 15:34; Isa. 53:10; JN.

1:29; 3:1; Acts 2:23; 4:28; Rom. 8:32

341. JN. 18:37; Like 19:10

342. Gal. 3:21-25

343. Renald E. Showers; What on earth is God doing? Loizeaux Brothers-Neptune, N.J.1989

344. Rom. 2; 4:3, 9; 10:4; Gen. 12:3; 15:6

345. Strong's Bible Concordance; James Strong, LL.D., S.T.D.

346. John 3:18; Gal. 3:10, 13; 4:5; Matt. 20:28; Luke 24:21,18; Titus 2:14; 1 Peter 1:18; Rom. 3:24; 8:23; 1 Cor. 1:30; Eph. 1:7, 14; 4:30; Col. 1:14; Heb. 9:15

347. Lev. 6:30; 8:15; 16:20; 1 Sam. 29:4; 2 Chron. 29:24; Ezek. 45:15, 17, 20,; Dan. 9:24; Matt. 5:24

348. 1 JN. 2:2; 4:10; Rom. 3:25; Heb. 8:12; 9:5; Luke 18:13

349. Strong's Concordance of the Bible

350. Rom. 3:9

351. Rom. 11:2-27

352. Matt. 25:31-46; Isa. 60:3; 62:2; Rev. 21:24

353. Gen. 3:15; JN. 3:16; 10:18; Rom. 3:25, 8:32; Gal. 2:20; Heb. 9:14

354. Rom. 5:1; Phil. 4:6-7

355. Col. 1:20; Isa. 63:1-6; Ps. 2:1-3, 8-9; Matt. 25:31-46; 1 Cor. 15:27-28

356. Rom. 8:20-23; Heb. 9:23-28; 11-12; Rev. 12:10

357. Strong's Exhaustive Concordance

358. 1 Cor. 10:11; Phil. 3:17; 1 Peter 5:3; 1 Thes. 1:7; 2 Thes. 3:9; JN. 13:15; Heb. 4:11; James 5:10

359. The History of Christianity – Fortress Press- 1977 p. 262-382

360. The History of Christianity- Fortress Press – 1977 p. 368

361. Benjamin B. Warfield, Studies in Theology (New Your: Oxford University Press. 1932, pp. 289-97

362. Isa. 42:1; 65:9; Rom. 8:33; Col. 3:12; 2 Tim. 2:10; 1 Thes. 1:4; 1 Peter 2:6; 5:13

363. Synod of Dort –1618-19

364. Rom. 8:30

365. Ezek. 20:33-44; Dan. 12:1-3

366. Jer. 31:34; Acts 15:14, 15:16-17; Amos 9:11-15

367. JN. 16:8-11

368.JN. 16:7-11

369.Eph. 2:8

370.History of Christianity Dr. Tim Dowley – Fortress press-Minneapolis 1977-pp 358

371.Rom. 8:28-30; Eph. 1:3-5, 11-12; JN. 17

372.Romans 8:33-34

373.Romans 3:21-5:21; 6:1-7:25; 8:1-39

374.Rom. 4:4-5; 11:6; Gal. 5:4; JN. 13:34; Cor. 10:3-5; Eph. 4:30

375.Titus 2:11-14

376.Phil. 3:20-21; 1 Cor. 15:42-57; Eph. 5:27

377.Rev. 21:4-5

378.JN. 17:22, 24

379.Eph. 1:17-21

380.Acts 9:31; 14:23; 15:41; Rom. 16:1; 1 Cor. 1:2; Gal. 1:2; 1 Thes. 1:1; Matt. 16:18; Eph. 1:22; 3:10; 5:23-25, 27; Col. 1:18

381.Ps. 103:20; 148:2-5; Col. 1:16; Matt. 24:3; Luke 15:10; Heb. 1:14; 12:22; Rev. 21:12

382.Isa, 2:4; 60:3, 5, 12; 62:2; Acts 15:17; Eph. 2:12

383.Acts 10:45; 11:17-18; 13:47-48

384.1 Peter 1:10-11

385.Ps. 22:1-21; 89:34-37; 69:20-21; 2 Sam. 7:16-29; Acts 2:25-36; Zech. 9:9; Matt. 21:5; Rev:15-16

386.Eph. 2:7; 3:5, 9; Heb. 1:2; 7:11-12 JN. 1:17; 5:21-22; 2 Cor. 3:11;

387.Matt. 24; Rev. 19

388.PS. 72; Isa. 2:1-17; 11; Jer. 33:14-17; Dan. 2:44-45; 7:9-14, 18, 27; Hosea 3:4-5; Zech. 14:9; Luke 1:31-33; Rev. 19-20

389.Ezek. 40-48

390.Isa. 65:17, 20; 6:22; Zech. 14:16-19; Rev. 20:7-9; 21:1-4

391.Jn. 1:17; Rom. 4:9-16; Gal. 3:19-25

392.Ex. 20:1-17; 21:1-24:11; 24:12-31:18; Duet. 28:58-62; Rom. 7:7, 14

393.Jan. 1:17; Rom:14; 7:2-; 10:4; 2 Cor. 3:6-13; Gal. 3:23-25; 5:18

394.Ex. 20:12; Matt. 24:36-51; 25:13; 1 Thes. 1:10; Heb. 11:16

395.Dan. 11: 36-45; 12:1-3; Isaiah 26:19; John 11:24; Heb. 6:1-2; Eph. 2:6; Col .3:1-3; 1 Cor. 15:23; 1 Thes. 4:16-17

396.Jer. 31:36; 33:21;Gen. 13:15; 2 Sam. 7:16; Ps. 89:36; Dan. 7:14

397.Acts 7:38; 9:31; 1 Cor. 10:32; Eph. 1:22; 5:23-25, 27, 29; Col. 1:18; Heb. 12:23

398.Acts 15:13-18; Amos 9:11-12

399.Eph. 2:14; Acts 15:7-11

400.1 Peter 1:10-11

401.Matt. 16:18; 1 Cor. 3:11; 1 Peter 2:4-8

402.Acts 20:28; Rom. 3:24-26; 4:24; Col. 1:13-14; 3:1-3; Eph. 1:19-23; Heb. 7:25; 1 JN. 2:1

403.Matt. 13; Rev. 2-3

404.Matt. 13:3-23

405.Ps. 23:1; 74:1; 79:13; 95:7; 100:3; Jer. 23:1; Heb. 7:25

406.1 Cor. 3:9; Heb. 3:6; 1 Peter 2:5

407.Rom 8:34; Heb. 4:14-1; 7:25; 9:24; 10:19-22; Col. 4:12; 1 Tim. 2:1

408.Eph. 4; John 17:21

409.JN. 5:25-26; 10:10;-18; Acts 2:24; 1 Cor. 15:45

410.1 Cor. 15:45; JN. 20:22; Cpl. 2:12; 3:1-4; 1 Thes. 4:13-18

411.Matt. 28:18; Rom. 6:3-4; Phil. 4:13; JN. 15:5

412.Eph. 5:27; 1 JN. 3:2; Jude 24

413.Gal. 4:9-10

414.Hosea 2:11; Isa. 6:23; Ezek. 46:1; Matt. 24:20

415.Peter Alexandria, Canon 15, Ante-Nicene Fathers, ed. Alexander Roberts and James Donaldson, 6:278

416.Justin Martyr, First Apology 67, in Anti-Nicene Fathers, 1:185-86

417.Ignatius, Bishop of Antioch, to the Magnesians 9, Anti-Nicene Fathers, 1: 2-3

418.Epistle of Barnabas, 15,7, Ante-Nicene Fathers, 1:14

419.Isa. 54:5; Jer. 3:1, 14, 20; Ezek. 16:1-59; Rom. 7:4; Eph. 5:25-33; Rev. 19:7-8; 21:1-22:7; Heb. 12:22-24

420.Eph. 3:17-21; 5:25; JN. 13:1; Rom. 8:38-39; Cor. 5:14

421.Matt. 17:1-8; Mark 9:2-13; Luke 9:28-36; JN. 17:5; 24; Romans 8:17; 1 Cor. 15:43; Col. 3:4; Phil. 3:21; Rev. 1:13-18

422.Acts 9:31; 11:12; 15:22; 1 Cor. 12:12-13, 27; Eph. 1:22-23; 4:15-16; Col 1:18; 2:19; Rev. 2-3

423.Matt. 28:19; Col. 2:9-12

424.Matt. 3:16; Acts 8:39

425. 1 Tim. 3:1-7; 7-13

426. 2 Sam. 7:12-1

427. 1 Kings 1:28-30, 43; 2 Chorn. 36:11-14, 15-21; Luke 1:32; Rev. 1:5-7

428. JN. 13:34-35; Matt. 5:43-46; Gal. 5:22; Rom. 5:5, 9:1-3; Isa. 42:6

429. JN. 7:37-39; Acts 1:8; Rom. 7::;6; 2:29; 1 Cor. 12:4-7; 2 Cor. 10:3-5;
     Gal. 5:16; Eph. 6:10-11; Phil. 2:13; Col. 2:6

430. Gal. 6:1; 1 Thes. 5:14; 2 Thes. 3:6, 11-15; 2 JN. 9-11; Rom. 14:1-4, 15-
     23; 16:17-18

431. Systemic Theology. New York: Charles Scribner's Sons, 1892, III, p.
     790

432. The theocratic Kingdom. Grand Rapids: Krekel Publications, 1952, I,
     p. 13

433. Dan. 9; 1 Thes. 4:18; JN. 17:17

434. Daniel 2, 7-8

435. Deut. 28-30; Psalm 2; Daniel 2, 7

436. Num. 11:25, 29; 24:2; 2 Kings 2:15; 3:15; 1 Chron. 12:18; 2 Chron.
     24:27; Isa. 11:2; 42:1; 61:1; Ezek. 1:3; 3:14, 22; 11:5; Joel 2:28-29

437. Daniel 11:1-35

438. Gen. 12:7; 15:13-14; 49:1-28; Deut. 28:1-67; 30:1-3; Lev. 26:3-46;
     Ps. 10:1-48; Jer. 9:16; 18:15-17; Ezk. 12:14-15; 20:23; 22:15; Neh. 1:8;
     James 1:1

439. Gen. 15:13-14; Lev. 26:32-39; Duet. 28:63-68; Neh. 1:8; Ps. 44:11; Jer.
     9:16; 18:15-17; 29:10; Ezek. 12:14-15; 20:23; 22:15; James 1:1

440. Deut. 30:1-10; Isa. 11:11-12; Jer. 23:3-8; Ezek. 37:21-25; Matt. 24:31

441. Rom. 11:25; 1 Cor. 15:51; Eph. 3:1-6; 5:25-32; Col. 1:27; Thes. 2:7;
     Matt. 12:1-50; 13:25-48; 2 Thes. 2:1-12; 1 Tim. 4:1-3; 2 Tim. 3:1-5;
     3:13; James 5:1-10; 2 Peter 2:1-3:8; Jude 1-23; Rev. 3:14-22; 4-18;

442. Romans 9:4-5

443. Rev. 13:1-10; 19:20; 20:10

444. Gen. 12:1-3

445. Deut. 18:15, 18-19; JN. 1:45; Acts 3:22-23

446. JN. 7:16; 12:45-50; 14:24; 17:8

447. Heb. 7:25; 8:18; 9:23-28; JN. 17:1-26; Rom. 8:34; 1 Peter 2:9

448. Ex. 20:1-31:18; John 1:17

449. Gal. 3:19; Matt. 11:29; John 1:17; 17:6-8; Titus 2:11-13

450.Dan. 9:4-23; Jer. 29:10

451.2 Chorn. 36:22-23; Ezra 1:1-4; :1-5, -12; 7:11-26; Neh. 2:1-8

452.Gen. 4:10-12; 7:1-8:18; 8:21-22

453.Genesis 9:2-17

454.Genesis 9:17-27

455.Genesis 10:6-13; 12:10; 21:21; Matt. 2:13-15

456.Dan. 7:11-13, 2-27; Rev. 19:11-21

457.Rev. 17-18

458.Dan. 2:33; 7:7

459.Dan. 9:27; Rev. 13:5; Dan. 7:23; Rev. 13:7

460.Jude 6; 1 Peter 5:8

461.Dan. 9:24; Rom. 11:26-27; Isa. 11:3-4; 2 Peter 3:13; Rev. 21:27

462.Daniel 7:7-8; 11, 20-21, 23-24; Luke 4:5-7; Rev. 13:2

463.Rev. 7:14; Matt. 24:21-22

464.Ezekiel 38-38

465.Revelation 6-18

466.Ps. 2; Isa. 24; Jer. 30:7-9; Dan. 9:27; 11:40-12:1, 11; Matt. 24:21-30;
     Mark 13:24; 1Thes. 2:4; Rev.3:10

467.Rev. 12:1-6; Matt, 24:16-22

468.1 Kings 17:22; 2 Kings 2:11;4:35; 13:21; Matt. 9:25; Mark 5:42; Luke
     7:15; 11:44; Acts 9:40;Gen 5:24; Heb.   11:5; Dan. 12:2; JN. 5:28-29;
     Acts 24:15

469.Matt. 24:15-30; Rev. -18

470.Ezek 20:34-38

471.1 Cor. 3:11-1; 4:5; 9:24-27; Rom. 14:10-12;

472.Heb. 12:23; Rev. 21:12

473.JN. 10:11; Eph. 5:25-27; 1 JN. 2:2

474.Rom 6:1-10

475.Gal. 5:24; Eph. 4:22-24; Col. 3:9-10

476.Gen. 3:15; Luke 4:1-14; Rev. 12:7-12; 1 Cor. 15:25-26; Rev. 20:1-3; JN.
     12:31; 14:30; 1:11; Col. 2:14-15

477.1 Cur. 11:30-32

478.JN. 3:18; 5:24; Rom. 8:1, 13-17; 2 Curs. 5:10; Rom. 14:10-12; 1 Cor.
     3:9-15; 4:5;9:24-27; Eph. 6:8; Rev. 22:12

479.Matt. 24:32-25:30; Ezekiel 20:33-44; Dan. 12:2-3; Mal. 3:16-18

480.Rev. 20:11-15

481.Luke 16:19-31; 23:43; Eph. 4:7-10; Dan. 7:9-10; 1 Thes. 4:17

482.Dan. 12:2-3; Ezek. 20:33-44; Matt. 24:37-25:30

483.Matt. 24:50-51; 25:10-12.

484.JN. 3:18; 8:24; JN 17:21-23; Eph. 4:1-4.

485.1 Cor. 15:24-28; Isa. 9:6-7; Dan. 7:14; Luke 1:31-33; Rev. 11:15; Heb. 12:22-24.

486.2 Chron. 33:6; Jer. 7:31; 18:9; 23;15, 33; Mark 9:43, 45, 47; Luke 12:5.

487.Greg Gilbert – Senior Pastor of Third Avenue Baptist Church in Louisville, Kentucky. September/October issue of Crossway, 2010, www.9Marks.org.

488.2 Cor. 5:8; 12:1-9; Acts 14:19; Phil 1:23.

BIBLIOGRAPHY

A Companion to the Greek Testament and the English Version. Harper and Brothers, 1883.

Alexander, W. L. System of Biblical Theology. Edinburgh: T & T Clark, 1888.

Anderson, Leith. *Becoming Friends with God*. Minneapolis, MN: Bethany House, 2001.

Barnhart, C. L., Editor. *The American College Dictionary*. New York: Random House, 1966.

Cunningham, William. *Historical Theology, Vol 1*. London: Billing and Sons, Ltd, 1960.

—. *Historical Theology, Vol 2*. London: Billing and Sons Ltd., 1960.

Dort, *Synod of*. 1618 - 19.

Dowley, Dr. Tim. *History of Christianity*. Minneapolis: Fortress Press, 1977.

Ed Uthman, MD, Diplomat. *"The Elemental Composition of the Human Body."* American Board of Pathology, February 14, 2000.

Ellis-Christensen, Tricia. *"Arian Heresy."* Conjecture Corp., May 20, 2011.

Feinberg, Charles L. *"Bibliotheca Sacra 92."* October - December 1935.

Gilbert, Dr. Greg, Senior Pastor of the Third Avenue Baptist Church. *"What is the Gospel?"* September/October 2010.

Halley, Dr. Henry H. *Halley's Bible Handbook (New Revised Edition).* Grand Rapids, MI: Zondervan Publications, 1965.

Hodge, Charles. *Commentary on the Epistle of the Romans.* New York: Armstrong and Son, 1909.

Holy Bible; KJV, NIV, NASB.

Levy, David. *"The Uniqueness of God's Word."* Israel My Glory, 2011.

Lightfoot, John. *Chronology.* 1642 - 1644.

Miley, John. *Systematic Theology.* New York: Hunt and Eaton, 1892.

Muller, Julius and Strong, *Augustus.* Theology Today, July 1987.

Ryrie, Dr. Charles. *Balancing the Christian Life.* Chicago: Moody Press, 1969.

Schaff, Philip. *The Creed of Christendom.* Grand Rapids: Baker Book House, 1983.

Schleiermacher, E.D. 1768 - 1834.

Shedd, W. G. T. *Comprehensive Discussion of the Sin Nature.*

Showers, Renald E. *What on Earth is God Doing?* Neptune, NJ: Loizeaux Brothers, 1989.

Strong, James LLD, S.T.D. *Strong's Exhaustive Concordance of the Bible*. Thomas Nelson, 1984.

Systemic Theology. New York: Charles Scribner's Sons, 1892.

The Theocratic Kingdom. Grand Rapids: Krekel Publications, 1952.

Thomas, Derek W. H. *How the Gospel Brings Us All the Way Home*. Reformation Trust, 2011.

Tozer, Dr. A. W. *The Tozer Pulpit*. Harrisburg, PA: Christian Publications, Inc., 1968.

Unger, Merrill F. *The New Unger's Bible Dictionary*. Chicago: Moody Press, 1984.

Ussher, James. *James Ussher Annales Veters Testament*. 1581 - 1656.

Walvoord, John F. *Jesus Christ Our Lord*. Chicago: Moody Press, 1969.

Warfield, Dr. Benjamin. *Bibliotheca Sacra 51*. 1894.

—. *Christology and Criticism*. New York: Oxford University Press, 1929.

—. *Studies in Theology*. New York: Oxford University Press, 1932.

Westcott, B. F. and Hort, F. J. A. *The New Testament in the Original Greek*. Cambridge: Macmillan and Col, 1881.

Westminister, *Confession of Faith*. The Constitution of the Presbyterian Church of the United States of America. Philadelphia: Presbyterian Board of Publications and Sabbath-School Work, 1907.

—. *Westminister Shorter Catechism*. Inverness, Scotland: Free Presbyterian Publications, 1981.